JACK RUBY

Previous Books

JACK RUBY

GARRY WILLS
AND
OVID DEMARIS

SEO Library Center
State Library of Ohio

40780 Marietta Road, Caldwell, OH 43724

NAL

THE NEW AMERICAN LIBRARY

First Printing

Published by The New American Library, Inc.
1301 Avenue of the Americas, New York, New York 10019
Published simultaneously in Canada by General Publishing Company, Ltd.

Library of Congress Catalog Card Number: 67-29996

Printed in the United States of America

To Natalie and Inez

Contents

JACK RUBY

"Taking the Play"

i

At 1312½ Commerce Street in Dallas, across from the Adolphus Hotel and just down Commerce from the Baker and the Statler, there is a stairway up to a second-floor warren of rooms and corridors. The sign on the locked door reads:

DALLAS POLICE
GYM
For Golden Glove Boxers
Sponsored by
DALLAS POLICE ASSOCIATION

As before, the place is open only at night; but now its stairs temper the welcome rolled down them in thick red carpeting. Only two officers have a key to the gym, and a rubber treadway is clamped into the carpet with metal strips. The run of stairs, broken by a short landing, is capped with a dusty, unused box office. A door on the right takes one into a low room widened, on both flanks, beyond ceiling traces of thin walls removed. Back in the Thirties, Benny Binion ran his book out of these rooms, from a club called Pappy's 66, but for two decades number 1312½ gathered dust until, in 1960, S & R, Inc. (Slatin and

Ruby) opened The Sovereign Club (private clubs are not subject to the Dallas ban on public sale of mixed drinks). The club had its troubles, and Slatin's interest in S & R was soon taken over by Ruby's friend Ralph Paul, who insisted that the club be opened to the public and strippers be brought in. That is how The Sovereign Club became The Carousel, managed by Jack Ruby. Paul owned half of the club, and Ruby's brother Earl owned most of the other half; but for Jack it was the fulfillment of a dream.

Today, a boxing ring is built out from the stage where blue lights cooled the strippers' writhings. Only one of Ruby's short runways still projects beyond the ring's lip ("The Only Club in Dallas With Three Runways"). In the girls' dressing room, cops shower after their workout. Down the hall from dressing room to stage, one walks past scribbled-over walls: "Number four girl goes first." Eleven musicians' names are recorded in fading pencil: Tom Piesnor and Bill Willis top the list. Traces of the nightclub look dingy in the gymnasium's hard light. Tinny chandeliers are tied aslant. The pasteboard star on Jada's dressing room shrivels at its corners. A sequiny gold horse in bas-relief is punctured at two points and shows its papery insides. There is more (and more efficient) punching than in the club's old days, but less fighting. It is still, as in Ruby's lifetime, a policeman's world, but no longer a girl's world. Ruby's club was electric with the violence of exploited women.

Dingy as it seems, it marks the top of a ladder. The rungs, each laboriously reached, were: The Singapore Club, The Silver Spur, The Bob Wills Ranch House, The Vegas Club, Hernando's Hideaway, The Sovereign Club, The Carousel. In 1947 Ruby came to Dallas to help his sister Eva, who had taken over The Singapore Club. This was in South Dallas, a prowling ground of tough outcasts, of Texans with an oil millionaire's temperament and a janitor's pocketbook. It is a Dallas that was forgotten when the city's thin wedge of skyscrapers reared itself, after World War II, to yodel challenges across the continent at New York. But Jack and Eva were used to tough neighborhoods. They grew up in a Chicago ghetto; every step outside it was dangerous. "Jack was the girls' protector," Earl Ruby says; if anyone picked on the Ruby sisters (there were four of them), Jack would hunt him down. On Dallas' South Ervay Street, he was still protecting Eva — though the two squabbled like fishwives when they were together. (If Eva called Jack at his office, he would put the receiver on the desk and go about his business, checking every now and then to see if the indignant static had died away.)

The brother and sister changed their Singapore Club to The Silver Spur, specializing in hillbilly Western music. The club bruised along and became known as Dallas' "bucket of blood." Ruby needed no bouncer; he had been a scrappy admirer and hanger-on of Barney Ross in Chicago, a haunter of fight circles, known for his own flare-ups and nicknamed "Sparky." Bill Willis, Ruby's drummer in The Carousel, says: "Jack grew up in the same kind of neighborhood I did. If you have our background, you learn to be a jungle walker; you *sense* a fight coming on. Jack used to tell me, 'You have to take the play away. If *you* don't take the play, the other guy will.' Jack was a reactionary." A what? "A reactionary — he reacted fast." (A stripper who worked for him told us, "Jack was a spastic." He was? "Yes — he acted suddenly.")

At The Silver Spur, there were many plays Jack had to take away. He was not a big man — five-foot-nine, 175 pounds — but he was brawny in the arms and shoulders, and fast, and deft at his tactic of the seized initiative. We found no memory, in the jumbled fight stories from his "bucket-of-blood" days, of his ever losing the play. He struck fast. Once, though, having struck, he left his hand too long in an opponent's face: "Dub" Dickerson chomped down on his finger and would not let go. By the time Jack shook him off, the flesh was mangled and one joint of his left index finger had to be amputated. Typically, Jack and Dickerson were friends when they met after this.

Even on South Ervay, Jack maintained strict, if eccentric, standards of decorum. "He didn't let no 'characters' in," one character told us. ("Characters," in Ruby's world, is the truncated form of crime-story phrases, like "suspicious characters" and "questionable characters.") "He threw me out four or five thousand times." The speaker is a wry young man with a sullen pout, Gilbert "Corky" Crawford. "I have a record, you see" (a five-page record of arrests, to be precise, often on charges of pandering), "and police would come in and sometimes take me out and sometimes take me to jail. So Jack said he didn't need my business." Did he ever throw you out physically? "Oh no!" Buddy Walthers, one of Sheriff Bill Decker's most promising young understudies (one of those who wear Decker's Dick-Tracy-style hat, not a Stetson), snorted at this. "He beat the hell out of Corky." Ruby, who despised "punks" and "characters," rarely found other ways of expressing disapproval. He moralized with his fists.

Decorum meant a great deal to Jack Ruby. He did not smoke or drink (his father was a drunkard). He rarely talked Yiddish (the language of his childhood); he was intent on perfecting his Bottom-the-Weaver English (his mother could not write her own name). But the only verbal mastery he achieved was in the realm of imaginative obscenity. ("He could cuss straight on, like saying his prayers," one of his friends said admiringly.) And his ardor for decorum manifested itself primarily in a readiness to flatten any patron who put his feet on the table. His determination to run a "clean club" made many strippers wonder how they could find protection from his protection. One girl told Jack she had been given her black eye by a cruel husband, and she was leaving him. The next time the poor fellow appeared at the club, Ruby pitched him down the stairs, though the couple had been reconciled and the girl was pleading, "Jack, I don't *want* you to hit him."

In 1952, Ruby tried to open a new place, and lost both it and The Silver Spur. It was the first, and the harshest, of his business failures in Dallas. Eventually he got The Silver Spur back, but by now he had his eye on the "respectable" downtown clubs. His major advance toward that goal came when he went in with Joe Bonds at The Vegas Club — which meant a switch from hillbilly music to rock-and-roll. He ran dance contests to bring in the young crowd, and kept the place even cleaner of "characters" — especially after his partner was sent to prison for sodomy committed with a minor. "Oh yeah," Corky says, "he threw me out of The Vegas, too." Jack lived for this club — as manager, bouncer, advertising agent, promotor, M.C. — until the day when he took his farthest step up and moved into the center of town, right next to Abe Weinstein's Colony Club, back at 1312½, where "Pappy" had started in the Thirties. In 1961, he opened The Carousel, which he thought of always as his "high-class place," his first club with strippers and a real "show." He left the old club for Eva to manage; Bob Larkin, a giant blarneyer, became the "houseman" (polite for bouncer) of The Vegas.

"He carried a lot of money," Larkin told us. "That's why he kept a gun in the bank bag. I often carried the gun. At the end of the night, Jack would take the money out of the cash register and put it in the deposit bag; that's when he took out his piece and put it in his pocket. Whenever he was carrying the money, he kept his piece handy. Sometimes he had me tote money from The Vegas to The Carousel, or to the bank, so I had the gun." Did you put it in your pocket? "No. I didn't want it. I just left it in the bag." But Jack put it in his pants pocket? "Yes." Ready, if anyone reached for the money bag or asked for his roll, to take the play away.

Was Jack a good fighter? "Sure. He never hesitated. Once he dropped by the club while I was at the door. I had to handle a troublemaker, and before I even got started, Jack stepped between us and nailed him. I asked him, 'Jack, why did you do that? That's what you pay me for.' 'Don't ever stop me,' he said; 'I might lose my nerve.'"

Did you get along well with him? "Sure. He was good to me. When I left him and went to work next door [at Abe's Colony Club], I got stabbed three times up in the Colony's telephone booth. By the time they got me down to the ambulance, Jack was there, leaning over and asking me how I felt. He followed the ambulance and came into the emergency room. A priest was trying to give me the last sacraments, but Jack shouldered him aside and came straight at me: 'What the hell, Bob! Freddy Bass had to pick his guts up and carry them after he got stabbed. You're as good a man as he was.' I tell you, it was the best medicine I got in that hospital. When I went into the operating room, he came right with me. They told him he couldn't stand there. He said he could watch through the door, couldn't he, and they let him. He was with me all through, in the recovery room and everything. He even offered to give me blood. When my own boss came to see me, there was his next-door rival already there. In fact, Jack told me I should sue Abe for getting stabbed in his club. I said, 'Aw, Jack, what would I do with all that money?' 'Come in as a partner at The Carousel.' He was always figuring the angles.

"He was a stickler for the law. He thought of himself as a kind of cop. He liked to do their job for them. If people came in after hours, he would frisk them to make sure weren't still carrying their bottle. He'd even frisk some of the girls. Other times, he'd have his girls take lie-detector tests if he thought they were hustling out of his club. We had one girl who liked to tell everybody her troubles; she kept Joe Johnson at the club till four one morning. When Jack and I came in from the restaurant, Jack hit the ceiling. 'This isn't a goddam bedroom.' The girl swore they had just been talking, but he took her over to Fort Worth to take the lie-detector test. He liked those tests and things the police use."

As Bill Willis, the drummer, puts it, "Most of my neighborhood friends became hoods or cops. When I started playing in clubs, old pals would drop by to say a raid was coming. I just got up and left my drums behind, while the old pals went after their paddy wagon. Jack was the same: he thought of cops as friends, as the ones who made good, who stayed out of the gangs." Jack made quite an impression on the police at the out-set: on South Ervay, he came to the rescue of two policemen — Officers Blankenship and Carlson — who were being beaten by three toughs.

When Jack was at The Vegas, his bandleader was the shy, proud Negro musician, Joe Johnson. Joe now plays the piano at a supper club before lugging his saxophone over to The Pretty Kitty Kat Klub, out by Love Airport, where his band is playing. This is the kind of club Ruby moved up to from The Silver Spur. It is a small place throbbing with the amplified beat that keeps dancers at their puppet-jerks in the cramped area left them for maneuver. At intervals, a pomaded young man takes the microphone and grunts back at the drum — five feet of silk suit and half a foot of elevator heels, mouthing syllables as un-shaped as the drum thuds. At unmercifully briefer intervals, two bovine girls make bare-limbed efforts at the spasm and lurch called "go-go dancing." It looks like a preternaturally vio-lent form of hiccuping. Patrons shout ill-mannered "requests" at Johnson, who keeps his smile determinedly in place.

There is no talking to Johnson (or to anyone) in this club; but Denny's is just across the highway, and by one-thirty Joe can escape the inexplicable cries for more of the same ("same" being one of this exaggerating crowd's rare accuracies). Joe carries himself with a pained deference; Texas long ago "taught him his place" — or thinks it did. But he is accepted at Denny's, which, from one to five a.m., is taken over by "show-business folk." "They are night people," says Bill Willis (who does not join them but goes home to his wife, an interior deco-rator). "If success has to be bought by working from eight to five, they don't want it. It's a grimy world, but it has the prom-ise of glamour, and they live on that. At Denny's or Brinks — in Jack's day, at Lucas B and B Restaurant, right next to The

Vegas — you meet the table-hoppers, coming to tell you that so-and-so is thinking of taking them into their act, or so-and-so is writing them a song."

The diner is crowded: aging charmers, male and female; sculpted coiffures, male and female; self-consciously "casual" outfits, girls with Tower-of-Pisa hairdos, raspberry-popsicle pants, dragonfly eyelashes. These fine-featured, rough-skinned girls, their eyes framed in velvet, their figures not good enough for the tight pants that proclaim them, are treated to elaborately gallant leers. This is the world Ruby aspired to when he came to Dallas. He was on the outskirts of it for years, got one foot in it with The Vegas, moved into its center with The Carousel.

Denny's is at its rush hour, and we cannot get a seat until Bob Larkin comes in and cons a booth from the diner's "mayder dee." Larkin is now a private investigator for a team of lawyers who have to know what is going on in this world. Bob knows. He moves from table to table, histrionically hugging girls and ducking a short punch at each man's arm. A Baby-Face Nelson type toddles adoringly behind him — sinister cherub with muddy skin. He has an orange sherbet sweater beneath his sport coat, to match his sherbety socks. When he slithers away for a moment, someone asks Larkin, "What's with The Creep?" Bob shrugs, a man explaining the obvious: "He's got money." We heard later that night people think The Creep is a professional burgler.

Bill Howard, an old friend of Ruby's, arrives Thunderbird-wafted to talk about his renovated Stork Club ("I was the first to bring the go-go girl to Dallas"). Howard invests in oil, and once got Jack out of a disastrous venture in Oklahoma wells ("He plunged into things. Jack was always a first-puncher"). Howard ran a club in Miami for a while, where Jack stopped by to visit him while traveling on a gift ticket to Havana. Sam and Joe Campisi, who run the Egyptian Lounge in Dallas but skip over to Las Vegas whenever they can, come into Denny's after their own restaurant closes. Joe Campisi liked to go to The Carousel to watch Ruby in action: "He was the best goddam show in town."

For this crowd, Dallas is partly a tryout town for Las Vegas, the new world's New Haven. Members of the Bottoms Up troupe, when they mince in, stir widening ripples: they have just played Vegas and are haloed with its neon. Anyone with a Vegas connection — especially if the connection carries a perfumy hint of the expensive underworld — is a celebrity. People who were children when Benny Binion and Herbert Noble ran the gambling in Dallas claim to have been their friends. Even now, when a man with a "reputation" — like R. D. Matthews, who claims to have been in on several gangland killings — stops by Denny's, the night people eat their scrambled eggs in awe. Just before the small-time Dallas gambler Lewis McWillie moved on to Vegas, he played the *padrone* to his old pal Jack Ruby, sending him that gift ticket to visit Cuba. In an expansive mood, McWillie once thought he would acquire a gun like Jack's; but when Jack obligingly sent him one C.O.D. to Vegas, McWillie's wife would not let him pick it up; the package came back unpaid for. Disillusioning, no doubt; but the night people are still dazzled by the town Jack's "second club" was named for.

Joe Johnson does not talk except in short answers. Yes, he worked for Jack a long time. Yes, Jack frisked customers. Yes, Jack took that girl to Fort Worth for a lie-detector test. Yes, Jack liked to show his club off to the cops. But what kind of man was he? "He made me part of his family. He never made me feel ill at ease because I'm a Negro. He always remembered to throw a party for me on my birthday." How would you compare the Kitty Kat to The Vegas? "Well, my band is more versatile now. We're getting so we will be able to play *all kinds* of engagements." Always the promise of glamour.

ii

For Ruby, the promise was fulfilled in The Carousel. "This is a fucking high-class place" he would assure doubters as he threw them down the stairs. To get some idea of that club, one must walk the block from Commerce Street to Jackson — from the dust of the Police Gym to the smoke that final-filters cellophane-dyed lights in Barney Weinstein's Theatre Lounge. It is a place still amused or made uneasy by memories of Jack. Every member of the band once worked for him — drummer Bill Willis, "Mr. Texas" of 1952; trumpeter Johnny Anderson, once in Stan Kenton's band; pianist Billy Simmons, who wrote the "Em Eye Crooked-Letter Crooked-Letter Eye" song. In this world men reach the top of their short ladder rapidly and take, without strong feelings of loss, the short fall down. It is a world of reputations won and lost, or never lost because not won; claimed anyway, and enjoyed as if bestowed by crowds enthusiastically.

Crammed backstage in a tiny dressing room, Bill Willis looks like an overgrown adolescent. A mild-mannered, non-smoking, non-drinking gymnast and devourer of books, he wears black suede boots and has long blond hair his hands mother and his eyes seek out in this wall or that wall of the mirrored room. "Hell, man, Dallas is still a shoot-out town. When I was wrestling as 'Mr. Texas,' I had people see me on television and pile in the car to come over and whip me. I knew the signs. 'Oh-oh,' I'd say, 'what can I do for *you?*' There are people who go out on the streets here looking for someone to 'draw' on them. They have the look. You stare it down; or, if that won't work, take them on. A smirk means they are confident you won't even draw. There's nothing to do with the smirk but mess it up, right now."

We asked Bill, an amiable mountain with the reflexes of a trapeze man (which he has been), whether any of these challengers ever "outdrew" him. "Nah. The only man I ever met who could beat me is my friend. People try to egg us into a showdown, but he thinks I could beat him, and I'm afraid he might beat me, so we plead our friendship." You really think you could not beat him? "Well, I'd have to take my lunch." How come? "Because" — he shudders a broad parody of fear — "it would be an all-day job."

And Jack understood this shoot-out code? "He had to *live*, didn't he?" What about the view that he fought in sudden fits, not knowing what he did? "Well, the girl who said that is not very trustworthy. No, Jack knew. He didn't *want* to hesitate. He had to take the play. One time a rough boy started trouble, and the M.C. hit him, then Jack hit him, but he kept getting up. I went over and put a pin on him, and we were at the top of the stairs, this boy kicking at Jack and Jack cussing him, when some well-dressed people started coming up the stairs. Jack instantly said, just as cool as you please, 'Come right up, folks! Step right over them! Just a couple of bums!'"

We told Bill a story given us by one of Jack's waitresses. She had just begun working for him, and was underage. When a drunk got boisterous, Jack took her back into the kitchen. "Stay here," he said, "there's going to be trouble; the police will come." He went out and pounded the fellow, then held him for the arrival of the officers. Does that sound like Jack? "Oh, yeah! One night he had two Vice Squad men at a table by the old hallway (he tore that wall out later and moved the box office forward, but the hall used to lead to the stairs). There was a guy at the bar who wouldn't pay and wouldn't leave. Jack went over to him several times, but got nowhere. So Jack grabbed him, rushed him right into the hall past the Vice men, quietly beat the shit out of him, and threw him downstairs; then picked up the conversation with the Vice men, who never knew anything had happened."

What made him fight so much? "He used to say, 'This is my

home. I don't want people spoiling it.' He wouldn't let anybody get away with anything." But his club became known as a rough place precisely because he fought so much! "Yeah, well, Jack tried to please, but he usually did the wrong thing for reaching his goal. It's like his big words to impress you. They always came out wrong. He'd say things like, 'It's been a lovely precarious evening.' Or he'd tell a girl, 'You make me feel very irascible.'" (Another of Jack's acquaintances told us he would say, "In lieu of the situation, let's do this.")

He was a Mr. Malaprop? "Yeah, he always did the very thing he was attacking. Like the time when Frank Fisher, our trumpeter, was lousing up his part and shouting insults back at the audience. Jack called out to him across the club, 'Frank, you cocksucker, you got no *class!*'" (One of Ruby's employees told the F.B.I. that Jack beat him up because he had ordered the employees not to fight and this fellow got in a brawl anyway.)

Didn't Ruby's antics drive customers away? "No! They came to see *him*. The strippers would be working away up front and people would turn around to watch Jack. Man, we had a *club*. We had a *show*." Was it enjoyable for the employees then? "Sure, we all liked Jack. There was a circle of us, the steady ones. Tammi, and Andrew, and Alice the washroom attendant, and a couple of the waitresses: Diana the dingbat, and Alice, and Nisi, and Bonnie. Jack was hard on some, like Jada; but they asked for it. They were tough customers."

"Bill!" The M.C., a man named Benny, sticks his face in, a sad-eyed greenish face, wearing the greenish appendage that, out under lights, is only mildly unconvincing as a cigar — at any rate, more convincing than the slab of black moss he covers his baldness with. "Time to go." The intermission is over, and Bill must climb to his balcony seat out in front of the piano, behind his drums.

The Theatre Lounge is owned by Barney, one of the Weinstein brothers who monopolized the downtown strip business until Ruby came along. The Weinsteins like to pretend that

Ruby was not a competitor; but, looking around Barney's club (which is bigger than Abe's), one finds many veterans of The Carousel: all of the band; this week's star stripper; one of the best champagne girls; many of the "professionals" who drop in. The Theatre Lounge has a U-shaped balcony which is, technically, a "private club" — making Barney's the only strip joint that can serve mixed drinks. The lights are low; it makes the motions of the champagne girls less obvious. Up on the left there is an iridescent murk of bottles and a robin-breasted bartender. To the right, the glitter of metal on his drums marks the spot where Bill Willis is nested in darkness. On the stage, the first of the evening's four strippers is flouncing through her garmented overture ("Number four girl goes first"). There is a fringe of oglers around the runway, but most of the tables are empty. Back from the stage, below the overhang of balcony, things brighten near the cashier's lighted cranny (*her* motions are not to be obscure). An all-American college-boy type, the bouncer, takes us around through the kitchen into Barney's office.

Barney does not think much of Ruby's business practices. "He was unethical. He used to go and give out Carousel passes to people lined up in front of Abe's club. Besides, he raffled off turkeys, or dishes, or anything to bring in the customers." (This, in some way Barney takes to be obvious, sullied the purity of Strip.) "Jack had seven fights a week. I've had three fights in thirty years." Not that the business is without its risks. Abe Weinstein told us of the time when some hoodlum type was dating a young stripper, back in the Thirties. It was the girl's first job, her mother had asked Abe to look after her, and he told her to break it off. "So this character came in one afternoon while I was in the office alone. 'Abe,' he says, 'I'm going to kill you.' 'Well,' I said, 'I understand how you feel. But killing me won't do any good. I could see it a lot better if you just beat the shit out of me.' That got him, so he sat down, and we talked a while. But that cured me. I never messed in the lives of my performers after that. They're not worth it. Do you know a moral, Christian, God-fearing girl who'll stand up there and take her clothes off?" Did Jack get involved in the girls' lives? "He was all mixed up with them. He had to be in on everything."

Barney agrees with his brother. "Jack had to *be* there, even when he wasn't wanted. I put on a benefit for one of our performers who died, and he came offering to sell ten tickets. But he never let well enough alone. He met people as they came in that night and tried to get them to buy *more* tickets. I said, 'Jack, leave them alone. They already bought their tickets.' So then he wanted to sell *special* tickets for the best seats; he wanted to be my usher; he wanted to help, and he only got in the way. Once he dropped by when my houseman had not come in. He said, 'Don't worry, I'll stay and take care of any trouble.' I told him, 'I don't *want* you to, Jack.' You know, he doesn't stop trouble, he starts it. But he stayed anyway. He had a wonderful heart. When he hardly knew me, he read about my mother's funeral in the newspaper and came to it. He just had to get into everything, including the excitement of that weekend Kennedy died."

Do you think that was his attitude? "Sure, that's where the limelight was. He always wanted class. That's why he would hang around here. He said, 'Someday I'm going to buy a Cadillac and a Jaguar in the same week, like Barney.' That was his idea of class. But these are nothing to me. My idea of money is investing in the market; and my idea of a good time is going to Las Vegas. Jack never used to go there."

Barney is tolerant of Jack, counting his foibles mere clumsy attempts to be Barney. It is a tolerance shared by others. Milton Joseph for instance, a jewelry store on the hoof, put it this way: "He wanted to be able to do this" (out comes a big roll, hundreds arranged around the outside as big strawberries are scattered on top in the supermarket). "He had one?" (Out with his gun.) "I have five." (We fear he will turn out pocket after lethal pocket to display this arsenal.) "He always wanted to be at the openings and closings of shows. But I was at more. He wanted to know the visiting movie stars. Face it, Jack was jealous of me. Now, you just met me, right?" Right. "If you were to see me again, would you remember me?" Undoubtedly. "Why?" It's hard to say. "The characteristics, perhaps?" (He shoots his cuffs with wide-flung hands as if stabbed from behind, then folds his arms with giant watch face flashing at us — a Victorian clock stand, china "Artful Dodger" from a line portraying Dickens' characters.) "The characteristics? The cigar? The star sapphire?" Yes, probably that. Did Jack shoot Oswald to be in the limelight? "Sure, I know. As soon as I heard Oswald was dead, I went down to help Tom Howard, Jack's lawyer. I became Tom's bailiff." His what? "I mean, if you came into his office, I would ask your names. 'Mr. X and Mr. Y? Writers? Fine, step in this room.' And then I would guard the door." Would what? "Guard the door. There was no telling what was going to happen. So when Jack's sister Eva came with the newsmen Tony Zoppi and Hugh Aynesworth, I showed them straight into Tom's office, and stood guard. But Eva was just like Jack — she said I would have to leave." You were guarding the door from the *inside*? "Yes." What did you do when she told you to leave? "I guarded it from the outside." Would you say you and Jack were much like each other? "A little. So they tell me. But Jack had no class." Mr Joseph ponders a mystery: "Jack got mad at people who told him he looked like me." (Henry Klepak, a lawyer who handles much of the Dallas club business, told us he was convinced, watching television that Sunday morning, he had seen Milt Joseph shoot Oswald.)

Barney takes us out of his office, which contains exotica like nude jigsaw puzzles, back into the kitchen. The atmosphere is homey; Barney's wife is giving out her cookies; no one drinks anything but coffee. Even the family pet is here, a forty-year-old parrot named Panama — one "exotic" whose wardrobe never dims. Pampered and taught bad words by the envious

girls, he shifts his shot-silk eyes complacently and ruffles velvet
feathers. He is the Weinstein bird. "It is time for Nikki." Barney takes us out to see his star, Nikki Joye, who is now working
second billing. She cannot, for a while, turn fast on her athletic
knees; a surgeon has just mined them for the cartilage ground
loose when she works hard. She remains Barney's favorite,
though she is disillusioningly thick below the waist. She has
been with him twelve years, from the time she lied about her
age at fifteen and bared the breasts that have been her visible
means of support ever since. She twirls warily tonight, relying
more on winks, pouts, serpenting tongue, mimed kisses than on
drumbeat spasms. Makeup and shifting light do not blot out
the incisions under each kneecap. Out at the end of the runway
she whispers "Ouch" to her fond employer, who runs his thumb
reflectively across a house matchbook (nudes on the cover,
with little cardboard bosses for the breasts).

Above, in his aerie, Bill Willis concocts hysteria on his drums.
"That's when I write my plays," he told us. What plays? "Oh,
there is my *Bug in a Sycamore Tree.* A man is whittling on his
porch one morning when something black splotches his hand.
'Son,' he says, 'what are we breeding in the bug way these
days?' 'Wa-al,' says the boy, looking up, 'in that tree I see a
ladybug, a cicada, and a Volkswagen.' The VW is driven by a
candidate for office who wanted a divorce. He figured on holding out till after election, but his wife ran off the day before. He
thought what-the-hell and took off with his girl. But a strong
wind drove them off the road, off a cliff, and into the tree. The
candidate, you see, is now parked illegally close to a voting
booth. But they cannot take him away without chopping down
the tree, and the tree is the last sycamore in Sycamore Junction." He winks at us, "How's that for a dramatic dilemma?" He
was known for pulling Jack's leg, too. When Jack said he would
match whatever his employees gave to charity at Christmas-
time, Bill (the one chosen to hold the money because he does
not drink) came to him and said, "Here it is, Jack — four hun-

dred dollars." Jack had his four hundred counted out before Bill told him they had only scraped up fifty.

Nikki has spun herself to a controlled climax, arching her upper torso out while, deftly, she veils her stomach bulge — a true pro can fake it. It is time for the penultimate thrill — the M.C.'s Al Jolson routine (it had to come, sooner or later; better sooner, so it comes later). Bill Willis leads the "spontaneous" applause when the lights go out and Benny moves around with tie, gloves and shoes lit up, a walking jukebox, Al Wurlitzer. Benny dampens the effect, of course, by his preliminary bustlings — turning on the amplifier, moving out the glow spot, starting the Jolson tape. It is like watching Houdini put the rabbit in his hat beforehand. Benny never gets far beyond the obviousness of his wig.

Number one girl goes last: tonight, Tammi True, Barney's present star and Jack's alumna. She is short and energetic, throwing herself orgasmically back and back against the drive of Bill Willis' drum. Nikki's action was all above the waist, Tammi's is mainly below: she has what Jack called a "loose ass," which her act is designed to mix and stir with maximum agitation. One of Jack's waitresses, in a catty moment, accused her of having a *creased* ass. The next day Tammi came in with net stockings sewed to her G-string (which is waist-high in back). She pulls that G-string far out in front and shrieks surrenderingly (a trick brought to Dallas by Jack's last star, the meteoric Jada).

Back into the dressing room with a perspiring Bill, followed in a moment by a blonde perspiring Tammi. She is smaller than she looked oscillating under lights. She blinks dark half-stars of eyelash down (chiming silently with the pasties that star her breasts), sets her tired doll's face (rosily mummified in makeup), and says: "I won't say anything against that man." Why not? "I understood him. I'm like him." How so? "I have a quick temper too. I don't normally do what Jack did; but when the time comes — did you hear what I did to Alice?" No. "Well,

I caught her in the john and beat her into the trash barrel. I told her that was where she belonged." We hear Jack fired you that night. "Yes. I *told* you I understand him."

Bill levers his shoulders out of the room. Tammi, glancing after him, says in her gravelly warble, "A good boy, Bill. But he takes liberties." The Victorian locution sits oddly with this girl's truck-driverisms — until she makes it clear that Bill dreamily makes her throw, in mid-grind, an unprepared bump or two: "He's writing plays again." When we ask her about the story of Bill holding a man down at the top of the stairs while Jack welcomed customers and told them to ignore the bums, Tammi remembers it with great concern for the dancer left onstage when Bill abandoned the drums: the poor thing had to work her pelvis without acoustic punctuation.

What kind of man was Jack? "A good man." Why? "Well, he found out I was living with my children in an apartment house full of gay boys. It was $25 a week, all I could afford. He was shocked. He said, 'You shouldn't be living next to queers.' He paid the deposit on my apartment in the house where he lived." Did he have any designs on you? "No." Why not? Wasn't he interested in girls? "He laid some, and he liked the others." And he liked you? "Yes. Of course, we had our clashes." For instance? "Well, he never let an M.C. tell racial or religious jokes — not about any race. One time he thought I was off base. In December, I stitched 'Merry' across the net on one butt, and 'Xmas' on the other. He came backstage and said, 'I don't think it's good for you to have Christ's name on your ass.' I told him, 'For Christ's sake, Jack, it only says X-mas. Do you want me to put Yom on one butt and Kippur on the other?' That finished him. He just mumbled something about thinking it over."

Tammi had never been hit by Ruby, nor seen a woman hit by him. "Of course, he used to talk big. He was always going to beat our ass, but nothing ever came of it." She thinks him capable of hitting a woman. "*They* are ready to hit — I was — why shouldn't he be?" The girls Tammi works with are a tough crew; at the first hint of trouble, they have one shoe off, their weapon. After Tammi beat up her good friend Alice, they went on being good friends — like Jack and "Dub" Dickerson.

Did he ever talk to you about politics? "No. But he liked that picture of Caroline in high heels. And he always turned the TV on in the back of the club when the President spoke — an Inaugural Address or State of the Union Message. The press asked me whether Jack was a queer. I said no, and they took that as if I had been *proving* he wasn't in bed. It wasn't true, but I don't care what they say about me so long as they don't lie about Jack so much."

Time for the mummy-doll to dress again (so she can undress) and put on her stage pout. Shortly after she leaves, Bill returns. Tammi is loyal to Jack, isn't she? "She's a good girl. She's steady and hardworking, and keeps a good home for her grandmother and children. At least she's not a lesbian." Are most of the strippers? "Well, many. You should see them fight over the green girls who come in." Why is this? "Oh, it's narcissism, I guess. They're making love to *themselves* out there. The only bodies they're interested in are women's." (In the other Weinstein club, Buddy Raymon, an emaciated comedian turned bartender, gave us *his* interpretation: "When they have been pawed so many times by so many guys, they begin to think there *must* be something better." One of the strippers told us she amuses herself by dreaming up tortures; she is the one who supplements her income with labors to titillate an impotent old man.)

What did Jack think of these girls? "He worried about them. He said he wanted no prostitutes working for him. But he didn't know what went on. He was generous when they got in trouble, bailing them out, loaning them money to get home or come back to work. A girl named Bonnie called from New Orleans and asked for money to get out of a hot-check charge and back to Dallas. He said, 'Who the hell is Bonnie?' We told him, and he sent her the money; but he didn't remember who she was."

Did he ever talk about politics? "Nah, he wasn't really interested. He was patriotic and everything, but he would have been that way about any President. What impressed him about the Kennedys was that they were in authority *and* they had glamour. Just like movie stars, he'd say. One day he claimed he saw an actress out at Love Airport — I think it was Rhonda Fleming or Arlene Dahl — and went right over to join her for lunch. He came home happy as a lark. Another time, I had gone to see the American Ballet Theatre with my wife, and we showed him the program; in it Jackie Kennedy was posing with members of the troupe. He said, 'Isn't that wonderful? Her as famous as a star, and going to see something cultural like that!' He asked me later, 'Do you think she *really* cares about ballet?' 'Sure, Jack,' I said. He seemed relieved: 'Isn't that wonderful?' He would come up and ask me things like, 'Is Leonard Bernstein really that good a musician?' I told him he was, and he was happy. He didn't like phonies, and he didn't trust himself in sizing up the cultural ones. He knew I read a lot, and he used to ask me about them — or ask me what some big word meant.

"The night before Kennedy's assassination, he was up on the stage to demonstrate a twistboard he was promoting. 'Even President Kennedy tells us to get more exercise,' he said. A heckler shouted, 'That bum!' 'Don't ever talk that way about the President,' Jack shot back. The next day, when he called me all broken up by the assassination, he said, 'Remember that man making fun of President Kennedy in the club last night?' "

What else did he say? "Well, he was crying and carrying on: 'What do you think of a character like that killing the President?' I was trying to calm him down. I said, 'Jack, he's not normal; no normal man kills the President on his lunch hour and takes the bus home.' But he just kept saying, 'He killed our President.' "

"Pappy" Dolsen pokes his head into the little box where we are cramped perspiringly. He eases in, vested, suit-coated, overcoated, and stays for some time without visible discomfort. He is about seventy, a night animal, mothbally with age and wearied by a thousand petty violences; but under the *livor* of his skin is the bone-blueprint of a handsome man. In the Thirties he ran glamorous, dangerous places, was like a club-owner from some Bogart film — the gentleman tough, on equally good terms with the hoods and the cops and the leading citizens. But after giving up his partnership with Benny Binion (at Pappy's 66) and Abe Weinstein (at the Colony Club), Pappy lost his ambitious clubs out in the suburbs to the creeping local "dry" laws of Texas. Now he is a theatrical agent, booking girls in and out of the strip joints — not really needed around the two Weinstein clubs, but every night making the circuit of those cheap clubs that spread like brushfire along the edge of Dallas — places where the girls strip on the floor, not onstage; where the lights can work little of their magic; where they have little enough to work on in the first place. Pappy goes in, flirts with the studiously coy beginners, creakingly clark-gables them, takes the mike from young M.C.'s. Backstage now at the Theatre Lounge, he tells us how he keeps toughs off with his fists — or with *this* (with many fumblings and snags, he pulls an ugly toy out, a tear-gas gun). Could you beat Jack? "Hell, no. He hit you quick, and never backed up. Even if it wasn't his fight, he would step in, in a second. I remember once I was outside the Baker Hotel and there was some kind of demonstration over the Hungarian revolution. One guy was going to poke me for nothing, but Jack came along just then and in no time flattened this guy and someone else who came up to help him."

You were friends then? "Hell, no. He was always mad at me for not getting him bigger stars. He said I was favoring the Weinsteins, and he tried to get A.G.V.A [the strippers' union] after me. But I got him his best star, Jada; and he cut me out of my commission on her."

Did that end your dealings with him? "Until the assassination [Jada left him a couple of days before it]. On the day before he killed Oswald, he called me and said, 'I did you wrong, Pappy; but I'll make it up to you. I'm going places in show business, and when I do, you're going with me. I'll call you back tonight.'" That was Saturday? "Yes." Did he call you back? "No." Have you told anyone about this? "Only Barney, on the day after Jack killed Oswald." (Barney confirmed this, but Pappy's memory, we were told, tends to get mixed with his imagination.)

Time for the third show out front. Bill suggests we talk to Diana. Diana Hunter is a champagne girl who worked for Jack five years. She is lustrous-eyed, teen-age-awkward, disheartingly experienced, with a little-girl voice and fingernails cruelly gnawed; mother of four children, survivor of eight miscarriages, and just out of the hospital from a suicide attempt. "I did the pill bit — seventeen sleeping pills, a pint of whiskey, and twenty kidney pills. My husband left me. I was in Parkland Hospital when they brought Jack in with his cancer. Eva came to see me, crying and hysterical."

Diana is a good champagne girl. No one can help pitying her, doing things for her, helping her in immediate terms (thereby, over the long run, sinking her deeper in voracious spiritual acids). Jack used to say, "Alice, what can I do with Diana when she turns those spaniel eyes on me?" She knows her power, laughs at it and uses it even as she tells us of it. She has a kind of silly innocence that makes her always the seduced one, even for the thousandth time.

The economics of the champagne girl is vital to running a club in Dallas, where the law keeps strip joints like Jack's from serving liquor. The house can supply "setups" — expensive ice-and-mix accommodation for those who bring their own bottles in a bag. (If you arrive without the canonical paper bag, you are given one at the door.) But setups and beer will not give the clubs a working margin of profit; that must come from the second part of the "beer and wine" permit — from champagne. The clubs pay $1.98 a bottle for it, turban the label in the customary towel (never more welcome than here), and sell it for

$18.50. The $1.50 change from a twenty usually goes to the waitress as her tip. The champagne girl gets $2.50 for every bottle she persuades "her fellow" to buy. It is her job to get rid of the bottles fast and move on to a second or third with this fellow, or to a second or third fellow. The indispensable instrument for this process is the "spit glass," a frosted glass of "ice water" (i.e., ice) frequently changed. The girl's mouth is simply a ladle for moving the cheap commodity from a thin-stemmed glass to a tall frosted one.

"I was so dumb," Diana tells us, "when I began. I was really *drinking* the stuff. I thought it dishonest not to. Jack had to take me aside and tell me: 'Diana, you're not going to make any money that way. All you'll do is ruin your kidneys. I like you, and I'd like for you to make me some money. So remember: selling champagne is a game, just like chess. The man wants to go to bed with you, and if he does, he wins. You want to get his money, and if you do, and don't give him anything in return, you win.' I've worked in a lot of places since, and that's the best advice I was ever given."

When did you go to work for Jack? "When I was eighteen. I had tried out in Barney's Amateur Night for strippers, but I couldn't dance, so I answered Jack's ad for a waitress. But I was so stupid, like a scared rabbit, I wasn't making any money. Then one day I had to bring my oldest girl into Dallas to the eye doctor." How many children did you have? "Three." You were eighteen? "Yes. I was married at fourteen. I told you I was stupid. Anyway, I knew Jack had Cokes and some food in the kitchen of the club, and I had no money to buy lunch for Lila, so I took her up there in the afternoon. Jack loved children. Children and dogs. He gave her grape soda and pie — Lila remembers that pie to this day. She wrote him a letter to thank him for it. Finally, he said to her, 'Go to the kitchen, honey, and play with the dogs,' and he took me over to the bar. 'Diana, we've got to do something about that girl. Her eyes need to be fixed.' 'Why do you think I'm working here, Jack?'

'How much are you making a night?' 'Seven to ten dollars.' 'You'll never make it. Now, I saw you at Barney's, and you'll never be a dancer; and even if you could, I don't need a dancer. But if you go out on the strip circuit you can make $150 a week. I'll get you some lessons, and a wardrobe, and an agent. Then you'll be able to pay me back.' 'For what?' 'How much will your kid's operation cost?' 'Three thousand dollars.' 'I haven't got that; but here's fifteen hundred.' He wrote me a check, then acted as if he were angry: 'Now get the hell out of here and take care of that kid!' So I went out and made enough to pay Jack back." No interest? "No." No favors? "No."

"When I made enough to get the operation out of the way, I could quit dancing; so I came back to Jack as a waitress. I knew how to make them buy me champagne now. I learned a lot on that trip — what I'm trying to *un*learn now. I became a good champagne girl — along with Alice, the best — and I brought a lot of money in for Jack. But he never could have known that when he loaned me the money."

Did you get along with him? "Oh, we fought. He blew up at everyone. He fired me at least three hundred times — seven times in one night. But it didn't mean anything. Once a new girl named Bonnie, dumb as I had been, was following Jack's rules on who got what table. The rest of us ignored them, we had worked out our own system. But she tried to take a table away from me, a champagne party of twelve. So I slugged her. Jack stepped in and stopped us, and then fired me." Why you? "Because she was the new girl, the dumb girl. He always took the side of the underdog. Anyway, I was pregnant; Jack didn't know it, but Alice told the other girls, and they cut Bonnie out of everything. At last she asked them, 'What have I *done?*' and they told her about my three kids, and my going to college in the daytime, and not eating when tuition came around, and being pregnant and all. So she went to Jack and asked him to give me my job back. 'Welcome to the club,' Jack said; 'she got to you, too, eh?' Then he told Andrew to call me; he would never make up after a fight himself.

"When I got back, I was hemorrhaging. I've had eight miscarriages. I needed to go to the hospital, but I didn't have any money. Andrew heard about it and he took a collection for me at the bar. At the end of the night he gave me $150 for the hospital. But at home that night I lost the child — a boy, my first one; I had to cut the umbilical cord myself with a razor. Then I collapsed back into bed, but the afterbirth hadn't come out, and at five in the morning I woke up gushing blood all over the place. I lost four pints by the time they got me to the hospital. I'm Rh-negative, and they needed two more pints than they had; so they called the place where I worked and Jack came right over. It was such an emergency they took both pints from him. He gave blood to lots of people. He went out and never visited me. When I tried to thank him at the club, he just swore at me." How was that? "He wouldn't let us sit down unless we were drinking champagne, but my first night back I was still weak, so before the customers came in I was sitting there and I heard Jack coming up — you could always hear his dogs thumping up the stairs ahead of him. We would all jump up then and pretend to be busy, but this night I figured what-the-hell, and he stormed right over to me: 'Diana, if you're so tired you can't stand up, then get the hell out of here, you're fired.'" Did you go? "Sure, it was his way of saying I wasn't well enough to work yet. He had a soggy heart, but he covered it up with bluster."

Did he ever hit you? "No. I never saw him hit any girl." He hit Winnie, the girl who operated The Sovereign Club before he took it over from Joe Slatin. "Well, I have my doubts about that. Anyway, she was not one of his girls. He was proud of his girls. We fooled him. He liked the police to come up, to see what a clean club he ran. But I sure got him mad at times." For instance? "Once he was stuck on a Saturday night with only two dancers. He said, 'Diana, I know you're not much as a dancer. You're the only stripper I ever met who needs padded pasties. But I'm really stuck tonight. Can you go on?' I told him I only had my Diana the Huntress act — I did a Greek ballet, then a hunting scene, then a victory dance with one breast bare; I wrote the script myself, that's how I got my name. He said it would have to do, and I went home to get my bow and arrow. After I did the first show that night, Jack came back and said he loved it. He thought it was an act with class. Face it: falling on the floor and rolling around and sticking your tongue out is simply not class! It might be sex, but it's not class. Anyway the bandleader came to me, very apologetic, and said, 'When you shoot your arrow down the entryway, you're scaring Bill Willis to death. He sits right by that door.' Funny, isn't it? The bigger they are, the more scared they are. But I said I would aim my bow somewhere else. In the second show, I shot it at the back of the stage, and it hit a big gold plaque with a horse on it. Remember, it was Saturday night, our big night, a full house, some standing at the bar; but when Jack saw that, he let out a scream and came shouting across the floor, onto the stage, up to the horse; he pulled out the arrow — I'm dancing all the time — and raged at me: 'Of all the *goddam* dancers in the *goddam* world I have to get a *goddam* huntress!'

" 'Alice' could tell you more stories, but I don't think she will talk to you. Her family didn't know where she worked, and she went away as soon as Jack killed Oswald so no one would talk to her. I don't think anybody ever did. Still, I'll try to get her for you." After much cloak-and-dagger negotiating — phone calls (for which others did the dialing), meetings on neutral ground, refusals, and a final knock on the door at two in the morning — Diana got her to talk to us: no name was to be used but "Alice."

Alice, it turned out, is a shrewd, cool woman who did the real managing of Jack's waitresses while he blustered. Just as there are romantic and realistic *managers* (Jack and the Weinsteins), so are there romantic and realistic *waitresses* (Diana and Alice). A conversation with both girls is tugged continually two ways.

Alice: "Jack was a fanatic about 'my girls.' Now let me tell you: *we* had a *bunch.* We had some who did and some who didn't; we had some who went for girls and some who went for money; we had all kinds. We had some who went for Jack, and if they did they lasted no more than a week. He made us miserable for that week! But we managed to run them all off, because once he got it, that's all he wanted, and they went out the door. All you had to do was hold out against him to stay with him. If you put out with him, you didn't get anywhere. We'd just sit back and smile, and say, 'Well, three more days and two more pieces and we're rid of her.' "

Diana: "Jack expected us to be virgins."

Alice: "Well, not virgins but not hustling out of his club, either. He thought if they would sleep with him, they weren't good enough to work in his place. The time that man took us all to the Ports O'Call for dinner, we got to work drunker 'n skunks, and all dressed up, but he couldn't get it out of us where we'd been."

Diana: "He only wanted us to go to church picnics."

Alice: "That was the night he fired Tammi for hitting me."

Did he ever set you up with men? Diana: "Never!" Alice: "Well, it was like his putting the make on you himself. He would introduce you to men as if daring you; but I said no, I would get my own men, and I think he was glad I did."

Diana: "He never set me up at all." Alice: "Well, he would introduce you if he wanted to impress people; but he wasn't promising one side or getting paid by the other, he was just getting people together." (Others told us that if a male patron in one party and a female in another were "odd men out," he would try to move them to the same table; he had to be arranging things, matchmaking, meddling.)

Did Jack, wanting class so badly, realize he could never have it as a strip-joint owner? Alice: "No. He thought he ran a very beautiful place." Diana: "He thought that *horse* was beautiful!" Alice: "He couldn't understand it when some people turned

down ads for his place. He wanted it to be perfect. He even
had his girls followed to make sure they weren't making arrangements to meet the patrons outside."

Was this because he was afraid of the Vice Squad? Diana:
"No, it was the class bit." Alice: "He checked us beyond the
point of protecting his license." Then why did he introduce
girls to policemen who were interested in them? Diana: "He
didn't." Alice: "He did too. But he never thought of that as
hustling. Not if *he* did it. That was just getting 'my friends'
together." Did he do many favors for the police? Alice: "Sure,
he gave them free drinks, even after hours. He couldn't do
enough for them — including some of the ones who belittled
him after his arrest. He thought cops gave the club class!"

Was it a good club? Alice: "Everyone was going up there at
the end, even those from other clubs when they got off. Jack
was so determined to come up from the bottom and beat his
competition." The Weinsteins? "Yes." Was he doing it? Alice:
"He was on the verge, at the end." Diana: "Oh, we were beating hell out of the other clubs!" But they say Jack was in financial trouble. Alice: "I guess he was personally, but we were
packing them in. We sold an awful lot of champagne. I used to
make $500 some weeks. It was a bad night for us to make under
$60." Diana: "Jack just liked to see that room fill up. And we
had a team! Jack would fire one of us, and we'd all quit. We
moved the bus-station girls right on back to the station." How
would you do that? Alice: "Get them to sleep with him. If one
refused, we'd kick in and *pay* her to. We paid them $50 or $100,
and that finished them." Diana, did you donate to these funds?
"Of course! That was the only way to keep things stable around
the club. We all knew how to please Jack and get our way."
Alice: "Sure, buy him a piece. Then, the first time she did something wrong in her work, he'd say, 'Get your ass out of here!
We want high-class girls.' "

Weren't there any girls who refused to sleep with him and
refused to go along with you? Alice: "One. But I fixed her. I

asked a friend on the Vice Squad to tell Jack she was a prostitute. Jack had told me I would go before this girl did: she was a nice girl. But pretty soon he came up and said, 'Alice, did you know that girl was hooking?' 'No!' 'Yep, she was. I had to let her go.' "

What's this about his drifters? Diana: "Oh, he'd help anyone who came along and needed food or a place to stay. He'd put them up on the cot in the club." Alice: "He would cuss them out for not working, but he fed them all the same. And if he read about anyone in trouble, he used to send things to the victims."

We hear you could egg him on. Alice: "Oh, I was *good* at that. One man had been ugly to the girls, so I grabbed his money out of his hand. He said he was going to kill me, but I got to Jack first and said this fellow was being nasty. If they asked for trouble, we would make them buy us champagne or get Jack after them. He would stick up for his girls." Diana: "We called it planting the seed. Just suggest something to him, and he jumps to conclusions. He was so suspicious. He was always afraid someone in the next group was talking about him."

Alice: "One time he came in and those dogs had messed all over the club. It was near opening time, and I said, 'Jack, you better clean up after your dogs. I'm not going to.' 'Okay.' Then Buddy, the young M.C., said he'd help; 'But you take the soft ones, Jack. I'll help you with your dog shit, but only the hard ones.' Jack reared up and roared at him, 'Don't you ever talk like that around these ladies. Don't you *ever* say that!' 'My God, Jack, what did I do? I just said dog shit. What am I *supposed* to say?' 'Use a little finesse! Say. . . .' He snapped his fingers in the air, reaching for a word. 'Alice, tell him what that word is I'm thinking of . . . oh yes, I've got it. *Crap.* From now on you say dog *crap.*' "

Did you know Jada? Alice: "Sure. She tried to horn in on our fellows, and sell champagne, and take our men. One night she sat down where I had been and collected the tabs for my sales. I told Jack, but he only said, 'The waitress gave her the tabs. That's your fault.' So I was plotting against her, but Jack got rid of her before I had to." How much money was involved with these tabs? "Oh, not much." Two-fifty? "No, more than that. But not much." It was the principle of the thing? Both together: "That's right!"

What happened to Jada? "Well, she would get down on that tiger skin of hers and she'd . . . well, she'd lay it." That's right! What's that word? Oh yes — say *lay!* "Yeah, wouldn't Jack love my finesse? Anyway, she would lay the rug, then climb up against her pole and lay it, and then 'flash' — pull her G-string way out; till Jack finally cut the lights out on her. She yelled *so much* at him that night!" Right from the stage? "Right there. And he yelled back. And pretty soon he'd cut the lights on again to see where she was." What were they yelling? "Oh, motherfuckers and what have you. He fired her, and she took him down to Judge Richburg on a peace bond."

Diana was fired three hundred times. Alice, how many times were you? "Not many. I could handle Jack. He could throw the rages; but I threw them just as good. Once he really blew up at me and told me to clear out forever. I went out and sat on those damn stairs, crying. After a while, he started down them. I expected him to throw me out, but he just went on by. In a little while, he came back up with a pizza and gave it to me. 'I thought you might be hungry.' It was his way of apologizing."

We understand he used to take coffee to the boys in the parking lot and sandwiches to the men at the dry cleaners where he got his shoes shined. Alice: "Yes, he always wanted to feed people. He would never let anyone else pick up the check when we went for coffee. Once, though, George Senator was cooking hamburgers in the back of the club and he put one on for me. Jack came into the kitchen, bitchin' as usual. I loved him dearly, but face it, if he ever came into the club and he wasn't bitchin', we would have rushed him to the hospital. So he saw the hamburgers, and he said, 'What the hell, George, are we running a restaurant?' 'No, but I put one on for Alice.' 'Well, take it off.' Then he saw me standing there. He mumbled to George to go ahead and cook it, but I told him where he could put his hamburger and went out into the club. He followed me and said would I please eat that damn hamburger, and when I said no, he shouted toward the kitchen, 'George, put on hamburgers for everyone in the house!' Poor George had to cook hamburgers all night.

"Once he threw a party for us after the show. George cooked up the big turkey we couldn't raffle off — no one who won it wanted to lug it away. Jack had rented a hotel suite for the night, and here comes George down the corridor with the hot turkey. But Jack stopped him, because Milt Joseph had crashed the party, as usual. 'I'll be damned if I'm going to feed that character,' he said. So we all had to wait till Milt left before we ate our cold turkey. He couldn't stand Joseph, who came from his old neighborhood in Chicago."

It is after one in the morning. Benny has become fluorescent for the last *Mammy* of the evening; now Tammi is doing her one-side twitch (the "Xmas" side, not the "Merry" one) to Bill's sustained drum roll. We get our coats from the all-American boy.

Out on the streets of Dallas, it is good to breathe air instead of champagne or smoke. Diana, back inside, is emptying her life into a spit glass; Benny is becoming the human equivalent of his own green cigar; Nikki and Tammi try to forget the day when a stomach becomes un-veil-able, a "loose ass" un-net-able; and Bill Willis "takes liberties" up in his drummer's perch — meditative bug in a dismal sycamore.

...

iii

Out on the streets of Dallas, one encounters a city of promoters. The main industry is banking, and the main bank has a fourteen-story neon sign. It is a town full of imaginative middlemen scrambling for the big one. Jack Ruby was, to the bigtime promoters, a "foreigner." But he was not out of place on the Dallas streets. He always had a new scheme brewing — pizza ovens, British blades, twistboards, a new entertainer, a new club, a new advertising campaign. "He was always a-churnin'" we heard from many as their impression of Jack Ruby nodding and handshaking his way down the street. Bill Willis put it this way: "What did I think of him? Well, before you could summarize Jack, he was out of sight."

"He never stuck with any of these projects," Barney told us. "The pizza oven he was pushing went over well. I've got one here. But he had moved on to something else by the time it became established." Ruby cruised the streets expectantly; if one angle does not work, and work fast, try another. Rebuffed here, go there, keep moving. The big deal is somewhere out there if one only gets in its way. Meanwhile, make contacts. "Whenever I drew up a contract for him," said Henry Klepak, the lawyer who managed his club purchases, "he wanted to know what my *connections* were. He thought law was a matter of who you knew. I tried to tell him I don't draw up contracts to please connections, but he thought I was just being modest."

Most of his bustling was done to promote his clubs, especially The Carousel. "You can't write about Jack's life outside the club," Andrew Armstrong said. "There *wasn't* any. Even when he was outside, he was at the newspapers or the radio

stations trying to get more publicity; he was handing out passes
to the club, or thinking of some new scheme to push it."

Andrew is a slim sober Negro, articulate, immaculate; Jack's
bartender, second-in-command at The Carousel. "He wanted
me to be the manager when it came to firing someone — not
when it came to making decisions." Didn't he ask your advice?
"Oh, yes, he would stand at the bar sketching ads for the next
day's paper, and he asked my ideas then. He put a lot of time
into those ads, he thought he was pretty good at them. Taking
them in was a big thing for him." (Bill Willis says that when
the show was finished Thursday night — actually Friday morning, toward the dawn of Kennedy's visit — he asked Jack if he
planned to see the parade. The answer was: "Maybe. I don't
know. I have to get some ads in.")

"He was proud," Andrew continued, "of his ad for Tammi.
Barney had billed some girl as 'The Teacher Turned Stripper,'
and Tammi was suing a man at the time, so Jack wrote an ad
for her as 'The Stripper Turned Teacher' — teaching this guy
not to break the law. When a new act was going on, he would
get too nervous to watch it. He went off in the back and asked
me, later, how it went. And, as I say, he tried to have me do the
firing. 'What do you think of so-and-so?' he'd say. 'I think she's
all right.' 'Well, I don't. Cut her loose.' '*You* cut her loose; you're
the one that doesn't like her.'" Why did he want *you* to fire
them? "He didn't have the heart to take a person's job away.
Half these people, if I had fired them, he would have taken them
back." (There was a drunken pianist he could not get along
with but could not fire; the band told Jack his toes had been
frozen and amputated in a Korean prison camp. Jack shook his
head and said, "Just like the Jews in the concentration camps."
The tipsy musician was untouchable after that.) "Then, when
Jack had fired someone, he would get to thinking about it and
want them to come back, but he would never call them. He
made me do it." We hear he used to make up arguments with
food. "Well, he was always bringing food to people. He'd come

up here every other day with sandwiches for me. I told him, 'Jack, I don't want these.' I never ate a one of them. But he kept on bringing them to me anyway."

Jack went out with the night people after his club closed around two in the morning. He often ended his day, near dawn, at the *Times Herald* office, reworking his next day's ad. After such a night, Jack rose late; but he would get to the club around noon to meet Andrew and check the last night's receipts. "He was never satisfied. If we had a thousand-dollar night, he would still say, 'What can we do to bring more people in?' If he couldn't get to the club, he would give me a call to see how things were. I would say, 'Okay here; where are you?' Sometimes he'd be way out in some Negro district where there had been a flood or something. I'd say, 'What are you doing out there?' 'Oh, nothing, just driving around.' But I found out what he did those days from one of the bums who slept on the cot in back. He told me he had been picked up by Jack way out somewhere. 'And what do you think he was doing?' the guy asked me. 'He was giving money to some kids that had been burnt out.' Then I began to notice that, after Jack read a newspaper, if you picked it up the way he left it, there would likely be news of some local disaster on that page."

Such excursions were not usual for Jack. After he came to The Carousel around noon, he normally spent his afternoon "a-churnin'" up and down Commerce Street. The nucleus of Dallas is very small. Once he had parked his car in the garage under the club and taken Sheba upstairs, he could go almost anywhere he wanted on foot. Down at one end of the street, he might drop in to see Max Rudberg, a bail bondsman Jack met ten years before the assassination when he was getting one of his girls out of jail. Since then, Max's wife and Eva have become good friends. "I used to see him at the Sheareth Israel Synagogue," Rudberg said. "He was a great admirer of Rabbi Silverman."

Rudberg, an imperturbable little elf, is wedged in a cubbyhole office which a plug-in heater makes an oven. A processor of little miseries, he floats on his sense of humor above the shabbiness around him. Dilapidated humans are lined up in the hall outside his hole, men who cannot make bond for their petty crimes, men glad to sit there in the darkness. Rudberg knows what it is all about, that it is a matter of the little blows, delivered one by one, unintermitted. "Jack had a good heart. If any of his girls ever called on him, he came. He put up money for the worst sort of risks. He was a soft touch.

"He used to stop in all the time. Whenever he came to the courthouse, just around the corner, he would 'make the rounds,' dropping in to see everyone he knew. Just a few days before the assassination, he was down here to fix some bad checks an employee had passed, and he came in here. He was all excited about Jada, his big-name stripper. She had hauled him in on a peace bond the night before, claiming she was afraid to go back to the club and get her clothes. There was a lawyer in here with me at the time, so Jack gave us a blow-by-blow description of his appearance before Judge Richburg. 'Didn't I do right?' he would say. 'Could a lawyer have done better?' He wanted us to praise him. He had to be accepted. He was a *meshugana.*"

Judge Richburg is a specialist on peace bonds — the story in Dallas is that he granted one woman a bond against her husband for breaking wind. He hastened to correct that story for us: "I gave it to her because her husband wouldn't bathe but three or four times a year." His most famous recent bond was Marina Oswald's against her second husband. Andrew told us about the night he and Jack had to appear before the judge: "Jada claimed Jack had hit her, but Alice, the washroom attendant, was right there, and she said no such thing happened. Judge Richburg was a circus, finding everybody in contempt every other sentence, talking on and on about his farm. We all came back to the club *howling* at him." Even Jada? "Sure. Jack fired her a little after that."

We asked Rudberg why he thought Jack killed Oswald. "Well, everyone was saying the sonvabitch needs killing, and Jack was anxious to please. He happened to be by the City Hall, sending money to that stripper, just like he always did, and he was bound to poke his head in and see what was happening. Wherever there was a crowd, he couldn't possibly pass it by. Then, as I say, he made the rounds wherever he was. After that, it was just a question of two nuts being in the right place at the right time." (Bill Willis said: "At the club, after the first shock, we all said, 'Well, it figures. Jack thought while he was downtown he might as well kill Oswald.' So — he made his TV debut.")

Moving up Commerce Street from the courthouse, Jack would stop in at the Doubleday store; he liked to check the new diet books and visit with a man there who patronized his club. Today, the man says that he hardly ever went to The Carousel; that Jack came in because he admired his education; but that he himself did not like to associate with a person like Ruby.

Up near the club, Jack would put himself in the way of temptation against his diet at a nearby delicatessen; he usually left with sandwiches or rolls, which he carried to the Enquire Shine and Press Shop with him. He would glance at the papers lying there while he had a shine, and give out buns to his friends — if there was anything left, he ran it up to the club for Andrew. Still making his rounds, he stopped by the hotels; he knew all the doormen, wanted them to direct men to The Carousel.

He haunted the newspaper offices. A. C. Greene, of the *Times Herald*, told us that when Jack came in with his advertisements, he would visit the columnists and the entertainment editor, trying to pass off items from his ad as bits of news. "He even came to us in the editorial section and tried to persuade us that his stripper, Jada, deserved an editorial because she had a college degree. I don't think she had one; but even if she did, what editorial point could be made of that? I guess he thought it would prove that education leads to success!" He was always looking for "publicity angles." When the Kennedys drew attention to fifty-mile hikes along the Potomac, Jack tried to drum up interest in a fifty-mile walk his M.C. would make. He couldn't understand the papers' lack of interest.

Jack liked to visit the office of Gordon McLendon, who bills himself as "the old Scotchman" and plays teen-age atrocities on his "top forty" radio station, KLIF. Jack thought McLendon one of Dallas' great intellectuals; he had been especially struck by a radio editorial McLendon put on the air after Stevenson was spit on in Dallas. This, said the editorial, had put a blot of shame on the city. Jack, who had an unreciprocated passion for Dallas, used to quote that broadcast reverently. Asked, after his arrest, to name his best friends, Jack put McLendon among the six he mentioned — along with Andrew Armstrong and George Senator.

Mitch Lewis, McLendon's assistant, says he tried to protect Gordon from Jack's clogging attentions. "But he did get to Gordon, I forget how, with his damn twistboard. In fact, when I met Jack in the crowd of newsmen outside Captain Fritz's office, the day Kennedy died, he came up to me and wanted to know what Gordon was going to do about the twistboard idea. I remember thinking that was a hell of a thing to talk about at the time." Wasn't Jack interested in what was going on at City Hall? "Oh, he was excited by the cameras and lights. He liked to hang around newsmen. When Marina and Marguerite Oswald came by, I was jostled up close to them and so was Jack. I happened to see him when he first looked at them, and his eyes *glazed*. I think he was impressed that these frumps, one of them in a babushka, could suddenly be made the center of attention."

Did you know Jack well? "Yes, he was always pestering me, when I was with the Dallas *Morning News,* and even more when I came here. He wanted us to advertise his strippers on

the air. I tried to tell him our station is all disc-jockey shows for
the young folk. We can't plug burlesque shows to teen-agers.
But he said his club was different. His star, Jada, was trained
in ballet. He said she had studied psychology, and was a de-
scendant of John Quincy Adams, and I don't know what all."
(Bill Willis said he helped Jack frame an ad claiming Jada was
a granddaughter of Pavlova.) " 'Mitch,' he would say, 'you're a
writer, and she's a good subject for a book.' After she quit Jack,
Jada came around to ask me if I would ghost a book about all
the famous men she had gone around with. When she heard
what Jack had done, she came running back to town to grab
some of that publicity. She had quit a week or so too soon."
(We asked Bill Willis if he thought Jada an opportunist. "Man,
she'd cut up Christ's robes and sell them for napkins. She knew
all the angles. She couldn't dance worth a damn, so she paid
me $10 a week for the privilege of bawling me out in public
whenever she missed a step — as if it had been my fault." She
was called Jack's girlfriend by the papers; was there anything
to that? Bill's friendly sullenness breaks up in laughter: "Well,
they were not about to move to a suburb and settle down!")

Did Mitch Lewis like Jack? "No, he was always glancing
over my shoulder to see if there was some bigger name he
could talk to. He was a small-time whiner, whining because we
didn't give him enough publicity. His suits were always ten
years out of style."

McLendon's office is just a couple of blocks from the Statler,
which was one of Ruby's favorite spots. He knew all the front
personnel; he liked to drive up with friends — sometimes in
Jada's gold Cadillac — and be greeted by the doorman. His old
pal Leo Torti now runs the men's shop in the basement of the
hotel, and his close friend Joe Cavagnaro is sales manager.
Cavagnaro is brawny and well-dressed, soft-voiced but em-
phatic. "I met Jack in 1955. I had just come to Dallas, and I ate
in the Lucas B and B Restaurant next to The Vegas. One day
Jack walked in and said hello; we talked awhile, then Jack

picked up my check. We became very close. I used to help him out at The Vegas, taking the cover charge at the door on Fridays and Saturdays. I even took the club's money over to the night-deposit slot, so I carried his gun, which was in the money bag. I never took it out, though." Where did he keep the money bag? "When it wasn't in the club, it was in his car trunk." Were you on his payroll? "Oh no, I did it as a favor to Jack. I just liked being with him. So did other young fellows who have become quite successful, like Heinz Simon and Leon Nowak. We were his friends; still are. We used to go around with him, servicing his pizza ovens, getting things for his clubs. He was fun to be with. He would take us to breakfast after the clubs closed, and treat us all. It was a good dance club, The Vegas, a bit tough but fun. Trini Lopez sang there when he was just getting started.

"Jack made his customers toe the line. I had a friend go to The Carousel with his wife. Jack had a gimmick — he would put a man up on the stage and have the stripper start undressing him. It didn't get very far; when the fellow's coat and tie were off, the M.C. would take a Polaroid picture and come on later threatening to blackmail him. Eventually, he would hand over the picture. Jack chose the men who were put up there carefully — they were ones he knew, or who were with their wives; not drunks. Even so, when Jack pushed my friend onstage he whispered to him, in a cold voice, 'Don't touch.'

"After I married, I didn't go to his clubs, except when my wife and I happened to be downtown at night; but he came out to visit us often. My wife would make him cheeseburgers — he loved them. And when my boys were born, he became very fond of them. He would bring his dogs out to play with them. He gave us one of Sheba's puppies; we called it Henry. The boys still think a lot of Jack." What did they think when they heard he had killed Oswald? Cavagnaro grins, a bit embarrassed: "They were proud of him. We tried to explain to them that what he did was wrong, but they were glad that Mr. Ruby got the man who killed the President. You know how kids are.

"When my mother and her sister came to visit us, Jack took them out to lunch. They were crazy about him. He was always very polite and gentle with them. And with his girl friend, Alice Nichols." Who was she? "A secretary at an insurance company; she's still there. Jack dated her, on and off for eleven years. She was a very nice, handsome woman, and he had an almost exaggerated respect for her." Did she love him? "I think so." Why were they never married? "He told me he promised one of his parents, I think his father on his deathbed, never to marry a gentile." (Mrs. Nichols, a shy widow, told the F.B.I. that Jack said he could not marry her because he was not worthy of her.)

Did you see many fights at The Vegas? "Sure, some people come to clubs like that itching to start trouble. If that's what they wanted, Jack took care of them. But he never looked for a fight. I only saw him hunt out a fight one time. The Hilltoppers were out at Memorial Auditorium, and I went to visit an old schoolmate of mine, Eddy Crowe, in the troupe. When I got to the dressing room, Jack was waiting outside the door, ready to jump Eddy. I asked him why; he had seen the show and he was going to beat up the guy who told the Jew joke. I told him there was no malice in the inoffensive Catholic and Jewish stories the Hilltoppers told, but he didn't like *any* racial or religious jokes. I finally got him cooled down.

"Though I didn't see him much at The Carousel, he dropped in here at least three times a week to have coffee with me. Once a week or so he would ask me to help him phrase a letter — he was writing a lot to the strippers' union claiming the Weinsteins violated union laws. When we finished working over the letter, he would dictate it to my secretary. He came in for coffee the day Kennedy was shot. He had been at City Hall, and he was writing an ad to say his club would be closed for three days. He asked me what *we* were going to do. I told him, 'Jack, you can't just close a hotel! People have to have a place to eat and sleep.' But he expected the whole city to close down. He was upset that Dallas would be shamed. I remember his telling me how much the Stevenson incident would hurt the convention business.

"When I was asked to testify at the change-of-venue hearing, there was some talk that the national corporation wouldn't be happy at my calling Jack a good friend there in the courtroom. My wife and I talked it over, and decided I had to give up my job if it would help Jack. He would have done the same for me." Do you think others in Dallas had this kind of pressure put on them? "Sure. I saw some important people in his clubs, people who would now deny they ever went there."

Was Jack's word good? "Like steel. Of course, you couldn't believe him when he said he was going to meet you at a certain time. He was always late. He would get caught talking to someone; and if he stopped talking to one person, he would start right up with someone else before he could get out the door. He seemed always to be on the run — glancing at a paper (he always had one with him), jumping up to leave, saying he was late for another appointment (he probably was) — but he hated to break off any conversation. He was a compulsive talker, even about the most personal things."

Would he boast of sexual conquests? "No. He was concerned it would get back to Alice. He never did anything that might hurt her." How did you hear about his murder of Oswald? "I had brought my two boys downtown to go to the Cathedral. We pulled up at the hotel — I was going to give them some milk and doughnuts before Mass — and we could see the crowd just up the way. The people were kept across the street, which was blocked off, and there was an armored car in the City Hall driveway. My boys — they were three and four then — wanted to go see what was happening (we had been listening to the car radio); so we started walking. Just as we came up, we heard the shot. It could have been a backfire, but someone came out shouting, 'He's been shot!' I grabbed up my boys to get them out of there. If only I had been on the other side of City Hall!"

Sometimes Ruby would stop by at other clubs — ones that

opened in the afternoon. Pat Morgan, an insurance man who has backed several clubs, says Jack was one of the first to call on him when he came to town in 1961 and opened Pat Morgan's Club Dallas. "It was just around the corner from The Carousel — on Browder Street. He came up and welcomed me and gave me all kinds of advice on running a downtown club." What kind of advice? "What kind of cover charge to make; which cops would play it straight with you, and which would try to screw you; and he told me all the 'characters' I should keep out of the club if I wanted to avoid trouble — the DG's, as he called them" (degenerates). Who were these DG's, in his eyes? "Oh, panders, queers, deadbeats." Was he accurate in this advice? "Perfectly. I never knew him to be wrong." Why was he so helpful to a rival? "Jack tried to be helpful to everybody — I guess it made him feel important. I never went into his club without his getting up on the stage and giving a little pitch for my club." What would he say? "Oh, something like 'Ladies and gentlemen, it is a great pleasure to have Pat Morgan here tonight. If you haven't been to his Club Dallas, you haven't really seen the city. It is one of the nicest places in town.'" Did you have strippers? "No, legitimate acts — it was more a lunch and dinner club. Jack was only really competitive with the Weinsteins. He would go up to Abe's, pretending he wanted to talk to Bob Larkin, and he'd count the audience. Then he'd run back to The Carousel, and if he had more people that night, he'd go all over town the next day boasting about it. He got Abe so mad at him! — Jack put posters for The Carousel in the window of a store just below The Colony Club. He was very proud of that."

Did you go to The Carousel much? "No, only to see Jack. We became good friends. Eva would come to me about advertising matters; and Jack and I swam together at the Continental Apartments, where a friend of his lived." Did you see him get into fights? "Only if somebody started trouble at his clubs. Once Wally Weston, his best M.C., needled a heckler in the audience so bad that the guy pulled a gun on Wally. Jack went right over and took it away — I saw him — and then threw the customer out. He was a fearless little guy. Of course, he shouted a lot at his sister and his girls and the other employees. But I don't think he was very angry when he did that — it was just a way of life with him. And in other circles, with those he respected, he could be very quiet, and he was always very polite. Around my wife, he always was. In fact, around me — he was impressed that I had a college education. He used to say, 'What does a nice guy who went to college need to go into the clubs for?' "

Did he think the clubs were not respectable? "Well, yes and no. He used to tell me he wanted to get into some higher form of business — but he would have been miserable without the clubs. He loved the excitement. He liked to take the mike from the M.C. and act the host and talk to stars." Did many celebrities come by? "Sure. I used to take Chill Wills up to see Jack. Jack was proud of all the people he knew. When I first came to town, he took me to a big 'Italian Night' party that all the important people of Dallas attended. He took me over and introduced me to Mayor Cabell, and to Judge Joe B. Brown, who later tried his case. They were sitting with Joe Campisi. I don't think he knew these people except to shake hands with — but he knew them all at least that far. He used to say to me, 'You know, Pat, considering my background, it's really amazing that I have come so far.' "

Jack offered unsolicited advice all over Dallas, not only to men who ran clubs. We talked with a girl, Dolores Elkins, who was hostess at a health spa newly opened in a luxury apartment building. "Jack Ruby came in when we opened and talked about membership. I showed him around, but he said he didn't want to join himself — he belonged to the Y's Health Club — but he would give me some advice worth a lot more than the money for one membership. He told me not to accept Milt Joseph or he would drive off our respectable clientele. I couldn't believe someone would come in just to say something like that!"

As the day wore on, Ruby sometimes drove to The Vegas and "made the rounds" there — B and B Restaurant (though he had been feuding with Pete, the owner, just before the assassination weekend), Phil's delicatessen, Kaye's liquor store. The Kayes, old friends of Jack, said he would bring his dogs over and say hello; he was known in the neighborhood as a soft touch for bums and winos; he let people who didn't even have enough to pay the cover charge come into his club and hear the music, though they could buy nothing. The Kayes believe he shot Oswald to become a hero.

One afternoon a week, Jack made it to McLean Hair Experts for a treatment. "He was always late; and he stayed a long time, past closing, to get more attention from the girl who was working on him. He always wanted me to reassure him that he could keep what was left of his hair."

By six in the evening, Jack was at the Y.M.C.A. He belonged to the Health Club, which some men join to avoid being approached by homosexuals. Jack was not known at a neighboring fairy-rendezvous, and he did not linger at the Y. He worked out with the weights, showered, and was ready for a night at the club by seven.

He liked to attend local affairs. Perhaps his favorite entertainment was boxing. A policeman friend said he used to come down the aisle just as the lights went up between preliminaries and the main event, shaking hands, greeting people, handing out cards, telling jokes. He had a bantam-cock way of carrying himself; he tilted his head to one side, or perked it up, or nodded with a pecking motion, like some bright-eyed bird. "He always thought his next deal would be the one to make him a big man."

iv

Sunday morning, November 24, 1963: 223 South Ewing Street — a concrete-block barn decorated at each end in the pastels that paint stores seem to unload on motel owners. Wings are built out at right angles from both barn ends, enclosing a swimming pool. The second-story rooms are reached by a gallery, so that every room opens on the court. The modern motel is much like a Shakespearean inn, with a swimming pool where the stage was.

This "apartment house" is a half-motel for slow-motion transients, mainly young working girls who share a two-bedroom apartment ($125) until they move on to marriage or a better job. The manager is a young girl too, Doris Warner, who lives in the ground-floor apartment nearest Ewing Street. Up the stairs, on the gallery, the first apartment one reaches is 207, where Mr. Ruby lives. He was drawn here by the swimming pool (where he splashes in a bathing cap, since Mr. McLean has warned him about chlorine in the hair); before this, when he wanted to swim, he visited a friend whose apartment house had a pool.

Ruby has brought other tenants in. Tammi True, one of his strippers, came for a while, with her children. George Senator, one of the hard-up people who lived on the cot in back of Ruby's club, moved here when his British blades began to catch on. At first he roomed with Stanley Corbat in 206. But Corbat got married, and Senator's chronic money troubles came round again, so on November 1 Ruby let him move in with him. He has let others use the extra bedroom in 207, including homeless strippers. Ruby is rarely "at home." His home is the club; and it is part of his bustling, oddly impersonal benevolence to find people places to live. If you needed anything, you mentioned it at your risk to Jack Ruby. He would press suggestions on you till you found your home, or car, or whatever — or until you feigned you had.

Sunday morning, at eight-thirty, the phone rings. George Senator is not in the apartment. Ruby paws his way out of sleep toward the phone and answers muzzily. Sheba stirs, too, and jumps off the bed. There is a picture of her dachshund sire, "big Clipper," over the bed. Ruby is having bad luck with his sleep these days. Yesterday, he got to bed at six a.m., only to have the current transient at The Carousel, Larry Crafard, wake him with an eight-thirty phone call. He answered that call so blisteringly that Crafard put what little he owned in his pockets and moved on — to Michigan, as frenziedly searching F.B.I. men later discovered.

With this caller, Ruby is more patient. His voice flares up, irritated, but gentles again when he remembers he is talking to a gentle, aging Negress.

"This is Elnora" (Elnora Pitts, who cleans his apartment on Sundays).

"Yes, well, what — you need some money?" Ruby has loaned money to "Eleanor," as he calls her, and she thinks he is referring to this. But he went to sleep with money on his mind. Sunday is payday for his employees, who get paid when they come to work. The Carousel has been closed since Friday — the only dark nights in its history — and his staff will not come in at the regular time. These are people who cannot go an extra day without their thinly distributed money. Two of the girls have already been after him for money, last night, when he was too disturbed to come to grips with the problem. And all the Vegas staff has to be paid, too.

"I was coming to clean today."

"Coming to clean?" What has that to do with payrolls?

Mrs. Pitts always calls ahead, so Ruby can clear the dogs out;

she fears dogs. Today she tells him she cannot come in the morning. Should she come later?

"Well, yes; you can come, but you call me!"

"That's what I'm doing now, calling you so I won't have to call you again."

"And you're coming to clean today?"

"Yes." (Long pause.) "Who am I talking to? Is this Mr. Jack Ruby?"

"Yes. Why?"

"Shall I come around two?"

"You call me before two, before you start."

"Well, what do I have to call you again for?"

"Well, so I can tell you where the key is and the money."

Ruby leaves change and bills scattered all over the tables and bureau tops, and Mrs. Pitts refuses even to touch those: "I don't dust them because I don't — by him being a Jewish man, I don't want him to say I taken the money." She is very sensitive on the point. Ruby has to tell her which money is set aside for her. (He owns antennae for sensing others' fear of racial rebuff.)

As usual, he cannot sleep after the call. Others, this morning, want to linger underwater in their sleep world, but Ruby is anxious to break the surface. He feels History all around him; he has been a demon of energy ever since that moment on Friday when the announcement momentarily stilled him (he sat in the *Morning News* building, numbed and staring fixedly).

First, to the paper; George brought it in before he left. Are the ads there? Yes. Carousel closed, Vegas closed. How about the other clubs? You might know! They are reopening. There should be some way of forcing them to do the decent thing. They want to take advantage of the flow of people into Dallas — reporters, TV crews, investigators, the curious, the photographers — all those people he has been giving Carousel passes to since Friday. (When will they ever be used?) It is frustrating. The assassination has made people unwilling to talk about the twistboard, too, though he did get the *Times Herald* staff interested in it yesterday. There should be some way of riding History's wave to success. But all it has done so far is make Ruby and his partner, Ralph Paul, lose their money. (Ralph was right about one thing — losing a weekend is serious for a club like ours. He wanted me to stay open, and it *is* his money I am losing. But I just couldn't — not after what happened.) What happened comes back to him like a blow. Of *course* he had to close the clubs; why didn't everybody else see that? Why are *they* open?

Coffee. Squeeze a grapefruit (his current health food). Turn on the TV. What is happening? He has not floated any private schemes this weekend, but he put *himself* well forward. He got those scoops for KLIF. Gordon will *have* to notice that; he was credited with it on his own station. Already Ruby is getting known!

At what cost? The careful masks and thin controlled voices on the television screen remind him of the numbness that washes, periodically, across his buzz of opportunistic instincts and drowns their chatter. What else is in the paper? The funeral arrangements for Kennedy (*"He read about my mother's funeral in the newspaper and came to it"*). A picture of the motorcade; the rifle; the rifle's wielder — who had stood not three feet from Ruby Friday night, put on exhibit for all the reporters. (I would have thrown him out of my club, the smirking punk; yet here he is basking in attention, enjoying it, *enjoying* what he did to Jackie. And to Caroline.)

"My Dear Caroline" (the letter in the paper begins):

"Caroline, you must have a lot of courageous blood in your veins." [Like the Jews; Jews have guts.] ("You will cry. My children did. My wife did. And I did.) . . . Mentally sick and acutely evil men are very difficult to understand. . . ."

Yes, sick and evil, the kind Ruby roughs up and throws out; the kind he has grown up with, been forced to clear endlessly from his path, his besieged escape route from the ghetto. They would have smothered him, the sneerers, had he let them, coming at him from all sides. But he rose above them, took the play from them, hit out always at that sneer. He throws the newspaper down, too blur-eyed to read further. (*"If you picked it up the way he left it, there would likely be news of some local disaster on that page."*)

Poor Caroline, poor Jackie. (*"He was the girls' protector."*) Coming to Dallas for this. How can she ever face Dallas again; at the trial, for instance? How can Dallas face her? (*"The Stevenson incident would hurt business."*) God, that sonvabitch needs killing! That's what they all say. Harry Olsen is right. He should be cut in little bits. (*"We called it planting the seed. Just suggest something to him. . . ."*)

It is after nine, and City Hall is swarming with newsmen. Chief Curry told them last night they would not miss anything if they came by ten in the morning; but few believed him. They thought he was moving Oswald early, and meant to throw them off the track. Yet nothing has happened; maybe he *was* telling the truth. Inside Captain Fritz's office, question after question chips at that smug facade but cannot splinter it. The sneer acts as a bulwark here. In certain company, it could be a bull's eye.

George Senator returns — a puffy man of fifty, with a whipped-cream fluff of curls on top. Unlike Ruby, he was married, and has a son — the marriage, like everything else in his life, failed. Failure lends to his natural geniality the compliance people feel protective toward. No one dislikes George; nor respects him. They feel sorry for him. At the moment, he comes in carrying freshly tossed laundry; he has been working the laundromat machine downstairs.

Ruby shows him the letter to Caroline; says Jackie should be spared a return to Dallas; says that punk should be killed before he gets to trial. (*"Of course, he always talked big. He was always going to beat our ass."*) George nods sympathetically. It is a comment he has heard many times in the last two days, from many lips. The TV drones mercilessly on, making the incredible inescapable. It *did* happen: look at the world telling itself, over and over, that it did. Ruby goes into the kitchen for more grapefruit and to scramble eggs. Senator cooks for people at The Carousel, and is considered an excellent chef. But Ruby is delicate about his food, accustomed to fixing minimal fare for himself on small stoves or hot plates. He has always lived in "a room" or rooms, not caring much which rooms. He has risen when others are at work, slept when they are getting up. South Ewing is simply a cot for him, or a dressing room attached to the swimming pool. His "home" was a place of raving foreigners who could not even speak English — a crazy mother, a brutal, drunken father — a place to get out of. He has been getting out ever since. He wants no "home."

Ten-nineteen a.m. The phone in the apartment rings again. At this very moment Chief Curry is telling the newsmen that Oswald will be moved in an armored car (the urgent call went out to the Armored Motor Service half an hour ago, and the driver has been hauled from the Sunday School class he was teaching). Ruby answers, "Hello." "This is Lynn again." In Fort Worth. He gave her five dollars last night, when she came over to work and found the club still closed. She has no salary coming; it was all advanced to her long ago. But she and her husband must pay something on their rent and groceries or they cannot stay, cannot eat. They *have* to have twenty-five dollars.

Ruby remembers how angry he got, last night, at her phone call for money — how could she think of anything but the President's death! (He said this to her on the same day he demonstrated the twistboard to *Times Herald* employees. He used to get angry at Eva for being so unpatriotic as not to pay her poll tax — which Ruby had not paid for four years.) He remembers, too, his storm of anger at poor Larry. He is angry at the world these days. (Larry! That's right! There's no one to feed the dogs. Sunday is Andrew's day off. I have to feed them. Poor Clipper.)

Lynn needs the money at once. They can't eat till they get it. All right. Can she get to the Western Union office in Fort Worth? Yes. "It will take me about twenty or thirty minutes to get dressed, and then I will go on down. I have to go near there anyway, to feed the dogs and let them out."

It is almost ten-thirty. The newsmen are getting restless; they had come to believe the ten-o'clock moving time. Ruby stretches his weight-lifter's arms, lifting the weight of full consciousness. Like many night people, he wakes up slowly, at no set time, against no regular deadline. He is used to dressing leisurely. This is the last morning he will be able to. Every morning after this, for the rest of his life, he will rise early, prodded against his protests to face increasingly empty days from their very outset. Today, though, not even Lynn's call can hurry him. Not even the thought of his hungry dogs.

First, a shower. Ban deodorant. McLean's hair lotion. (Eva will pick it up for him the next three years.) He studies and rubs, combs and studies. Disposing his remains of hair almost strand by strand, he achieves a slightly off-center part — a hairstyle very popular with the men of Dallas. The elaborate asymmetry of these few lines that cross his scalp rears thin barriers against the Enemy — Baldness, an enemy all the more dangerous because comic. The one thing Ruby does not want to be is a clown. One of his recurrent key words is "dignified." Dignity is at issue as, after scrutiny, he moves two hairs across the divide, right to left, strong side to weak.

Must be at one's best when meeting History. He lathers up and shaves, once; British blade, the kind George was pushing; good product. He lathers again, and shaves slowly back and forth from every angle. Ruby has a heavy beard; any shadow of it would accentuate his jowliness. Even in jail, he will shave twice every day (still with a British blade, locked into the razor with a key the guard retains). His hands are hairy too, battle-scarred; chewed off at one point, that stump on his left hand. He has a ring on that hand, winking at him as he pulls his face back and forth to turn curves into planes for his blade's razing; not a big ring by Texas standards, though it has three diamonds in it. A recent acquisition. No one will remember a star sapphire among Ruby's "characteristics."

He studies himself in the mirror, challenging, hoping, asking approval from that face as he does from all other faces. He has brows that hood his eyes — Lloyd Nolan brows. Nose too big for Nolan, though; and too many chins, despite his sweating in the Y. (Chin up, eyes down, tie the Windsor knot, silk tie.) The eyes keep returning to his face. They do not rest easily on one thing, but slide on, always, wary of blows and wistful for "the big one." Eyes of someone forever being moved on (*"He was always afraid someone in the next group was talking about him"*). Eyes of a promoter (*"He was always glancing over my shoulder to see if there was some bigger name to talk to"*). Eyes ready for challenge (*"You learn to be a jungle walker"*). Always in motion, they belong to a man always moving, looking for the next spot to jump, watching where the play is, ready to take the play away.

Flitting eyes, distrustful — fixing other eyes desperately in his conversation, loath to break off, lonely but afraid. Apprehensive about tenderness, which he shows provisionally, where it seems most safe, with a self-protective grouchiness (*"Get the hell out of here and take care of that kid"*). How much can he risk? Not much: surly benevolence toward bums; sex with the bus-station girls; love for brothers and sisters, as long as they are absent (too near, *they* too are dangerous, and must be abused); extravagant devotion to his parents — from the very moment that they died; vaguely warm companionship with a widow kept safely at a distance by "respect." Love slows the reflexes of jungle walkers. Even bums and bus-station girls can mock. Only the dogs stay loyal. It is safe to love them. Or is it? Leo Torti remembers the time when Ruby said, "Look at that dog. I actually love him, do everything I can for him. I wonder if the sonvabitch hates my guts."

Move your eyes, moving man, time to move. Suck in the gut. Dark suit jacket. Glasses in the pocket. Neat gray hat, name stamped in gold inside. Home is what the hat is, a moving marquee, its message not reaching the outside. No overcoat. Ducking in here and there and back out, he would have to shed and don and carry and check it. A coat is like affection, too unwieldy, slowing everything; impedes the swing of tightened shoulder (*"Jack was a first-puncher"*). Ruby owns no overcoat.

He'll be needing money. There is some locked in the closet ($131.41), more scattered around the apartment ($124.87). Not enough to meet the entire payroll. Besides, I have to treat the boys — and many of the boys are here now, newsmen from everywhere. Need my roll. I can do better than the sandwiches I bought them yesterday, that's what I do *every*day for my friends. Get the money and gun from the car. (*"Whenever he was carrying the money, he kept his piece handy."*)

He is pacing the rooms and mumbling to himself. Hard to remember all he has to do today. Hard to get the load of consciousness up in one weight-lifter's snatch. Why should he? In everything there is to be done, what can he *do?* There is no displacing that dead center of his numbness. No bringing a dead man back. No way to un-kill, erase the memory from Jackie's mind, spare Caroline. Senator watches him pace, hears him mutter, but makes out no words. Ruby's friends, asked what actor could play him in a movie, turn invariably to types like Marlon Brando, Telly Savalas, Ralph Meeker — men with fists for tongues, who mush out *s* to *sh*, blunt *th* to *t*, *t* to *d*. Ruby's lisp bothers him; he tries to talk slowly, to correct it ("as if he had had a few drinks and was being careful how he spoke," says Andrew). In prison he will practice, over and over, pronouncing the names Shadrach, Meshach, and Abednego. But when he is excited, the lisp and the ghetto accent fill his mouth with the thickening bitter porridge of his past; syntax disappears; he babbles. This morning he paces and babbles a full five minutes, all confused plans (what do I tell Eleanor, how to pay Andrew and the others?) and numb hurt (poor Caroline, my hungry dogs) and hate (Dallas, the rifle, the punk) and excitement (a real reporter, "The Only Three-Runway Club in Dallas With Jack Ruby").

"George, I'm taking the dog down to the club."

Ruby's car is his traveling office; the "office" in the club is home to a succession of bums. Even his files and "securities" are wheeled and on the move. There is nothing fixed or settled about Ruby. He houses transients because he is one. The car is white — a two-door Olds, a 1960 model; mustn't be flashy with the I.R.S. after him. (As if jukeboxes were taxable "entertainment"!) Sheba takes the back seat, which she keeps in a proprietary shabbiness. Ruby pulls his little transistor out of the glove compartment and flicks it on; turns it down a minute to talk with a neighbor, out at the end of the drive; then enters the Thornton Freeway (which runs right by his apartment). It is almost eleven. The armored car is on its way to City Hall. Andrew is arriving at the club, despite the fact that it is his day off — things are too unsettled; he has to find out what is going on; he is shocked to see the dogs have not been fed. Joe Cavagnaro is putting his boys in the car for Mass. Forrest Sorrels, of the Secret Service, is being allowed to question Oswald.

Ruby does not stay on the Thornton Freeway, veers, instead, left along Industrial Boulevard to the point where it meets Main, tugged insensibly toward Dealey Plaza, as thousands will be in future months and years. Tomorrow, and for the next three years, Ruby himself will be one of the Plaza's attractions, when he lives above it in his prison corridor. He dips, now, under the Stemmons Freeway — where Kennedy, approaching from the other side, was hit. Rising out from the underpass, Ruby slows his car, snagged in the cobweb of trajectories already being spun by conjecture and hypothesis. It is scarred air he drives through. To the left, the wreaths. But up by Houston

Street, a crowd turns from the wreaths and is facing the jail (Ruby's future home, the most settled dwelling he will ever have). Oswald must be in there, transferred by now from Chief Curry's City Hall to Sheriff Decker's Courthouse. The radio is vague about the time of transfer, but Ruby heard yesterday it would take place at ten.

On up Main, still reversing Kennedy's course, past Sanger's on the left, Neiman-Marcus on the right. Ten blocks, to Harwood, where City Hall is — in the same block as the only Western Union that is open on a Sunday. There are four or five people talking to a policeman as Ruby drives past the rabbit hole in City Hall that lets police cars underground to park. On the other side of the building, an armored car has just jockeyed with difficulty backward into the small mouth of the exit. Ruby hugs the curb to see what is going on (*"He had to be in on everything"*). There is still something down there — TV crews perhaps, packing up their equipment (*"He liked to hang around newsmen"*). Now he must get back to the left lane; he wants to pull into a parking lot across the street. But a moving bus blocks the other east-bound lane beside him; he cannot race ahead of the bus or ease in behind it in time to make the turn. He slows till he is even with the lot, waits for the taillight of the bus to clear, then swings hard left into the lot from the far-right lane (*"He was a spastic — he acted suddenly"*). Ruby — who is almost superstitious about the law, reverencing it and tempted to break it and feeling remorse about it afterward — has just committed his penultimate infraction of the law.

The lot is on the corner of Main and Pearl, directly facing the Western Union office. Sheba jumps into the front seat, rustles in last week's newspapers (*"He always had a paper with him"*). Stay here, girl. He puts the transistor in the glove compartment. No need to lock the doors. He opens the trunk (his file cabinet and bank and transient home's attic), throws the keys down in the front part of this dreary treasure chest, and

rummages through it. Receipts, junk, money; a moldering holster he never uses (it came with the gun); brass knuckles in the
money bag, where he keeps his weapons. (Take the gun now.
God! How I'd like to use it on that character!) The money is in
two places. He takes the bigger amount ($2,015.33) and leaves
the smaller ($837.50). He puts the gun in his right-hand
pocket, the money in his left; it is one motion, the two go together. Slams trunk. (Damn! Forgot to pick the keys back up.
My head is a hurricane these days.)

It's all right, though — extra trunk key in the glove compartment. He keeps it there always, with his wallet. George Senator
has never seen a wallet on Ruby or in his room — it is good
only for the license he needs when driving. Ruby saves his
pockets for Carousel cards, and twistboard literature, and pictures of his girls. The glove-compartment key is there so Ruby
can get to his second key ring — farther back in the trunk, in a
box — if he mislays the first. Bill Willis remembers talking one
night in the garage under The Carousel: "I told him I keep my
extra keys under the hood, in case I lose my pocket set, and
Jack said he kept a spare set in the trunk."

(I'll get out the keys when I come back. Over the street. Still
those four or five people at the other end of the block. I wonder
why?) Into Western Union. At the long counter one customer
is ahead of him.

Oswald is pulling on a sweater in Captain Fritz's office. Ruby
adjusts his glasses — bifocals, he wears them as little as possible — and prints Little Lynn's maiden name on the form:
Karen Bennett. But he neglects the bottom of the form; Doyle
Lane, the clerk, must ask for his address, then write it in:
1312½ Commerce. Not the apartment house. That is not home,
there is no home; The Carousel comes closest. Lane copies the
address, and other information, a second time; this is the receipt he will give to Ruby. The minutes click by now. Lane
stamps the receipt: 1963 Nov 24 AM 11 16. Ruby puts his
glasses away, hooking one of their hornrim wings on his breast

pocket, while Lane writes a duplicate of the receipt, to keep in the office; writes it rapidly, with only a glance or two at the other slip of paper; copies the address the third time, wrong, 1313½; stamps the second receipt: 1963 Nov 24 AM 11 17. A new minute has cogged itself up in the machine, a controverted minute that men will haggle over and cling to and question. Ruby takes his copy and puts it in his pocket.

(Must get the keys out, drive Sheba to the club. The dogs need food and an airing; then leave Sheba with them; can't have her waiting for me in the car all day while I mix with the other reporters. But those people are still there, just down the street. Looks like the same ones, not just passers-by. Well, it will only take a minute to find out what's happening.) *"He always made the rounds."* He turns left, west on Main.

Something strange *is* going on. A car is nosing out of the ramp, and this is an entrance door only! Ruby quickens his stride.

History has broken her date with Jack Ruby before now, despite his efforts to arrange a meeting. In fifty-three seconds, she will keep it. A block over, on Commerce Street, Joe Cavagnaro has pulled up in front of the hotel, his boys in the car with him. "If I had been on Main Street, it would never have happened. The minute Jack saw my kids, he always picked them up. And he would never let them see violence." No, Jack saw too much of it when he was a kid. Cavagnaro kept him from hitting Eddy Crowe outside the dressing-room door. History will not be cheated, though; Joe is a block away when Ruby waits outside the door for Oswald.

The entrance to the ramp is narrow — twelve feet, six inches — just wide enough to let a car turn in (so narrow that the armored car eased clumsily into its counterpart on Commerce Street, and could not back down; low clearance blocked it). The policeman who had been in the middle of the Main Street ramp must move aside, and the knot of gazers with him. They back toward Harwood Street, to the driver's side of the car, away from the approaching Ruby. The car that is surfacing must turn left to circle the block and move up one-way Commerce Street. It is meant to lead the armored car in what, by a sudden change of plans, will be a decoy caravan. In Dallas, turning left on a two-way street is illegal for a car that comes out of a driveway or a parking lot. The policeman on guard here does not know what is happening. He leans down to the driver, just as the car's nose reaches the curb and points left, poised for the illegal turn. The driver tells the guard what he is going to do and, as they talk, Ruby arrives. The car's taillights have just cleared the entrance to the ramp. He will keep his date in less than fifty seconds (*"He was never on time"*). Ruby glances down, sees lights, does not break his stride (*"Jack was a reactionary — he reacted fast"*), but turns smoothly left, and down (*"He plunged into things"*). As he is about to reach the line of men at the bottom, he hears a cry: "Here he comes!" The brightest TV lights blink on, turn the glow in City Hall's belly to a glare (*"He used to come down the aisle just as the lights went up between preliminaries and the main event"*). "He's coming out!" He? The character? Ruby's shoulders tighten instinctively, a jungle walker's reaction when the natural enemy is near.

Just as he reaches the line of people, Captain Fritz's Stetson bobs into view, brilliant in the TV lights. At that moment, Ruby is looking straight ahead, on camera, though he does not know it. He stands in the penumbra of those lights (*"He always wanted to be at the openings and closings of shows"*). At the edge. How short a step to the center. Like Marguerite and Marina (*"His eyes glazed"*).

Detective Leavelle, a movie Texan, moves the human chain of handcuffed men toward the car. He wears a white Stetson and white suit — the good guy (*"Hell, man, Dallas is still a shoot-out town"*). He dwarfs the young man beside him, tense in his dark sweater — the bad guy, face logy with fatigue and bruises, jaws faintly dusted with morning growth. Tomorrow

Ruby will tell his old friend Buddy Walthers, "He looked just like Corky Crawford!"

The orange stab of light in this dark place turns Oswald's face to the side, for a moment — toward the dim figure just arrived. Some will later claim he looked at Ruby, looked *for* him — but he could not see in these first seconds of the dazzle. The glare makes him tighten his lips further, in a slight grimace (*"There's nothing to do with the smirk but mess it up, right now"*). Ruby pushes through the line (*"Jack shouldered the priest aside and came straight at me"*). No one has a chance of stopping him now (*"Before I even got started, Jack stepped between us and nailed him"*), but one policeman raises his arm (*"Don't ever stop me, I might lose my nerve"*). As usual, his first act is decisive — dead on target (*"Jack was a first-puncher"*). He mates in one move (*"You have to take the play away"*). The job is done.

Sergeant Pat Dean, who cleared the basement an hour ago, thinks, "My God, a cop has killed him" (*"He liked to do the policemen's job for them"*). When police swarm toward him, Ruby the scuffler does not try to take *this* play. They are friends, they'll understand (*"He usually did the wrong thing for reaching his goal"*). But why are they so rough? Don't they know he's on their side, just like on South Ervay, fighting along with Blankenship and Carlson? He came to their rescue. Why turn on him? (*"He wanted to help, and he only got in the way"*). They must know I did it for Jackie (*"Jack, I don't want you to hit him"*). For Dallas (*"Even if it wasn't his fight, he would step in, in a second"*). For Caroline (*"Diana, we've got to do something about that girl"*). They must see that: "YOU ALL KNOW ME!" (*"Mr. Ruby got the man who killed the President"*). "I'M JACK RUBY!"

"I Love This City, Joe!"

i

Like a stork or a flamingo, Bill Alexander has a crowded way of walking. He collects himself, with winced shoulders, moving forward but leaning back, picking his way, on guard. But a creased and pitted face belies his body's diffidence: his buried eyes seem to belong to another man looking out of this crinkled-putty mask. Alexander is the most energetic prosecutor in an active District Attorney's office, a man widely feared and hesitatingly respected — as a ticking bomb commands respect. Slumped in his chair, shoulders folding in under the watchful berry eyes while he plays with a letter opener, he arches a muddy rainbow of colorful, patentedly Texan phrases over his desk at visitors. A request that one keep things aboveboard becomes, in his idiom, "Don't pee on my leg, boys."

He was soliciting a candor he is himself famous for. When he brought a psychiatrist to Jack Ruby the day after his arrest, he said: "Jack, if you're crazy, you should be in the insane asylum; and if you're not, we're going to burn your ass." Ruby asked, "What should I do, Bill? You won't gin me, will you?" and Alexander replied, "I won't let thirteen years' friendship go down the drain just to fuck you around." Melvin Belli, colorfulest blur in the kaleidoscope of Ruby's lawyers, argues that his client was "buttered up and disarmed" by this exchange. But Belli is not a Texan. He could not imagine grown men playing the old Pat Garrett scene with a straight face: "Billy, there's nothing personal in it, but I got to take you in, Billy." It is a scene Alexander plays regularly, and never tires of. He likes and is fascinated by his prey; but he has a cruel mysticism about Law Enforcement that makes him a strange blend of tough guy and puritan (one of the things that bothered him about Ruby was that he went to bed when decent people were getting up). Ruby stopped by Alexander's office for a visit the day before Kennedy was shot; when he killed Oswald, he was carrying a permanent Carousel pass he had promised, on Thursday, to give "Bill." Alexander would not have used it.

Texas itself is a mixture of the prim and the crude, maintaining loose frontier manners alongside a frontier rigidity of "code." The ultimate compliment is to say a man's word is reliable: "If he tells you it's going to rain, run for your umbrella." Alexander prides himself on the fact that his word is good among criminals. If he says he will let them off or go easy on them in return for information, he does. If he says (as he tends to) that he will fry a man's ass, he usually fries it. Part of his regret over Ruby's sad end was caused, it seemed to us, by the fact that intervening nature kept him from making his word good. In a shoot-out town, you had better *make* the shots you call. It is the way one earns respect, even from "the bad guys" (as Alexander more than half seriously calls them). Ruby's lawyers could not believe in a real Pat Garrett; more important, they were unable to understand a real Bill Bonney — they kept asking Ruby, incredulously, why he was so friendly at all meetings with Bill Alexander. In the long three years of his ordeal, Ruby came at last to distrust everyone on his side, but never Bill. ("It's all right, Pat; you were only doing your job.")

Alexander's memories of Ruby are reservedly fond. "I only wanted to give him the death penalty. I hated to see Jack pecked to death by ducks." He liked Jack, without respecting him. "He already had three strikes on him in Dallas: he was a Yankee, a Jew, and a strip-joint owner." Spokesmen like Stanley Marcus (of Neiman-Marcus) assured us there is no prejudice against Jews or "outsiders" in their city (only to remind us, moments later, that neither Oswald nor Ruby were Dallasites); but Alexander is a connoisseur of Dallas prejudice — a virtuoso who knows all its stops and keys, and plays on them expertly in the courtroom.

Although Alexander's pity for the man done in by blunt instruments is partly humanitarian, his reaction was basically aesthetic — contempt of a hawk for ducks: "They *plumbered* his case." He does his own work with deadly efficiency, and has a real distaste for work he considers clumsy or unprofessional. He operates on a law-enforcement team whose unspoken motto is the Mounties' — a spirit expressed in the police force's "shotgun squad" which if it ever failed to get its man, almost always managed to get *some* man. Alexander estimates its toll at one criminal a month: "It sure does hurt Earl Warren's business when you kill 'em right on the floor. There's no appeal from that double-nothing buckshot." A. C. Green, caustic veteran columnist for the Dallas *Times Herald,* takes a less enthusiastic view of the squad: "When they decided there had been too many robberies in an area, they planted a few of the shotgun boys in the back of liquor stores and other likely places. Then, when a man tried to take money out of the cash register, they blew his head off. In those days it was a good idea to speak clearly when you went into a liquor store. If you asked for change and the men in the back thought you were demanding the cash, you were liable to find yourself without a head."

Alexander, no mean judge of such a matter, says: "Those boys are the coolest-eyed set of killers I ever saw. If they had been in the Presidential parade, where they were supposed to be, Oswald would not have killed Kennedy. They always ride with their guns out, bristling all over the car, and when that first shot went off, they would have stopped dead and hit the ground. The Secret Service has to *move,* and get the President out of danger. But it would sure shake an Oswald's second shot if he saw men hitting the ground at his first one and looking around for someone to shoot at."

Chief of the city police at the time of the assassination was Jesse Curry, a man pliant to suggestions from above — e.g., from Bill Decker, chief of the Dallas *county* police since 1949. Decker is too much the cowboy sheriff to dress like one. With one leg propped up on his desk, his Dick Tracy hat firmly set on his head as if with a carpenter's level, he watches callers out of his one good eye (the other is glass), through lids that ripple and puff and wink, as if he were squinting, through smoke, over the top of a winning hand. Now sixty-nine, he has the porcelain legs of the old, but the pottery face of an Indian. The dogma in Dallas is that Oswald would not have died if Bill Decker had managed the prisoner's transfer from Chief Curry's City Hall eleven blocks out to Decker's own jail. At the last minute, Captain Will Fritz of Homicide began to take control of the move, with his decision to send the armored car as a decoy. (Monday, Ruby made the same move his victim was beginning on Sunday; there was no notice of his transfer; he rode on the floor of an unmarked car.)

Three years after Decker's election, Henry Wade became District Attorney. One of six lawyer-sons of a judge who fought Texas lynch mobs with the creed that only the law should kill criminals, Wade has done his part to make the law perform its function. His record to date: twenty-five capital penalties asked for, twenty-four won.

The Wade-Decker-Alexander-Fritz team was informally commissioned by Dallas' invisible government to complete the long cleanup of the city's underworld. Wade's office conducted its war not only in court but out on the streets, where Bill Alexander cruised by night in patrol cars with a pistol in his belt. He went on raids and set up a network of stool pigeons, seining sewerfish into the court where Wade could flail them. Then as the bookie joints and whorehouses closed down, Alexander shifted his primary operation to the courtroom (though he kept his appetite for an occasional raid or arrest and continued to wear his gun) while Wade spent more time on the administrative side of his office than in trial work.

Oswald's death and a jailbreak during Ruby's trial have made the world believe that Dallas cops are clowns. That is an error no one in Ruby's world would commit. They know how efficient the force is, how tight they keep things buttoned, how swiftly they execute orders from on high. Clubs must be kept clean "for the sake of Dallas." As Bill Alexander puts it, "The club-owners have to renew their license every year. When renewal time comes up, no disorders are counted against the owner if he has called the police in himself — only if the police catch the trouble on their rounds. So the owners are quick to get on the phone if any rough stuff is in the offing. If 'characters' show up, or out-of-town people who look suspicious, they get the Special Service boys to come look them over." Ruby did this? "Oh yeah! Jack sure knew how to use that phone. It wouldn't be exactly true to say he was a stool pigeon, but it wouldn't be exactly false, either. He knew he had to stay on the good side of the police."

The club world was vividly reminded, in 1957, what it means to get on the bad side of the police. Candy Barr, a stripper who started in Barney Weinstein's Theatre Lounge and moved over to Abe's Colony Club, was getting nationwide publicity for her onstage and offstage acts (e.g., shooting one of her husbands in the stomach), for her theatrical personality, for her underworld friends, and for an undoubted ability to back up her florid-as-Tosca gestures — she would patriotically put a Stetson over her heart, then take her hand away and let it hang there. This was not the publicity desired by custodians of Dallas' "image," and it is assumed by all the club world that word came from the top to "get Candy Barr" — not surprisingly assumed, if one considers the following sequence:

Arrest-Day minus 20 (October 7, 1957): A detective from the Criminal Intelligence section of the Dallas Special Service Bureau rents, under an assumed name, an apartment just down the hall from Candy's. The apartment is paid for by "Billy Paul," a name used by the captain of Special Service when disposing his men on undercover jobs.

A-Day minus 12 (October 15): A telephone man is called to explain why Candy's signal is fading and generally "acting up." In the apartment's first-floor telephone box, he finds a "jumper" connecting Candy's apartment to the detective's (which, so far as the telephone man knows, has no phone). On the same day, the electric company's meter reader finds that electricity is being used in the detective's apartment, although no application has been made to the company.

A-Day minus 1 (October 26): This was supposed to be A-Day. Early on this Saturday morning, the head of Criminal Intelligence took an affidavit to Judge Richburg (who will later deal with another famous stripper, Jack Ruby's Jada). The complaint reads that "one Juanita Dale Phillips [i.e., Candy] and unknown persons did then and there unlawfully possess a narcotic drug, to wit: marijuana." The judge issued a search-and-arrest warrant; yet though the warrant said, "You are therefore commanded to forthwith search the place above named . . . and you will also arrest and bring before me, at said place and time, the said Juanita Dale Phillips and unknown persons," the detective did *not* forthwith arrest the said Juanita. Instead he parked his car across from Candy's apartment house all afternoon (one-thirty to four-thirty) and much of the night (nine to one). Meanwhile, early in the evening, a nineteen-year-old stripper at the Theatre Lounge — a girl who up till a month ago had been rooming with Candy but now was moving back with her mother — is given a tobacco tin full of marijuana. Another dancer gives it to her.

A-Day (October 27): The head of Intelligence again took up his post, alone, from one to four-thirty in the afternoon; but when he returned at six-thirty that same Sunday evening, he brought with him two other men, both from the Narcotics Squad. Shortly before this, at six p.m., the nineteen-year-old stripper had brought the Prince Albert can of marijuana to Candy and asked her to put it in some container less bulky. The girl was going home to her mother at last (she spent the previous night in a friend's house), and she did not want to take the marijuana there. She said she would pick it up again Monday, after Candy transferred it to something that would fit in a purse. At nine-thirty, a man delivering a telegram knocks on the door of Candy's apartment while she is on the phone. The three detectives are out of the car now and on the spot when she opens the door. They enter, search her apartment for fifteen minutes, find nothing. Then a man named George Owens knocks on the door and is brought into the room. While he is there, one of the detectives pulls a marijuana cigarette out from under a chair in the front room. Here were Candy and "persons unknown" and the "narcotic drug" all present and accounted for. But Candy wants George let off, so she agrees to show them the marijuana that was left in her apartment if he is released. After Owens leaves, she pulls an Alka-Seltzer bottle full of marijuana from the capacious hiding place where she used to hang her Stetson.

She was taken to jail around midnight. The captain of Special Service then went to the "Billy Paul" apartment in her building. About this time, the landlord of that house saw his detective-tenant (who had told him he worked for a bank) drive away. It was the last time he saw him until they met in court. The rent contract was terminated by phone early in November. (The day after the arrest, an affidavit showing what had been found in Candy's rooms was notarized by a man in Special Service, Detective Gayle Tippit. Special Service is the force that patrols the clubs, and this is the Tippit Jack Ruby knew. He is not the other policeman with the same last name — one of three Tippits on the Dallas force — who was later killed by Oswald.)

At Candy's trial, the defense tried to make a case that the warrant had been illegally obtained, executed, and registered; that only on the assumption of an illegal wiretap could the detective's streetside surveillance be explained; that the cigarette had been planted, the Prince Albert tin trojan-horsed into her home. But the prosecution — ably generaled by Bill Alexander and his most efficient colleague, Jim Allen, and aided by some helpful rulings of the judge, Joe B. Brown — said that the head of Criminal Intelligence had no dealings, on the relevant days, with that member of his six-man force who was living down the hall from Candy's room; that the telephone "jumper" (of a type not used by the telephone company's own repairmen) was probably left over from some earlier party line; that a respectable (unnamed) informer, at an unspecified time before the warrant was sworn out, had assured the force Candy "did then and there unlawfully possess" the drug that did not reach her till the next day. For the rest, the prosecution gave the impression that Candy was on trial for general naughtiness. They tried to get one witness to explain the term "exotic dancer," asked another one if he knew Candy as Juanita Phillips or Juanita Dabbs or Juanita Swanson; and they drew attention again and again to the obtrusive repository of the Alka-Seltzer jar — five times in as many minutes Alexander sang this forensic refrain:

"I'll ask you if the defendant pulled any object *from her bosom.* . . ."

"And what was it that she pulled *from her bosom.* . . ."

"All right, sir, did she tell you anything at the time she pulled this *from her bosom.* . . ."

"Is the person who pulled the marijuana *from her bosom* and gave it to you present here in the courtroom?"

"Will you look around the courtroom and see if you see the person who pulled the bottle *from her bosom.* . . ."

The prosecution was up to its old tricks, enjoying every minute of it. They casually placed the marijuana on the rail of the jury box; they harassed the defense by invoking the Texas court custom of remaining seated while addressing the witness. As usual, Bill Alexander did the shrewdest punching — as when, after asking about the man who called on Candy at night, and for whose release she pleaded, he nonchalantly inquired of the witness whether Mr. Owens was a white man or a Negro. The defense spluttered its objection and Alexander, his implication planted, mildly stork-walked away from the question.

The jury gave Candy fifteen years, an extraordinarily heavy sentence, despite the fact that this was her first offense. "Two years for her," grins Alexander, "three for Braecklein, and ten for Lester May" (her lawyers). She began a series of appeals, all unsuccessful, though her friend Mickey Cohen brought a very famous lawyer into the case, Melvin Belli of California, who fired off an angry telegram to Judge Joe Brown. Belli has a friend he regularly calls on for his transactions in Texas — Joe Tonahill of Jasper. Tonahill, too, got into Candy's case and clashed with his old pal Joe Brown, the easygoing judge who tried his hand at making motion pictures of Candy in the courtroom. (Things like this made the prosecution fear the judge as much as they enjoyed his willingness to be guided by their homework on the Texas laws.) After her appeals, after her defense by Belli and Tonahill, and after another marriage, Candy began to serve her term. Several years later she was out on parole, and a new strip joint had been opened in downtown Dallas. She could not dance yet, by the terms of her parole, but the new club's manager, Jack Ruby, wanted to get his bid in early. He visited her, sent gifts, and telephoned her at her home in Edna, Texas. If and when she went back to work, she could lend class to his nightclub.

The same team we saw at work on the Candy Barr case went into action on November 22, 1963. Henry Wade was at the Trade Mart waiting for the President to arrive, but Bill Alexander was on duty: "I went out to eat lunch early, so there would be someone in the office while Henry attended the speech. I had run some errands, and planned to get back just after the parade passed, so I could get into my parking spot. I saw a squad car running a Code Three — lights and sirens at maximum alert. I heard other sirens and thought there had been a big-industry accident. But then I saw detectives running in the street, and thought, 'Something has happened in that parade.' When I parked, a lawyer I know told me the President had been shot at. I reached my office around twelve-thirty-five, and heard the sheriff's office was questioning witnesses, so I went to see what they knew. Then, after setting up a command post at our switchboard, I went to the interrogation point Inspector Sawyer was maintaining at the School Book Depository.

"Around one-fifteen Sergeant Owens got an assist-officer call on his radio — a policeman had been shot in Oak Cliff, so Jerry Hill and I got in the car and went out to where Tippit had been killed. That was a pretty wild ride; but during it we listened to the radio and wondered if Tippit had recognized the man being described there. At first we thought it was a thousand-to-one chance, but by the time we got there we had half made up our minds the killings were connected. We were the first car there. There was blood on the street, and three pistol hulls. We searched an old house used as a furniture store. The call came out that a man had been seen running to the library, so we searched it. We had just shaken down a church, with our guns drawn, when a call said our man was in the Texas Theatre. I went to the rear and was guarding the back door when he was captured." The posse rides fast — so fast that conspiratorial theorists will forever wonder how the Dallas clowns caught their man so rapidly.

Alexander went for a search warrant, and took the Justice of the Peace with him to shake down Oswald's room: "We found his notebook and started checking out the phone numbers back here — one of them was for the Russian Embassy in Washington. There were about five of us looking over each other's shoulder seeing what we could find. There was correspondence to read, too — some of it with the head of the Communist

Worker." He took the Justice of the Peace into Captain Fritz's office and arraigned Oswald. "He was the most arrogant sonvabitch I ever saw. 'Arraignment!' he snarled. 'An arraignment has to be in a courtroom.' If one of us was haphazard in asking a question, he would pick that right up. He wouldn't crack; he was in complete control of the situation. He answered every question with another question.

"Cap Fritz and I had decided to file on him for Tippit, before some Communist lawyer tried to get him out on bond. Then Jim Allen joined us; he had gone into private practice, but he came down to help us out. He swung right into it, just like the old days. Cap and I have always worked well together, and about nine o'clock that night we went over to the Majestic café to eat dinner and discuss what we should do. We decided to file on Oswald for Kennedy's killing as well as Tippit's. When we went back to City Hall, I went after publicity for the first time in fifteen years. George Carter of the *Times Herald* asked me, 'Are you going to file?' I said yes. 'When?' 'As soon as I can draw up the complaint.' 'For what?' 'Murder.' 'How will it read?' 'Did then and there voluntarily and with malice aforethought kill John F. Kennedy by shooting him with a gun *in furtherance of a Communist conspiracy.*' I knew I couldn't draw up an indictment like that, but I wanted to kill all the talk about right-wingers in Dallas. I didn't know anything about plots, but I knew this sonvabitch was a Communist. Reporters are so afraid of libel they wouldn't run that as our opinion; they'd print it only if they could say it was our formal charge. Well, George took it and ran with it. In about fifteen minutes, Wade got the word from Washington to knock off this Communist stuff. But we had done our job."

As usual. Carter is the police reporter Alexander likes to work with. This D.A. knows he has a twofold mandate — to punish crime and to protect the Dallas image. He was working at both jobs that busy Friday. "I saw just enough of the television, while moving around, to get sick at my stomach and mad.

The announcer said, 'This is what Lee Oswald looks like — or at least this is what he looked like before he fell into the hands of the Dallas police.' " The press had to be shown that the Dallas force was doing its job properly. And they had to be disabused of the Dallas right-winger idea.

It was going well. The team was functioning, until a man tried to do their job even more efficiently. In the City Hall elevator just after his arrest, Ruby told the police: "Somebody had to do it, you guys couldn't." "I hope I killed the sonvabitch," he told his captors as they wrestled him to the floor, "I intended to shoot him three times. . . . You didn't think I was going to let him get by with it, did you?" Later he added, "When I saw that smirk, I knew who I was going for." He explained to Treasury agent Forrest Sorrels, the man in charge of security at the presidential parade, that he shot Oswald for Mrs. Kennedy's sake, to spare her and her children the agony of a trial; and that he did it "to prove a Jew has guts." He seemed calm in these early interviews, friendly to the police, puzzled that they were not as friendly in return. When Forrest Sorrels was brought in to question him, he asked "Is this for any magazine or publication?" He said to Captain Fritz, "I hope you will not hate me for what I did." He was the center of attention, explaining himself carefully. He told Dr. Manfred Guttmacher, one of the first psychiatrists who talked with him, "After I was brought upstairs in the elevator, I felt relieved." "Don't you think I would make a good actor?" he asked Captain Fritz. Late in the afternoon, he was fingerprinted by Ed Carlson, one of the officers he rescued in the South Ervay Street brawl. Jack chatted pleasantly with Ed, and asked after Blankenship, the other man he helped in that fight. When his sister Eva came to see him, he told her, "I have friends here, so don't worry about me." They all knew him. "I got lots of friends here, so don't make a scene and get hysterical." He was Jack Ruby.

Later, at his trial, Ruby's lawyers would fight to prevent the admission of incriminating remarks made to the police in these first hours of arrest. They went even further; they implied or asserted that these remarks had been made up by policemen, acting on instructions from the D.A.'s office. (They even claimed their defendant could not have used on Oswald the omnipresent Dallas word "sonvabitch" because — as two witnesses testified, to the amazement of Jack's friends — Mr. Ruby never used profanity!) But the first friends to reach Ruby were given the same explanations he voiced to the police and to Federal agents. Jack asked that Joe Campisi be allowed to visit him during his first week in jail and told the restaurateur when he arrived that "Somebody had to kill him." Ruby was pleased with the favorable letters he had been getting. "All the girls love me," he boasted. Though he had been ordered not to get in touch with newsmen, he was allowed to telephone members of his family and certain approved friends; he managed to call Tony Zoppi of the *Morning News* by catching him at a restaurant number. The chat was a lengthy one, the only extensive interview Jack had with a newsman after his arrest. (Conspiratorialists of the wilder variety believe that Dorothy Kilgallen had a private interview, one that caused her death. This tête-à-tête never took place: she leaned over the rail and talked to Jack in the open courtroom during a break in the proceedings. Lawyer Joe Tonahill, who hoped to collaborate with Miss Kilgallen on a book, arranged the brief exchange, and was present at it.) The phone conversation with Zoppi repeated themes from that first day of Jack's arrest — he wept for the widow, said he felt sorry for her, and added that he did it to prove to the world that "Jews have balls."

During the second week of his confinement, Jack was visited by a close friend, the nightclub comic Breck Wall, a star and co-producer of the show *Bottoms Up*. He told Wall, "I was right to kill Oswald." Andrew Armstrong, bartender at The Carousel, came regularly to the jail to report on the club's affairs and get instructions about running it. He told us, "Jack talked as if it would be no time before he was back running things." Ruby's lawyer Tom Howard, after a first interview with his client, was sure he did it to become a hero. Jim Martin, a lawyer who reached Jack even before Howard did, says "He never expected to spend a night in jail," and amiable Joe Brown must have agreed with this view — he granted Tom Howard a writ for his release on bond. When Alexander heard this, he hit the ceiling, and instantly got Brown to change it to a "dry writ" — one that demands a hearing before the prisoner can be let out.

Joe Tonahill remembers his client's first month in jail this way: "When I first saw him, he was way up in the clouds, exhilarated. I had an interview with him to satisfy myself he wasn't in any Communist plot. And after it was over, he got up and shook my hand very graciously: 'Well, Joe, you make a good impression. I'm glad to have you with me.' He acted as if *he* had been interviewing *me* to perform in his damn club!" How long did this euphoria last? "Till the change-of-venue hearing. When Mayor Cabell got on the stand and said Jack couldn't get a fair trial in Dallas because he had hurt Dallas so badly by his action, that hit Jack like a ton of bricks. 'Why, I love this city, Joe!' he would say to me. He never dreamed of hurting Dallas." Mayor Cabell told the Warren Commission he had known Jack Ruby nearly four years. Jack was very proud of this acquaintance; he liked to take friends up to the Mayor, at all public events, and preside over introductions (the same role he played with Henry Wade on the night of the President's death). When he introduced Pat Morgan to the Mayor, on "Italian Night," it was in the presence of Joe Brown. When, with Brown presiding and the Mayor on the stand, Jack heard the words of "my friend, the Mayor," they came as a complete shock. From that time on, the disillusioning blows came at him faster and faster, as the "good guys" he chatted with so fondly made it clear they meant to see him fry. And he had thought, at first, that he was *joining* this posse that would ride him down. One cop shouted, as he fired at Oswald, "Jack, you sonvabitch." It was a message that did not reach him until Mayor Cabell rephrased it in the courtroom.

The commands of the Dallas hierarchy, wafted invisibly

down from skyscraper aeries, are so mysterious that a man may
think he feels the raven's down of a passing order brush his
cheek — some knight of Henry II off, at a hint, to murder
Becket. Ruby thought he was only doing what a shotgun squad
does when the deteriorating image of law enforcement needs
rough refurbishing. Sometimes a citizen, attuned to the city's
needs, can do more than the officers can (*"You guys couldn't do
it"*). It is the logic of the Dallas rulers' non-official Citizens
Council.

Mayor Cabell had reason to resent Jack Ruby's action. It not
only thwarted the rulers' system; it did so by exemplifying, by
parodying it. Ruby wanted to do it "the Texas way," and nothing
much was working the Texas way that weekend. The shotgun
squad could not protect Kennedy (the "Feds" thought it would
look bad for a President to be herded down an American street
under cover of bared guns). Other newsmen in town were not
as cooperative as the Dallas reporters. Bill Decker had to wait
on the sidelines to keep up appearances. Harried Jesse Curry
had to expose his prisoner to prove he was not mistreating him.
The very efficiency of the police force — what, in other situations, makes them efficient: their short-cuts, their relation with
the Dallas papers, their squad-car-riding D.A. and J.P., their
quick talk to head off any rumors that might hurt Dallas —
turned against them. And the efficiency of the rulers — who
make their will known to subordinates in a manner that might
confuse an *amateur* vigilante — worked against *them*.

Well, no system is perfect. Last Christmas at Northpark
Mall, the grandiose Dallas shopping plaza with more than a
hundred plush stores under a single roof, all of them connected
by wide echoing indoor streets, there was a cage of smoldering-
red flamingos that moved on Giacometti legs; their hooked
heads, looping down sideways on long necks, turned berry eyes
askew at visitors. They were beautiful from a distance, but
whoever put them there must not have returned during the
season to see what they were like up close — not have heard

their Bronx-cheer voices buzz down corridors, nor seen that ventilators cannot cope with the olfactory problem of housed-in birds that size. Perhaps the man who put them there — if he understands the nature of responsibility in Dallas — would not admit he did.

ii

What to do about Joe Brown? In 1963, four Dallas judges divided the year between themselves: a case that came in during a man's three-month stint remained (unless he surrendered it) within *his* jurisdiction. November of 1963, Judge Brown was on the bench — to the consternation of all Dallas. It was remembered that, during a trial which men hoped would brighten the image of Dallas, he had been sidetracked into amateur photography. No one could guess what he would do in Dallas' "trial of the century." This apprehension deepened when men learned that formidable Melvin Belli would step in as Ruby's lawyer. "I could have cried," Bill Alexander says. Taking a case before Judge Brown seemed, at times, a mere "trial run" or preview for the D.A.'s office — ten of his thirty-four cases reviewed in appellate court had been reversed, for judicial error. (The two Dallas judges with comparable tenure had only four reversals in sixty cases reviewed.) "I went and pleaded with him," Alexander continues, "to give the case to another judge. 'Bill, you just don't like me,' he said. I told him, 'Joe, I love you like a brother, but you can't handle this case. You don't know your Evidence well enough.'" Others told us that members of the powerful Citizens Council tried to lever him silently out of the way, only to find that a judge who is determined to hang onto a case cannot be budged with anything short of dynamite.

Judge Brown does not remember any attempts at removing him — not even Alexander's. But the Ruby proceedings were to show he has a short memory. "He wakes up in a different world every morning," his friend Joe Tonahill told us. He even had trouble, the whole world was to learn, remembering that he wrote a book on the Ruby trial (*Dallas, Ruby and the Law*). At a hearing meant to prove his interest in the book invalidated the trial over which he had presided, this exchange occurred:

Q (by Ruby's lawyer, Phil Burleson) "Now, at any time after the signing of this contract back in July of 1964, did you deny that you were writing a book?"
A (by Judge Brown) "I probably did, yes."
Q "As a matter of fact, did you deny to me that you were writing a book?"
A "I probably did, Mr. Burleson, I was denying it to most everybody."

He tended as well to forget how much work he put into the book and how much was contributed by his "ghost" (Paul Crume, columnist for the Dallas *Morning News*). At the hearing he took this line:

A "Mr. Crume is doing the writing, I am not."

*   *   *

A "Mr. Burleson, please remember that I didn't write any of this. These are all Mr. Crume's conclusions that are written."
Q "Didn't he draw those conclusions from conversations with you?"
A "Not necessarily. I think he did a great deal of research on his own."
Q "Some of them at least deal with the trial?"
A "Maybe we did discuss some of the things in here."

*   *   *

Q "During the course of the book as you contemplated it and it now stands with the work you have done on it so far, did you comment upon or try to justify or explain any of your rulings or decisions during the trial?"
A "Well, I don't know, you would have to read the book to find out, I don't know."
Q "You have read it?"
A "I read it very briefly, Mr. Burleson, I couldn't tell you what is in it or anything."

But two and one-half months later, on the Mort Sahl TV show, Judge Brown answered a question about his forthcoming opus this way:

Brown: "It's the first time I ever tried to write anything, and it's difficult, let me tell you."
Sahl: "It's a lonely occupation."
Brown: "You read and read and read, Mort, and then you write one paragraph."

And so it goes. The Judge tells Joe Tonahill in court that he would not have let him continue on as Ruby's lawyer if he had known of an affidavit from Ruby's family asking that he be dismissed — whereupon Tonahill showed that Brown not only knew about the affidavit but had ruled on it. The Judge said he did not read accounts of the Ruby proceedings till after the trial — yet when Belli submitted a bale of newspaper clippings, at the outset, to demonstrate community prejudice, the Judge had it admitted into evidence, "promising to read and digest each piece." He said he had not read Belli's book on the trial — then answered a question about his own manuscript by saying, "That is a direct quote out of Belli's book." But his most spectacular lapse of memory occurred in a letter he wrote to Sam Stewart, an editor with Holt, Rinehart and Winston: he actually forgets, while passing from the first to the second of the paragraphs quoted, that he is *not* writing a book:

"About the book — It perhaps is a good thing that it is not finished, because they have filed a Motion to disqualify me on the grounds of having a pecuniary interest in the case. [*Another lapse of memory: the motion he refers to had been overruled four days before this letter was written.*] I can refute that by stating that there has been no book published or that I have not begun to write a book.

"We are coming along nicely. We have approximately 190 pages complete. I have been on Paul, trying to hurry him, have called him, gone to see him and everything else I could do to hurry it, but Paul has been sick and has not been able to do as much as he wanted to on it."

Another paragraph from this letter would survive to haunt him:

"As you probably read in the papers, the Court of Criminal Appeals tossed the case back to me to determine Jack Ruby's sanity and I have set the Sanity Hearing for March 29th, and don't know the outcome, but it is my opinion they will never prove Ruby insane, but the case is far from being over. Therefore, I ask your indulgence and patience as actually we may have a much, much better book than we had anticipated; but I do not want to put myself in the position of being disqualified."

This paragraph became the equivalent, in the Ruby case, of photographing Candy Barr:

Q "And did you express an opinion in that letter as to the sanity or insanity of Jack Ruby?"
A "Yes sir, it was an erroneous opinion, but it is in there nevertheless."
Q "What did you mean by erroneous opinion?"
A "I mean that I had no opinion up until the time I wrote that letter."
Q "Now, at the time you wrote the letter of March 12, you had, just as you say in your letter, had the case tossed back to you by the Court of Criminal Appeals to determine this very issue, is that correct?"

A "Yes sir."

Q "And in this letter you express your opinion, upon that issue that was presently pending before you, is that correct?"

A "That is the one of insanity?"

Q "Yes."

A "Yes."

Q "And then you stated that because of the pendency of the sanity hearing before you that the case was far from being over?"

A "Not because of that, no sir."

Q "Isn't that all in that same sentence in that paragraph?"

A "Yes sir, it is all in the same sentence."

Q "What did you mean when you said that you were going to have a sanity hearing, what was going to keep the case far from being over?"

A "Well, I don't know what I meant by the things, Mr. Burleson."

There are some who would give a less charitable name to these lapses of memory. Judge Brown is one of them:

Q "I will ask you if when you were asked how the book was coming along or of the status of the book, you made the statement, 'We are coming along fine, I am just about finished'?"

A "I probably did."

Q "Was it a true statement at that time?"

A "No."

Q "It is not?"

A "It is a flat-out lie, Mr. Burleson, if that is the way you want to construe it."

The whole book episode is a painful memory for Judge Brown now. It began offhandedly enough, though, with a phone call from Brown to his friend, oilman Clint Murchison. Joe said he was thinking of doing a book on the Ruby trial, did Clint know a publishing house that might take it. "Yeah, Joe, I think I own one, but I can't tell you the name of it right now. I'll have my secretary look it up and call you right back." The secretary called to say that Mr. Murchison owns stock in Holt, Rinehart and Winston, and Judge Brown soon had a contract with that firm — $5,000 advance to him, $5,000 to his ghost-writer. The two authors holed up in a Murchison motel in California to rough out the book; expenses for that trip were paid out of Murchison's office. After the hearing on his literary activities, however, Judge Brown "recused" (disqualified) himself in the Ruby proceedings, and the book died unpublished.

Only mavericks like Murchison and Brown would launch an "unauthorized" book in Dallas. Murchison has many ties with Dallas — including its football team (one of the things he probably remembers owning) — but oilmen are suspect in the city, kept out of its inner counsels. Judge Brown is charming, well-liked by Dallasites — he was reelected after the trial, despite his "bad press." For years he was a Justice of the Peace in Oak Cliff, where Ruby lived. Now his son, Joe Jr., holds that position. When a warrant was needed to search Ruby's apartment (after his arrest), Joe Jr. issued it. The apartment number on this document was wrong, so the police called the J.P. over to amend it. The pretty manager would not let them in. Joe Jr. took care of the matter, then watched them conduct their search. In this clannish city, Ruby's judge was not only an acquaintance of his, but the father of the man who helped search his rooms. Nonetheless, as Judge Brown's resistance to the Citizens Council proved, he does not have the true Dallas instinct for putting the city's welfare over everything else. He held onto the trial, which was bad enough — but writing a *book* was positively un-Texan. When Warren Leslie, a novelist-executive high in the Neiman-Marcus organization, wrote a critical book about Dallas, it seems to have been understood all around that he would quietly leave town when he published. After the assassination, an oil executive wrote an article in *Look* descriptive of shortcomings in the Dallas community. He had concrete blocks dumped in his swimming pool; he was criticized publicly by one of the city's most powerful men (Robert Cullum);

and the oil company demanded that his statements be cleared in advance. He resigned.

The printed word is severely controlled there. Both newspapers breath symbiotically with the power structure. The Citizens Council openly boasts of the way it "managed news" to bring about racial integration in a peaceful way. Others maintain that the news is as carefully managed all the time, in every area. Indeed, some of the city's hostility to "outside" journalists is mixed with sheer amazement that anyone could have the effontery to go away and *write anything he wants to*. This is considered "irresponsible." Dallas thinks of literary *responsibility* as the urge that fills shelves in that large alcove of the Cokesbury Bookstore devoted to celebration of Texas and things Texan. (Opposition to the press is common at all levels; the only one who seems to have taken the menace in his stride is Bill Alexander — "They were crawling all over during the trial, sticking those damn microphones in my face wherever I went. But I soon learned there are a couple of words that make them pull those mikes away as if they had got their fingers burned, and I just dealt them a few when I wanted to get rid of journalists.")

The whole time of Ruby's trial was a nightmare for those in Dallas who fear the rumble of "irresponsible words" disseminated through "unauthorized" typewriters. To have Joe Brown playing with such dangerous things — that was simply too much! The *Times Herald's* A. C. Greene says, "The whole Citizens Council went into mourning over Judge Brown. And their response was typical of Dallas — trying to solve a social problem with a business method. If a businessman runs up against something he can't handle, he disappears behind closed doors and sends his P-R man out to start explaining. So Sam Bloom was sent over to handle the publicity of the trial. He is not only a P-R man, but a member of the Citizens Council, he handled many of their operations. In fact, he has carried a lot of trash in this town." But there was not much Bloom could do. The Judge was irrepressible during the trial. He would shout "Fire!" to get through a crowded room, or declare a recess by saying "Go out and get a cuppa coffee or a slug."

Then, to top it all off, Melvin Belli came to town. The scourge of insurance companies came to the insurance center of the Southwest, a man bound to draw even more of those dangerous creatures from "outside" newspapers, a man who went instantly to war with the city and its rulers. "You know what really made them mad at me?" he asked us. "My saying that they do not even know what to use a bidet for — the one I saw in Dallas had flowers planted in it!" Belli has always been a crusader for "the little guy" against big companies. Dallas seemed a destined arena for him — an oligarchy, a nightclub owner who embarrassed it, a managed press, a subservient law-enforcement team. As soon as he hit town, he began to represent Judge Brown as the tool of Dallas businessmen and Jack Ruby as their natural prey — a picture of the city that Ruby, for one, would never understand. Neither would Judge Brown (the rulers were more anxious to "get rid of" the Judge than of Ruby at this point). The real anger of the "oligarchy" was directed at Belli himself, not the defendant (sad beneficiary of those enmities his lightning-rod lawyer attracted). Belli's was a crucial misreading of the situation, since defending men in Dallas courts is as much an exercise in sociology as in the law.

When the posse rides, there is no escaping it. But a breezy, boozy camaraderie of defense lawyers has learned one way to get clients off — by making them creep so low they are not worth the hunt. There is sporting instinct in the riders, it makes them loath to shoot at crippled rabbits. That is why, despite the awesome power of the police, there are so many murders in Dallas and so few convictions. The circle of defenders has perfected its arts — the "no-bill" (grand jury dismissal), the feather-light sentence in "nigger killings" (ones a Texas jury does not really care about, as when one Negro kills another). One of the acknowledged masters in this genre was Tom

Howard, a lawyer who "no-billed" a girl who had shot her lover ("Chicken Louis" Ferrantello), then took the lethal female as his bride. In twenty-five capital cases, Howard had not lost a client to the chair.

Howard was the first lawyer put in charge of Ruby's case. George Senator, Ruby's roommate, had gone to a lawyer friend of his named Jim Martin the moment he heard (on a café radio) that Jack shot Oswald. Along with Senator, Martin was the first to reach Ruby, but others were seeking legal aid as well. Comedian Breck Wall called his own lawyer, Phil Burleson, to see if Phil might do something for Jack (Burleson would become the only lawyer who stayed with the case). Joe Cavagnaro tried to get to Jack and recommend Charles Tessmer, a highly respected defense attorney; but the police would not let him in. Despite the obstacles, five lawyers showed up Sunday afternoon trying to arrange bail for Ruby. As he told Eva that day, "I got lots of friends." Taking his friend Ralph Paul's advice, he accepted Howard as chief counsel, with Jim Martin to assist. Howard's strategy was clear — to go for "murder without malice," a charge on which juries are lenient in Texas. He would minimize the case, ingratiate himself with Dallas by keeping the publicity low-key, and put Jack on the stand to say he lost control of himself from grief did a bad thing and is very sorry and please-don't-kill me. "Tom would have outpolited the State," Alexander says. Howard thought Ruby could not possibly get more than five years — "just another nigger case."

He was perhaps too confident. Not only was this a headline killing around the world; Ruby had shot a helpless man escorted by police. Many of those we talked to in Dallas had no objection to Ruby's killing Oswald, only to his killing a *handcuffed* man. (His old bouncer, Bob Larkin, said, "I can see him punching the guy, but not *shooting* him when he had the cuffs on.") Howard would have to appeal to the Texans' sporting attitude; but that very instinct would tell against him when the subject of the handcuffs was brought up. "The defense has a great advantage when there's any touch of shoot-out," Alexander admits, "but Oswald could not fight back. Plenty of people would *love* to have killed him, if only he had grabbed a gun or made a break for it; but Jack just plain gut-shot an unarmed, manacled man."

Still, the provocation was great; and Oswald was hated, in this right-wing stronghold, not only as a man who disgraced the city by shooting President Kennedy and a Dallas policeman, but as a presumed Communist. Congratulations flowed in on Ruby in his jail. An early poll showed that citizens were seven to one in favor of a light sentence for him. Every lawyer we talked to in Dallas agreed that Howard was taking the right approach. So do the two scholars, John Kaplan and Jon Waltz, who wrote an account of the trial's legal aspects. And Bill Alexander, who claims he could have fried Jack no matter who defended, concedes it would be difficult to beat the Howard strategy. "If you lay a great big ol' heart out there on the table and let it flip-flop around for the jury, and bleed for them, it's awful hard for them to send the man off to die. There's no better defense than the truth and an I'm-sorry." The nationwide team of distinguished lawyers that was in charge of Ruby's case when he died had chosen a strategy for the retrial that was pending: they would go for murder without malice — Tom Howard's case, without Howard to try it (he was dead by then); without Howard's knowledge of Dallas juries, prejudices, pride; his savvy for crouching low when the posse is out hunting.

Howard might have done it. But only by making it a "nigger case" — which is not what Jack Ruby bargained for. He thought — so did the hundreds sending thanks to him — that he acted hastily, perhaps, but against a man who deserved no better. Howard was aware of this feeling; he played upon it, said publicly men should "pin a medal on Jack cuz Oswald deserved it." But he knew that, in the last moments, up against a slashing Wade-Alexander attack, he would have to win the jury with a "nigger-murder" plea.

Jack could not stomach that. It was beneath his dignity. It offended, as well, his brother Earl (the most responsible family spokesman) and his sister Eva (next to Jack, the most volatile Ruby; but the one, in all other ways too, who was "next to Jack"). It had been a long, slow climb out of the ghetto for all of them. The idea of slinking back into a moral slum to play the lead role in a "nigger case" touched every Ruby on exposed nerves. Tom Howard's clientele was, on the most charitable reckoning, a seedy one (though Judge Jim Bowie, then on Henry Wade's prosecuting team, rightly said, "They forget that even though Tom Howard defends whores and pimps, he does it damn well"). Howard was married to a woman who had killed her lover. He had been in trouble with the law himself, over unpaid income tax. A coarse-tongued Texan, Stetson-wearing, shabby, tough; without a law library, with no secretary — definitely not "class."

The family looked elsewhere. As Jack explained to Jim Martin: "If I had some rare illness and all the best brain surgeons were willing to come and work on me, I'd want them. Well, I can have all the best legal minds." He was confident that his old friends, and all the new ones who were wiring or writing to him, would stand beside him. As one of the telegrams from a stranger said, IF YOU NEED MONEY YOU WILL GET IT BOY. YOUR DEFENSE WILL BE THE BEST.

The flood of telegrams was intoxicating. Alexander says of those days, "He didn't think we were going to do anything to him. He believed we were just going through the motions, because we had to. He was enjoying all that attention, just like a pig in slop." The Jack who "interviewed" Tonahill before admitting him into the case, who told Joe Campisi that "All the girls love me," was savoring messages like this one, sent from a woman who closed with LOVE before her name: I KISS YOUR FEET. His old dancers sent best wishes from their current dingy bookings, and a California stripper who had never worked for him said she would come and perform at The Carousel free of charge. More important, he had proved that "Jews have balls."

A typical telegram (from Florida) said, WE LOVE YOUR GUTS AND COURAGE. Another one said, THANK GOD THERE IS ONE MAN IN AMERICA WHO KNOWS HOW TO DEAL WITH PUNKS — a man who, in the words of other well-wishers, knew how to "eliminate the monster" with his "idiotic smirking face"; how to "kill a snake"; how to "eliminate a rat." These people understood. Most of the telegrams saluted his courage and patriotism, just the things Jack wanted to impress on others: CONGRATULATIONS TO A COURAGEOUS AMERICAN YOU HAVE DONE A REAL SERVICE FOR US ALL THANK YOU. A master sergeant sent this military tribute from Chicago: WELL DONE SOLDIER MISSION ACCOMPLISHED. At last he belonged. He was a "red-blooded American" who had the courage to do what others wanted to but would not or could not do; he did not let Oswald get away with it—Jack the avenger, the defender of women's honor, the squelcher of racial jokes, the one-man shotgun squad working outside the law for the purposes of law and order. Even Joe Tonahill, after the interview to satisfy himself Ruby was not a "Commie" in some plot or other, telephoned to Belli that "Jack and his brothers are, I am happy to say, true Americans — and, I might add, true Texans."

It was the supreme accolade in Ruby's world. He was the defender of Dallas, of Texas, of his country: AFTER 48 HOURS OF SHAME I AM AGAIN PROUD TO BE AN AMERICAN. His adopted city had at last recognized her son:

YOU DID WHAT MANY CITIZENS OF DALLAS WOULD HAVE DONE EXCEPT YOU HAD THE COURAGE.

GOD BLESS YOU FOR YOUR HEROIC DEED YOU HAVE VINDICATED THE PEOPLE OF THE GREAT CITY OF DALLAS AND OF THE NATION.

CONGRATULATIONS MR RUBY YOU REDEEMED THE STATE OF TEXAS.

They even realized how his devotion to President Kennedy had inspired him: YOU ASKED YOURSELF WHAT YOU COULD DO FOR

YOUR COUNTRY AND YOU FOUND THE ANSWER. Whole organizations sent their thanks and best wishes. Some wired money; others promised it; most said they would lend him any support he needed. The cascading yellow slips gave a glow to his bare cell. Jack Ruby, starved all his life for recognition and affection, was rolling in it at last, "a pig in slop."

YOU ARE OUR HERO.

CONGRATULATIONS HOPE YOU RECEIVE CONGRESSIONAL MEDAL OF HONOR.

When Breck Wall came to visit him, Jack was all "show business." Wall had just become local Council President of the performers' union, A.G.V.A. Jack's attentiveness to Breck had increased in the short interval between that promotion and his arrest — in fact, the day before he shot Oswald, Jack found out that Wall was out of town, found out where (Galveston), and called him there to let him know which clubs were staying open. He was anxious to pursue this matter on Monday or Tuesday, when Wall planned to come back to Dallas.

They did not see each other till the following Saturday, when Jack asked Sheriff Decker to bring Breck down to see him. His only comment on Oswald, during this visit, was that he had been "right in killing him." Aside from that, Jack was very businesslike. Breck asked if Phil Burleson had reached him. "Yes, he came to see me and I think he would do very well and I would like to use him if I can." Then Jack asked whether Breck would like to get into the case. Breck said no. Jack persisted: he was doing his memoirs, wouldn't Breck like to help? He described all the favorable mail he was receiving; wouldn't Breck like to answer some of it for him? No thanks, Jack. (Well, he had offered him the chance.)

The memoirs were pieced together from things Joe Tonahill and the family heard from Jack. (The "ghost," William Read Woodfield, wrote as if he had done the interview himself; he had not.) "My Life" — the first duty of celebrity:

"I'm so grateful for the opportunities I've had in Dallas. I'm a Jew from the ghetto of Chicago. I came to Dallas and was accepted and made a fine success."

Breck Wall is grateful to Jack for describing, in the article, his Saturday phone call to a *Buck* Wall and Joe *Feder* (i.e., Joe Peterson). He thinks it was Jack's way of honoring the request that Breck be left out of the case. But the whole account, as it appeared in the papers, is riddled with errors; at least half of the names given are garbled (e.g., "Andy Anderson" for Andrew Armstrong, "McWhiters" for McWillie, "Wes Weiss" for Wise). Nonetheless, one does at times hear the voice of Jack (megaphoned through Tonahill) — as when he emphasizes his acquaintance with that other celebrity, Candy Barr. (When he heard of the Woodfield contract, Jack tried to set aside $10,000 from the story for Officer Tippit's widow. His family dissuaded him, at last, by showing him newspaper accounts of the money she had received already.)

The sale of the Woodfield story gave the world a first hint of tensions in the Ruby camp. No one would tell inquirers how authentic the story was. Belli was righteously indignant; *Newsweek* (February 10, 1964) quotes him as saying, "Many writers have asked me to cooperate on stories about Ruby and I've told them all that it would be in bad taste and unethical [to take his case to the press before trial]." Nonetheless, the story was offered free of charge to the afternoon paper in Dallas — which turned it down. Belli also gave a hint of things in the offing and of his role in them: "This is just the beginning — everyone's writing books about this case. The District Attorney. The investigator. Ruby's brother. Ruby's sister. Even the judge. And I'm going to write a book too — with one chapter devoted to each of the other books." Of all the books he mentions, only one appeared. His.

Ruby could not make out the exact shape of the future through his dizzying haze of sudden fame; but he thought there was only one way to go from this new eminence — up. He told his guards about other Jewish entertainers who had made good, "men like Jack Benny." He thought he might lecture in all parts of the country represented by his sheaf of telegrams. He was working on his vocabulary and diction, surprising guards when he won at Scrabble. One of the guards says, "He would sit there dreaming absentmindedly and comb his hair for hours."

Smoothing his thin surviving hairs, he was ready to woo Dallas, his chromium-and-steel *inamorata*, poor Jack; oblivious to the chaplinesque futility of the courtship and — true to form — planning the one move that could make his situation worse. A "nigger-murder" defense was out of the question. He would get class, the kind sophisticated Dallas understands. He would get Melvin Belli.

Earl Ruby was in Hollywood, making arrangements with Woodfield for the sale of Jack's story, when the writer told him about Belli's spectacular career, one built on courtroom theatrics shrewdly exerted on a weakness in the old insurance contracts — insufficient reparation to the injured. There is no doubt that Belli's past performance makes him one of the century's greatest lawyers. And one of the saltiest — an old drinking pal of Errol Flynn, a lawyer often married, bouncy and peppery-tongued. He told a *Playboy* reporter how he used to cavort with his famous friend: "One hot afternoon in Paris, Errol took off all his clothes to be cool and lay down on his bed for a nap. I left him sleeping soundly and went downstairs to the hotel bar and sold tickets for five dollars apiece to about twenty women — Frenchwomen and tourists — whom I brought upstairs for a guided tour of Errol in the altogether." Shades of Bill Fallon and high jinks with Jack Barrymore!

When Belli appeared in the Dallas jail, in his resplendent tailoring, he seemed the embodiment of all things Ruby admired — bantam-cock of a man, nearly as short as Jack, but with a creamy head of hair; with a fortune in clothes on his back, a famous name, a gallery of "names" for friends, a poly-syllabic uninterruptibility, an earthy charm. This was no Jackie Kennedy, about whose interest in culture Jack had to ask others. Belli's friends were Mickey Cohen and Errol Flynn. Here was Las Vegas glittering through the dim aisles of the library — a mirror where plump short unimpressive and tongue-tied Jack Ruby was put magically face to face with the plump short impressive "Great Mouthpiece." Belli realized that "It made him feel good that I not only knew my law but was a sharp dresser and a great cocksman."

Only one thing gave Ruby a momentary bit of doubt. "He didn't know what to make of my boots," Belli says. "He asked if I thought they were the right things to be wearing." Jack wore cowboy clothes when he ran The Silver Spur, but had long ago shed them for dignified business suits. "I explained to him that I wear them because my father always wore them." He did *not* explain that their high heels gave him an inch or two on Jack, whom he refers to as "that little fellow." Ruby's apprehensions were well founded: Belli's footwear became famous during the trial after Bill Alexander referred to his opponent's "fruit boots." Perhaps Ruby later had doubts, too, about his counsel's magnificent vocabulary — when Belli published an account of the trial that refers, more than once, to "the ubiquitous conferences in the Judge's chambers."

When Earl Ruby asked him to take the case, Belli said he must have a Texas lawyer working with him and he wanted Joe Tonahill of Jasper: "Joe's father-in-law is Howard Smith, chairman of the House Rules Committee, so Joe has a lot of influence in Washington and Texas." In Tonahill Jack thought he was getting a bonus of "class." Tonahill is a huge man who cannot quite manage to look as big as he is. His skull seems narrow, almost lost in the flesh cascading down his collar — like the features from which gold spreads weirdly out on the "mask of Agamemnon." His eyebrows are tufted, brushed upward in the manner of John L. Lewis, yet thin-looking *because* they prompt this comparison. He comes from Jasper, which is East Texas — Old South, cotton Texas; plantation land, not frontier or prairie or oil land, with memories of Negro slaves not Indian enemies. "I wish," he joked to us, "some pickaninnies would fall into the fountain outside the Supreme Court so we could sue Earl Warren for maintaining an attractive nuisance." When Judge Brown threatened to cut the trial short before the defense could bring its last witness into town, Belli told newsmen, "Well, I guess Brother Tonahill will have to show you what an old-fashioned Southern filibuster is like."

Mr. Tonahill's legal terminology is wielded with considerable imagination — as when he told a reporter that Ruby should plead "patriotic insanity" in his second trial. His typewriter has a pamphleteering tic, and rattles incessantly with manifestos sent regularly off to newsmen. He handed us this sample:

To begin with, the emotion-laden atmosphere, not only in the South but within the four quarters of Red, White and Blue America, was such as to cause normal human beings to recoil beyond the norm, that black day — November 22, 1963.

Ruby shot the assassin Oswald no more for a place in the limelight than would his allegers along this line of belief have done the same thing for the same reason. The act of Ruby's triggered mind went deeper than this. Jack Ruby is a very unstable and emotional person who ran a striptease joint, engaged in fisticuffs on slight provocation, yet nurtured virtues within himself hardly to be associated with the public image of him. These paradoxical virtues were what triggered the act.

He felt, in fact, no animosity toward the assassin Oswald. He tilted in the list to preserve inviolate his own code of right over wrong. This necessitated the killing off impersonally of an insipid ideologist of no intellect, group with no motive other than a grandiose revolutionary compulsion, who shot the President.

Oswald was the one who wished to cast his image before the world, even if only an image of unbridled revolutionary tactic.

The entire world recoiled in sorrow and horror at the assassin of our beloved President.

But normal reaction was not for Ruby. The flywheel mechanism controlling his enate [*sic*] instability when face-to-face with his personal definition of a wrong when out of control and nothing mattered but that fingered by his own emotional storm — he did something (anything) to right in his own way a wrong to him as heinous as the "crucifixion."

Were Ruby capable of explaining himself in his own defense he would propose the morality of the lines "For whom the bell tolls? — It tolls for thee."

When qualifying jurors for the Ruby trial, Tonahill asked questions like this: "Could you find a sick GI guilty of killing a Communist?" After it was all over, Belli said, "I guess I did let Joe go too far with that cornball stuff." In his interview with us, Belli expertly mimicked the Tonahill drawl when he said, "Joe's favorite objection was, 'It is incompetent, irrelevant, immaterial, un-American and un-Texan!'"

Perhaps Ruby realized he had not got the "class" he bargained for when, during the selection of jurors, Tonahill angrily threw his pencil at Judge Brown ($25 for contempt). We had our own awakening on New Year's Eve when, accompanying him to a nightclub, we watched in fascination as he supplied the lack of a handkerchief in his expensive suit with, successively, paper napkins, the doilies under our drinks, the little envelopes containing sugar (their granulated contents first sandboxed into a pyramiding ashtray), and large linen dinner napkins brought by a waiter called in on the emergency — the detritus of this extraordinary sequence all the while gooily silting up, both sides of his chair, upon the floor. A large man.

When these dramatic lawyers entered the case, Jim Martin and, later, Tom Howard were eased out. Ruby had his specialists, "the best in the country." With his champions flanking him — on one side Belli, who looks like a pugnacious Liberace; on the other Tonahill, mild bulldog blimp drifted off from some Macy's parade — Ruby went into court to face the whimsies of Joe Brown, Henry Wade's efficiency, and Bill Alexander's hellforleather-hard pursuit.

...
iii

Ruby, now in custody, was taken away from that plunge of narrow driveway into dark garage where he killed Oswald; from that surreal pit of headlights, car horns honked, cameras, shouting, and a gunshot; from City Hall, where an innocent bystander was arrested Sunday — the posse's quick response — as he ran, frightened, from the sound of the gun. Ruby was driven through his Dallas — unable to see it, though, crouched on the floor — to a prison bordering Dealey Plaza. From scene of the crime to scene of The Crime. County jail is just inside the concrete tangle of thruway and "cloverleaf" that rings downtown Dallas. He did not pass through that cincture again. His few guarded trips took him north to hospitals — including the last trip to Parkland. From the courthouse where he was tried, one can see the spot where President Kennedy was killed.

To the south, across that concrete spaghetti rim, lies Oak Cliff, former suburb blanched now with metropolitan ashenness. There is an air of transience about it — middle-class, but in a city of fluid hopes and fortunes, a stop-off point for the *climbing* middle class. Or, for those unable to move on, a "settled" place that sinks with them, or is already down and stagnating. Here, near the freeway, are the "airline stewardess apartments" where Ruby lived, homeless in a homeless area. Here too, a mile or so from Ruby's place, Oswald stayed briefly at 1026 N. Beckley Avenue — a small-business ganglion in the residential area, where streets at odd angles leave pie-wedge corners, gas stations (in Oswald's time) islanded on two of them. Rootless enterprises litter the other wedges (even the stores are transient here) — a laundromat, a barbershop; small, necessary commerce of minimal living.

From this point Oswald walked nine blocks to a scruffy street corner without a curb and shot Tippit, in a neighborhood with old mattresses in the frontyards, old cars in the back. This is a grimy backyard to the stores on Jefferson Street, main thoroughfare for Oak Cliff. It was an easy sprint for Oswald, out along that Jefferson facade; in, occasionally, at the reverse fishbowl of receding display windows; then, after reconnoitering, out again; in finally, with a curious frightened clerk now trailing him, at the Texas Theater, fake-Spanish front curlicuing the facade (transformed now, after its rise to dubious notoriety, into a fake-Modern front). The color cartoon ended ten minutes ago. Now the Van Heflin war show, with a Tony Russell war show to follow. Lights; revolver; action. "Well, it's all over now."

Back at 1026 N. Beckley — low, brick, long porch with metal chairs and overarching flowerless trellis, "rooms" straggling along the side and climbing onto the garage — we asked the landlord if we could look into the shallow room where Oswald burrowed during his last days. "You'll have to wait for my wife. I never do anything right, it seems." When his wife arrives, she says we may indeed look in — for three hundred dollars. With commentary, five hundred. Neiman-Marcus is not the only place in Dallas that sells expensive oddities.

There is something in Oak Cliff more depressing almost than the dirt streets and squalor of West Dallas, above Oak Cliff, where Negroes and Mexicans live in huts just off the pulsing highways. This is a dirt-hazed, unrecognizable Dallas still innocent of air conditioning — and, in some places, of plumbing. Negro areas have housefront churches (a step out — and down — from the urban storefronts); Mexican territory has Spanish-dialogue cinemas and patches of color above the mud — store windows filled with plaster saints, bright populous heavens. Two varieties of saints — ceramic and celluloid, heaven and earth. West Dallas has, also, its patron sinners, remembered as fondly as the saints — this was home base for Clyde Barrow and Bonnie Parker, whose names give the dirt streets a livid glamor. Small heaven, and a skyful of earth.

In Oak Cliff, there is only earth. Not outright squalor, but a dinginess of burnt-out ambitions — like the stranded cars, run dead before their time by the distances and pounding heat and "saddle-up" rapidity of Texas driving. The cars, shredding chrome and rusty intestines, disemboweled so that other motors may run a short while longer to the same weedy end, resemble the Dallas men who, with unwitting cannibalism, disassemble them. Their skeletons are the carrion of this bustling desert.

Turning north, one seems to move into another country — curves pleasantly along rilled foliaged Rock Turtle Creek, with its sparkling new apartments or dim homes set far back in protective trees, veiled gardens given sanctuary from the sun; and, on a rise above the Creek, a large Frank Lloyd Wright theater, like an elbowed cubist mushroom. Farther north, then east, the car rambles around White Rock Lake — leafy scenes, and, through the leaves, pretty girls on horseback, houses striding far back into trees, prosperously dungareed men teaching their sons how to aim a gun. High on a treeless lawn, H. L. Hunt's replica of Mount Vernon. Gorgeous residences spaced out in "The Cloisters" behind a long stone wall, and signs on the wall: "Restricted Homesites." We discussed that sign with many Dallasites. Mayor Jonsson assured us it refers merely to zoning and congestion restrictions — which is legally true, no doubt; but the ordinary populace understands it in a more ordinary sense. And not only the average citizen: Stanley Marcus raised an eyebrow: "It says that? I thought that word went out with the Supreme Court decisions."

A city of extremes — not a wider spread, perhaps, than one finds in other large cities. But the gradations here are on a single standard, the spread is recent, the grades are supposed to be rungs; everyone is encouraged to climb, those who reach the top are lavishly rewarded, and the frustration of those who do not get there is proportionate. One expects this scramble to cause divisions, sector against sector. Even a close observer like Warren Leslie calls Dallas five cities, not one. But under all the differences, there is a strange cohesion and agreement. Success and failure are so clearly marked because everyone agrees on the norms for their measurement. Dallas has a single set of values, which makes it, not quite a single city, but something even more united — a singleminded enterprise.

While we were in Dallas, Eric Sevareid spoke his measured TV editorial on Dallas. The instantaneous closing of ranks made Dallas unite not only against Sevareid but against *all* outsiders — especially all newsmen. "Oh," people would respond to us, "some more Sevareids." This defensiveness was not restricted to the city's rulers. All Dallasites are defenders and promoters of their city. The young manager of Ruby's last apartment, who is now a secretary, pouted prettily, breathless with indignation, and said "I'll never listen to that man again." A normally gracious hotel man muttered, "We'll make him regret it if he ever comes back here." Up and down the scale, reaction was the same. Mayor Jonsson answered our question about Sevareid by saying: "I do not want to comment on our persecution by the press. You cannot win. They always have the last word." The city's most characteristic response, however, was dot-dotted in the 686 light bulbs of the Blue Cross Building sign, which spells public service messages in seven-foot letters out over the North Central Expressway, cheery mottoes to brace motorists for their day of service to Dallas. For a week after the Sevareid broadcast, the bulbs limned this message: HE WHO SLINGS DIRT LOSES GROUND. COURTESY PAYS — TRY IT. Everyone knew what — rather, whom — it was referring to.

Courtesy *pays*. A characteristic note of commercial outrage. Good business, good morals. Dallas is a fundamentalist state with its religious fervor partially displaced in the direction of succeeding — understandably enough: this is a city like no other. America's major cities owe their importance to phyletic placing on the water thoroughfares — coastal cities, or those clustered at the Great Lakes, or nodes on the network of great rivers. Inland cities grew where water crossed the land, all major cities but one (it has been doing things backwards ever since): Dallas was a ford, it marked the spot where land crossed water — a rock ledge slanting through the Trinity bed to give sure footing to horse and cattle. John Neeley Bryan found the ford in 1839; marked it with a driven stake; in 1841, returned with settlers.

It seemed a forlorn project; and Bryan, the "founding father" whose log cabin is enshrined just off Dealey Plaza, appropriately took to drink. Even now, there is not an oil well in sight. Wheat is grown outside the city, but irrelevantly. Cattle drives came through for a short time only. The Trinity shrinks and swells in useless tantrums. The climate is awful. Considering its background, it is amazing Dallas has come as far as it has.

Everything is wrong with it — and nothing is. The natives love to attack the land as a way of promoting the city. "We have nothing to offer but the people, and the people must be pretty good to create a great city in the middle of nowhere." The present Mayor, Eric Jonsson, is an engineer from New York who built up Texas Instruments. He told us, "I first saw Dallas back in the Thirties, and I knew then it was where I wanted to live." Wasn't it a different city then? "No, it was the same — the people were here."

An extraordinary people. Back in the 1870's, they had no navigable river; their town had faded as a cattle route; the population was less than 3,000. Yet they scraped together an offer of $5,000 and 115 acres to snakecharm in their direction the train tracks that were rising up from Houston. That is the Dallas style. Early settlers knew they must hang together economically or they would hang separately. The instinct is deep-seated still; civic service is almost a passion with them. And that railroad deal is forever being reenacted. Stanley Marcus,

in an office wallpapered with polyglot awards, puffed on fine ci-
gars (which he does not offer visiting journalists) and told us
how it works: "After the war, I told some members of the Citizens Council that the city's major need was for a big hotel, and
that the store would put up a hundred thousand dollars to
bring one in. The three bankers there" (of *the* Dallas banks —
Republic National, First National, Mercantile Trust) "said
they would put up four hundred thousand. Before the meeting
was over, we had one and a half million dollars to bring in a
hotel." The head of the Statler chain was summoned to Dallas,
lavishly dined, and driven over to look at the site of his new
hotel. Dallas is still luring the railroads into town. The city's
leaders decided they wanted opera, and (as they would put it)
decided to buy the best. New York's Metropolitan would bend
its tour toward Dallas, but only if a $65,000 guarantee were put
up beforehand. Businessman Arthur Kramer checked with
some friends, then told the Met to make it $100,000.

Only once did Dallas have to feign modesty. It was when the
Texas and Pacific Railroad was pushing laterally through the
state, moving "by the book" along the thirty-second parallel.
On this course, it would run fifty miles below Dallas, straight
toward the New Mexico state line (laid out along that parallel). Men from Dallas had to warp the tracks upward a full
latitudinal degree if Texas' north-south tracks and Congress'
east-west T and P were to intersect at the quiet cattle ford. The
city's whole future depended on its finding a way to slide that
junction fifty miles up the state's central plain. The only point
of leverage for them was the Texas legislature, which was
granting free land to the transcontinental line; but open dealing there was politically dangerous and beyond the finances of
the 3,000 Dallasites. What to do? Their shrewd lobbyists jockeyed an unobtrusive rider onto the land grant, providing that,
in this dry land, the line should pass by "Browder's Spring."
Only natives of Dallas knew this was a trickle of water outside
their town.

Dallas is a city based on such manipulated "image," on taking chances, on the pure cash offer. It has a great talent for institutionalizing risk, for the sublimated shoot-out. It is not an oil city, not even an oilman's city — the wells lie south, wildcatters are too vagrant for the artichoke mentality of Dallas chauvinists. But it is the oilmen's strongbox. The banks that jostle their fifty-story shoulders in competitive, corporate pride are the secret of the city's power — financier power; savings and loan, insurance, investment power. They gambled on oil still in the ground and on men determined to get it out — and they won their gamble. They had no natural resource to take out of the ground; they had to deal in that deracinated universal resource, the mobile "equalizer" with which they are quick on the draw, taking the play away — the biggest of big D's, the dollar. Dallas lives on dollars the way Cuba lives on sugar or Manchester lived on coal. It is a one-industry town. Dallas' business is Dallas.

On paper, the City Council runs the city (the Mayor is simply the ninth councilman). Mayor Jonsson says, "It is like the board of any big corporation" — not least in this respect: it is made up of wealthy men. The pay is $20 a week, and even that is contingent on attendance at the weekly meeting. The Mayor gets no more than his fellow councilmen. Not that it matters — all recent mayors have been millionaires. Not Rockefellers — born to money, looking now for private challenge and public service — but self-made men, honored as such. Six of the nine councilmen run from the six municipal districts, in the sense that each must live in his respective district. But they are voted on by all the electorate. In that sense they all run at large, these six as well as the three formally listed as "at-large candidates." A less favored district never gets a councilman who depends exclusively on its support. In fact, since voter registration is so low in the slum areas of West Dallas and South Dallas, those areas do not even get a *proportionate* voice in deciding who "their" councilman will be. One cannot, moreover, bring pressure to bear on the Council through party organization. City politics is nonpartisan. The Citizens Charter Association, an activist arm of the "non-political" Citizens Council, is operative only at election time. It puts up a slate of candidates, irrespective of party affiliation at the state or Federal level. Individuals who wish to oppose these selections had to file independently and go it alone until, in 1961, the Dallas Charter League began to offer alternative slates, operating, like the Charter Association, only intermittently as elections come and go, putting up candidates only for some offices. Mayor Jonsson says the advantage of this plan is that it prevents the pettiness, graft and corruption of ward politics. "Our city has no bossism or ward-heelers or party hacks put on the public payroll." The secondary result is that only the wealthy rule, which P-R man Sam Bloom counts a blessing: "They have the time, the experience and the staff to devote to the good of the city. To me, 'rich' simply means 'able to serve.'" Others, presumably, are *un*able, and need not apply.

This whole arrangement has been called undemocratic: the actual day-to-day ruling is in the hands of a City Manager, who is not elected, but appointed by the City Council. In point of fact, all criticism based on this council-manager plan misses the point. The formal machinery of rule is only a partially useful, partially obstructive bureaucracy for the real government, which is even less elected than the City Manager is. This is the Citizens Council, the non-political benevolent society of Dallas. "We are like the Elks," one of its members told us in his carefully textured and technicolored board room (which looked like the set for some Hollywood satire on plush life in corporations).

It is fitting that this city, which started its growth by tricking railway lines into an unexpected marriage at Browder's Spring, should have acquired its informal "Constitution" by luring another Texas enterprise its way. In 1935 Texas was gestating an outsized self-congratulatory centenary. Dallas was hardly the place for this historical commemoration. When Texas entered the Union, Dallas was not a city but a camp (it was not even incorporated for the first twenty years of Texas statehood). Yet, despite its exiguous historical claim, Dallas rose to the memory of its train-seducing forebears. Leading citizens, under the guidance of R. L. "Bob" Thornton, collected $3,500,000 in enticement money and marched with determination on Austin, where they cajoled the legislature into giving Dallas the centennial affair. The city was not content with raising this pledge money. It laid out an ambitious site which became the permanent State Fair Grounds (for the largest such fair celebrated annually), kept the Centennial running an extra year, and turned the Fair into the biggest channeler of people toward Dallas since the T and P tracks inched their way into Browder's Spring.

It took money. In 1936 and 1937, there were crises every week — meeting pledges, payrolls, upkeep. Bob Thornton kept the whole thing afloat by his incessant energy. He was a colorful uneducated banker — "I am a graduate of C M & M (Cotton, Men, and Mules)" — with a casey-stengelian English whose vigor compensated for its lack of polish: "I want dy-*da*mic men around me!" In his quest for ready cash during the centenary, he separated Dallas' wealthy class into those who responded to his pleas by reaching for their checkbooks (he called these "Yes Men") and those who said "I'll have to talk it over with my board" (these became "No Men," with a subtle implication that they were not only people who said "no," but were, in other ways too, no *men*).

In 1937 Thornton organized his picked Yes Men into the Citizens Council. It holds regular weekly meetings and special crisis meetings. A. C. Greene describes the latter this way: "Old Bob Thornton would invite six or seven men to lunch at the City Club and say, 'Boys, we're the only men in Dallas who can put up two hundred and fifty thousand dollars within the next hour. Now that breaks down to so much per man. If you can't meet that, you'd better leave right now, or we'll just embarrass you, and we don't want to do that. The rest of us will make up your part.' Well, by this time, they're all saying to themselves, 'Dammit, he can't say I haven't got the money to stay in this league,' and by the end of that lunch he had his money." This is what Thornton used to call a "Do Meeting." He refused to attend "Don't Meetings." This was the tradition behind Stanley Marcus when he opened bidding for a new hotel. There are many ways to hold a shoot-out. Money is manhood in Dallas. Without it, without a readiness to "draw" it, you are a no-man.

Men misinterpret the Council's actions if they neglect its unique Dallas roots, physical and psychic. It is wrong, for instance, to consider it a mere business operation; and even more erroneous to think it is a group with any real political philosophy. Though its decisions do lead to better business, the motives of those involved are frontier motives — the constant challenge and proving of oneself, the maintenance of "a reputation." They will show the world that bankers have guts, that they can take the play away from older, better situated, more polished cities and firms. The Citizens Council gives Dallas a new hotel the way Jack Ruby used to pull out his big wad and give money to bums. It is called "class."

Nor is the Council, in any principled way, a right-wing political bloc (though most of its members are financier Republicans or Southern Democrats). They have only one cause, the immediate good of Dallas as their arena of achievement. They are not doctrinaire about things like Federal aid, so long as it contributes something to Dallas; they are not diehard about any point of ideology. General Walker thought he was moving to a congenial place when he took up residence here, and in many ways he was. But his extremism was discomfiting to the Citizens Council, so he had no voice with them — which means he had no power. As a candidate for Governor, he ran sixth in a field of six. Texas does not like losers.

Congressman Bruce Alger disillusioned many of the Dallas

leaders by blocking Federal grants; but what finally turned
them against him was his part in the mobbing of Mr. and Mrs.
Lyndon Johnson outside the Baker Hotel. Dallas nurtures a
strange visceral dislike for Johnson, even more than it had for
Kennedy — "He's just one of them tire-kickin' boys who made
good," as a Dallasite expressed it to us — but Alger did the one
unforgivable thing: he disgraced the city. Mayor Earl Cabell
resigned his office to run against Alger in the next congressional
race. It was as easy as "getting" Candy Barr when she became
an embarrassment. In fact, the whole operation was in the best
Citizens Council manner. Some of their men on the City Council — five of the nine — went over one night to visit Eric Jonsson, and the city woke up next morning to find it had a new
mayor. "This place is just the Dallas *Morning News's* front
yard," according to Bill Willis. "They shout out of the house if
they think there's anything we should know."

Another mistaken notion about Dallas is that oilmen run it.
Oil money does — safely deposited in banks and insurance
companies — but not oil *men.* They lack one of the three essential conditions for membership in the Citizens Council. The
first, of course, is money. No problem there. The second is ability to produce that money on demand, to "put up or shut up,"
to be a Yes Man. Some oilmen can do this, though many have
their funds tied up in long-range drilling risks. Bob Thornton's
idea of Yes Men became institutionalized in this rule: a member of the Citizens Council must be the top executive in his
firm with a comparatively free hand. This has had several consequences. It means that even very wealthy men who are second or third in the line of succession are kept out of the top
cone of power. This, of course, has repercussions in the structure of the various firms. The importance of having a man on
the Citizens Council means that a company must sacrifice some
of its board control; Dallas enterprises tend to have single outstanding individuals who "run the show." The whole structure
is personal, honorific, and hierarchical. It saves its rewards for

the top guns. Though there are now over two hundred members of the Citizens Council, and twenty-seven men on its Board of Directors, the real power in Dallas pyramids sharply even within this group — up to seven men according to Carol Thometz's respected study *The Decision-Makers* (1963), to six according to Warren Leslie's *Dallas Public and Private* (1964), to nine according to an analysis in *Fortune* magazine (July, 1964). The lists are in substantial agreement. Eric Jonsson is high on all of them — as are Stanley Marcus, Robert Stewart (First National), James Aston (Republic National), C. A. Tatum, and Les Potter. The Thometz book omits Robert Cullum. No one would do that anymore.

Although some oilmen can meet the first two requirements for membership in the Council, most do not measure up to the third — active involvement in the community. Independent oilmen (the kind who do not need a board's approval before writing a check) tend to be loners, putting only steel roots down, moving on if the thrust of these roots does not meet the give, far below, of an oil lake. Dallas, on the other hand, is nothing *but* commitment to a place — a place unpromising in itself, kept prominent only by the imagination and spirit of those who are promoting it. That is why the despotism of the Citizens Council is so benevolent. Real power comes only to those who signalize themselves in community service. A. C. Greene says: "The highest accolade to a 'comer' in Dallas is to make him chairman of the United Fund drive. His appointment is announced at a big dinner, where last year's chairman gets up and says the honor proves there is no finer fellow in the whole world, and all that. Of course, when he says this, he is also praising himself."

Oilmen are not prominent in United Fund circles. H. L. Hunt lives in Dallas physically, but not in spirit. He is not even one of the two hundred and more who belong to the Citizens Council — far less a power at its core. The Murchison brothers have more ties with the city — they own downtown real estate, and they launched the Cowboys, a football team that Dallas hopes will act like a new state fair. But they are not among the real leaders of the city. (If they were, a protective municipal instinct would have warned Clint not to encourage Joe Brown in his dangerous flirtings with literature.) Dallas is a tight ship, and the few who walk its quarterdeck mean to sail it efficiently. Everything depends on that.

Even the lowliest crewmen realize that their rations depend on the maintenance of this ship's honor. Outsiders are surprised that Dallas citizens do not resent their rulers, the invisible navigations of their highly visible top men. But Dallas did not begin as a normal city, and it has not developed toward normality over the years. In some ways, it is not a city at all. "I've looked for the city for years," Bill Willis muses. "I've driven all over, searching, but it's never there." That is because he was looking for a *city*. Dallas' defenders think of their town as a brilliant commercial venture. Mayor Jonsson, trying to explain his duties as chairman of the nine-man City Council, told us the Council is the city's Board of Directors, and he is Chairman of the Board. Hardly. The real Board is the Citizens Council. Its six-or-so most prominent men are majority stockholders. City officials (Council, Mayor, City Manager, Chief of Police, etc.) are corporation officers, hired and fired by the Board (whose meetings are held behind closed doors). The citizens are all employees. Employees, however, with a very lucrative profit-sharing plan. They prosper as the city does. And the city prospers wondrously. Its labor market is excellent; its standard of living is high; and — lifting and lowering in a continual rhythm, weaving their vapor-trail pattern — the jets run on time.

The corporate spirit of Dallas is a corporation spirit — which explains its failures as well as its successes. The success one hears of endlessly, in Dallas, is its "final solution" to the problem of racial integration. Bob Thornton, still alive then, put it to his Yes Men: integration was inevitable, resistance to it (involving, no doubt, a little Texas gunplay) would hurt the city's image. So the men who bought Dallas its railroads and hotels and centenaries went out to buy it some integration. They launched a program to educate their employees. C. A. Tatum, of the Dallas Power and Light Company, was put in charge. Sam Bloom's P-R firm orchestrated the several stages of the program. Both newspapers swung into action. Bloom's firm made a movie that was shown to every group that could be called together in Dallas. Walter Cronkite donated his services as narrator. (Those services might not be accepted now; Sevareid delivered his hated editorial on the Cronkite show.) Stanley Marcus integrated his store's facilities. Schools mixed the token black judiciously in with compliant whites. It was all over but the shouting — which goes on constantly. The newspapers told and retold this story for the benefit of visiting journalists during the Ruby trial. We heard it from Mayor Jonsson, Sam Bloom, Stanley Marcus, and businessmen like Troy Post of Braniff Airlines. *This*, they are convinced, will vindicate the Citizens Council even with Yankees.

Even token integration is better than nothing; and Negroes, like other elements in Dallas, are by and large acquiescent to the way things are run. Nonetheless, this is the city of the "shotgun squad," and underneath the whole smooth operation runs a muffled thunder of the ultimate appeal. Bill Willis remembers the time when rumor of a Negro protest went through the community, and his friend's gun store was sold out. Bill Alexander is even more blunt about it. We asked him why there have been no Negro demonstrations in Dallas, and he grinned this answer: "They know we'd stack 'em like cordwood."

What even the Yankees will respect. That is important. Dallas is not Old South, conscious of a past and scornful of its conquerors. Its bristly uneasiness under Northern regard betrays the city's basic trait — envy — under its disguise of pride. Not money only, but "class." No Western architecture of horizons for them. They do not look west for their model, to California, nor south, to Mexico. There is only one rival, New York. The incongruous skyscrapers huddled together in their few downtown blocks — odd as five lighthouses stranded in a bundle far out to sea — are up there nervously eying Manhattan through the clouds. Neiman-Marcus does a brisk trade in tickets to Broadway shows. The airplane set from Dallas likes to drop in, frequently, and see how their rival is doing.

An outsider of any sort is presumed to be measuring Dallas against New York — presumed, indeed, to have flown in from there. We converged on the city from Santa Barbara and Baltimore, only to be assured over and over that the dangers of Dallas gun-toting and the high Texas homicide rate are nothing to what one risks in "our" subways or "our" Central Park. We asked Stanley Marcus if he thought the hyperbolic blue streak crackling through Dallas conversation helps create an atmospheric flammability. "Well," he said, "I don't suppose a tough Texan's speech is much different from a Brooklyn cop's." We asked Mayor Jonsson about the omnipresence of guns in Dallas. "Guns are useful here — one sometimes has to kill a rattlesnake. Besides, this is good hunting country. Maybe there aren't as many guns in New York. But think of all those knives on the subway!"

Nothing pleases Dallas more than one-upping New York. The papers crowed when Maria Callas broke with Rudolf Bing. New York did not have her anymore. Dallas did. But the *supreme* pleasure is to "leapfrog" New York, appeal across its towers straight to "the continent." Direct flights for Europe leave Love Field on a regular schedule. The city is proud of the French wines on its table, the foreign wares in its favorite store (Mr. Marcus'). And the rest of Texas is impressed. When we asked Joe Tonahill whether Belli's feathery flamboyance — cummerbund, fruit boots, red velvet briefcase — set any frontier teeth on edge, the man from Jasper replied: "No, I don't think so. Dallas is as cosmopolitan a town as you'd find anywhere. And Mel is just as sophisticated as Dallas. Besides, that briefcase is damned handy — it holds an awful lot!"

Those who think Dallas style runs to Stetsons and spurs should reflect on the fact that the city's arbiter of taste wears a continentally trimmed beard. "Yeah," chuckles Bill Willis, "I figure a beard is meant to say, 'I just got back and haven't had time to shave.'" The morning before we visited Mr. Marcus, we were in District Attorney Henry Wade's office. "Going to see Stanley? Ask him how his mustache is." His mustache? We heard he has a full beard. "Oh yes, he has mustaches all over his face." You sound bitter. "I should be. He blocked my appointment to a Federal judgeship."

The importance of Neiman-Marcus was expressed this way by its owner: "Many of these [Texas] millionaires never had the money to buy fine clothes. . . . They were willing to be guided, because they recognized an authority on which they could depend." Once he gets them a ticket to *Hello, Dolly,* Mr. Marcus must tell his clients what they should be wearing when they touch down at La Guardia. "Class" is style as seen by those who do not have it (*"Is Leonard Bernstein really a great musician?"*). It is style bought and used to impress others (as Bob Thornton put it, "I'll do anything for the Dallas symphony except attend"). It is the striving of uneasy men to be what they are not — Dallas masquerading as New York, Ruby affecting long words. Style is the achieving of identity, of a self. "Class" is devotion to some model, an envious rivalry of imitation, where there is no resting in a dignity achieved. Ruby, wanting "class," went to the appropriate spot — to a city yearning for it as visibly as its skyscrapers yearn up away from the plain; a city looking over its shoulder to see if it is being talked about; a city that adds towers and stories to beat its rivals as Ruby added runways.

It might seem impossible for critics of this vulnerable flawed town, turning their fire on Dallas, to miss the target, to use false charges when there are so many true ones ready to the hand.

But the blaming of Dallas has nothing, necessarily, to do with the faults of Dallas. Part of it, at least, has grown from men's need for solace at the death of John F. Kennedy. That abrupt inexplicable thing must be subsumed in some reassuring rhythm. Fate's patterns are consolatory. We are resigned if it *had* to happen, frightened if the act was arbitrary, almost whimsical. And so Dallas, bustling, trying to "belong," cohesive, one big firm, gets blamed for being the spot where the vagrant Oswald got his last best shot at a hostile world. Dallas was such a logical place for the assassination that men are loath to admit an Oswald does not fit their "logic." William Manchester, for instance, in his *Death of a President*, says that "establishing the precise link between deed, era, and locale is a hopeless task," but he argues that we must *assume* a link, since the alternative would be "absurd." The mind wants reassurance, not absurdity. He labors, therefore, at all the ties between Oswald and Dallas. In his short peregrinative life, Oswald spent off and on less than three years in the city; Manchester tries to suggest a much longer period and intensify its significance. He describes as an "atrocity" Henry Wade's contention that Oswald was not a Dallasite. He writes that "Oswald had lived in Dallas as a boy" (yes, for a year and a half, at age five to six) "and had landed at Love Field when he had returned from Russia with Marina" (yes, on the way to his brother's house in Fort Worth). In the last seventeen months of his life — between the return from Russia and his assassination of President Kennedy — Oswald tossed restlessly from home to home (his brother's, his mother's, Ruth Paine's several apartments, "rooms"), from city to city (Fort Worth to Dallas to New Orleans to Fort Worth to Dallas, with an abortive attempt at breakout via Mexico), from job to job, and even from name to name. Manchester presents that last period this way: "Dallas was especially anxious to forget that the assassin had prowled its streets, read its leading newspaper, watched the patriotic programs on WFAA, and listened to the anti-Kennedy stories of his fellow employees in Dealey Plaza." On another page, he reminds us that Oswald read the right-wing *Morning News* (in the mildly left-wing home of Ruth Paine). The implication is that the virus of superpatriotism got to him, that he became a super-American-Texan. But if the Dallas atmosphere *had* to trigger this crime, if the act was inevitable, surely so irresistible a primal cause could have found, somewhere, a more appropriate instrument. If it did not dispose a real Texan — a real right-winger, one open to *all* its pressures over a long period — to do the deed, then perhaps the crime was not inevitable after all. Only a rather fanatical antifanaticism, an oddly intense hatred of haters, can imagine that Oswald read in the *News* what he thought would please Ted Dealey and then tried to give it to him; that this misfit grumbling against every society he found himself in, even his chosen new motherland Russia, suddenly decided to ingratiate himself with the community — with *this* of all communities — and become "one of the boys," cracking anti-Kennedy jokes in Dealey Plaza; that the rebellious young man who hit his mother in the face became a backslapper with the Chamber-of-Commerce types who meet at the City Club to worry about widening the freeways.

Actually, it is lucky for him that Oswald was *not* hoping to ingratiate himself with Dallasites. Dallas is a shoot-out city, not a sniper's town.

But Dallas was caught in a comic dilemma. Its rulers could not convincingly make the case that Oswald did not belong with them, because it is precisely the *faults* of Dallas that marked him an outsider there — its tight, tribal conformism, its initiation rites and pride at "belonging"; its bustle and business and success, its shiny expansive efficiency — and Dallas is incapable of admitting its faults. The whole problem was further complicated when the numbness of Greek tragedy was followed, two days later, by the knockabout violence of Greek satyr play — when Ruby compounded Oswald in the popular list of Dallas crimes and pseudo-crimes. All the things that ex--

onerated Dallas of Oswald convict the city of Ruby. Ruby was just where he belonged — up from nowhere, proud of it, still rising; knowing everyone, gladhanding; amiably cutting corners, and no harm meant; all "image" and combed hair and puzzled-over "ads"; on the side of the law, convinced that this would put law on his side (a businesslike compromise, righteous and profitable); with a strict code, quick to defend it; admiring power.

Owning up to Ruby was as unthinkable for Dallas as taking the bum rap for Oswald. It is the whole point of scrambling up the ladder, that this permits you to escape — so far as possible, to forget — the lower rungs (as Ruby tried to forget his "foreign" home and childhood). The graceful duels at the top — Bob Thornton in a financial stare-down with his peers — seem parodied, seem somehow cheapened by cruder shoot-outs down in the street (or, below the streets, in night places that come to life only when the sun leaves the tops of the financial acries). "They don't even know the street is down here," Bill Willis said, looking out a hotel window at the tilted aluminum prow of Republic, the black Manhattan facelessness of sunproof glass checkerboarded down the LTV tower. The clubs at the foot of these buildings are the city's murky Id, Wurlitzer-lit and plangent. They crouch far below the cool glass scrutiny of the metropolis' Superego.

Dallas has what Faulkner called the "vicious depthless quality of stamped tin." The more energetically stamped and patterned it is, the more its malleable thinness shows. The higher these towers strain up, the more they emphasize the level plain around them. *Depthlessly* vicious, in a mindless sort of way; cruel without cruel intent. Ruby was not a malicious man; indeed, a notably generous one, open-hearted, open-handed. But a punch was his only exclamation point. Not a malicious man; simply one who killed — "poison, in jest; no offense i' the world."

Some try to equate Ruby and Oswald — pharisaically, for

the most part, as a way of saying "I am not as these men." But Dallas *is* as Ruby was. No one knows what went on in Oswald's mind; but many felt as Ruby did — people who, like Ruth Paine, or Justice Douglas' wife, shouted "Good!" when they saw Oswald killed, people who sent their heartfelt thanks to the jail. In Dallas, or anywhere, Oswald was driven out from the human settlement, off toward that edge of the spiritual map where medieval cartographers shivered to an end of their knowledge and confessed, in neat calligraphy, "Here be monsters." But Ruby was in and of Dallas for sixteen years; and — by contrast with Oswald, who was forever opting out, if we can believe that options were still his — "Jack" was always pushing in. Moving his club from the outskirts of town to its core, edging around polite suspicion into respectable parties, introducing others to vaguely puzzled men of power: "Pat Morgan, I want you to meet Mayor Cabell and Judge Joe B. Brown." He knew everyone. Quite a few knew him. "It's amazing I have come so far."

The nation tries to disown Dallas; Dallas, Ruby; each actor in that strange drama, all the rest. But these very energies of denial make the participants look similar. Ruby's life was polarized around "class" — a striving for it, set over against his lack of it; what he was, cruelly defined by what he wished to be. This was not a private drama, merely, but the theme for a whole canon of efforts set at cross-purposes because undertaken, from slightly different vantage points, for the same purpose — to maintain precarious dignity. The Ruby trial shows us a whole circle of men wincing, in a chain-reaction shudder, at each other's gaucheries: Ruby at Belli's boots, Belli at Dallas pretensions (the posies in the bidet), Dallas at Joe Brown's book, Brown at Tonahill's pencil-throwing, Tonahill at Ruby's fumblings after heroism. Judge Brown, a compassionate man after all, said regretfully that Ruby became the forgotten man at his own trial, as everyone scrambled for a vestige of dignity in the confusion. But that is precisely the point: Ruby set the theme, the musical pattern for everyone — *Tutto nel mondo è burla.*

Dallas is always disowning its Rubys. But that does not make them any less part of the city. They are simply its disowned part. There is every gradation of entry into the pyramid of Dallas power and of effort up its busy interior. After all, Joe Brown, the handsome and friendly and well-liked judge, did not belong to the "real" Dallas, to the aerie-dwellers. But, like Jack Ruby, he was trying. In 1959, the Judge won a lifetime membership in the Chamber of Commerce by signing up one hundred new members. One of them was Ruby.

iv

Belli, though he came (in cowboy boots) to indict all of Dallas, maintained friendly relations with some of his opponents, with Judge Brown, for instance, and Sheriff Bill Decker, and Jim Bowie of the prosecution team. But there was an immediate hostility between him and Bill Alexander, one that persists to this day. They did not address each other outside the courtroom or the judge's chambers. Their styles are in every way at odds, as are their characters. Belli, short and expansive, has a wide histrionic gamut, a rich drawl expertly violin-bowed, a polished affability. Alexander, tall and indrawn with a kind of frontier primness, twangs out blunt words stingily in a Wichita Falls accent that turns *ar* sounds to *er* (we thought, for a while, that when he mentioned "guards" taking care of Jack he was referring to Elmer *Gertz,* one of the lawyers who entered the case after Belli left it). His emotional range is from the slightly sardonic to very-very sardonic. At his desk in the hygienic new Dallas courthouse (built since Ruby's trial), his coat off, pistol visible, elbows on the chair pushing his shoulders high in a buzzard hunch, he remembers with grim satisfaction the weeks when he had Melvin Belli every morning for breakfast.

When the telephone rings, we cut off our tape recorder; he almost whispers his quick "yeahs" and "nopes" into the instrument; then, as the phone goes down, the recorder is flicked on again. But for the recorded phone ring, one would not know there had been any interruption. He returns to the exact point where he left off, never fumbling, never searching for names or dates or sequence in his complex story. He has a cross-examiner's mind even when he is the one being questioned. He does not get sidetracked by new questions till he says what he intended on the subject that is "up."

"We sure were scared when we heard Melvin Belli was coming — I'd been hearing about him since I was in law school. Then he came into town like God on a sunbeam, spouting words all over the place. He's a real talkin' piece of furniture. I tell you" (the putty face stirs with its one expression, a monkey leer), "we had an inferiority complex around a high-class-talkin' gentleman like that. Nobody was more surprised than we were when he started *plumbering* the case. He made things so easy for us, we thought it was a trap. We kept wondering when he would drop this psychomotor stuff and spring his real case on us. But he never did."

What did he do that was wrong? "Well, at the first step in the process — the bond hearing — he threw away the chance to pump our witnesses. Since at that time we didn't have 'discovery' of prosecution material to the defense (we do now), our defense lawyers around here used the hearing as an exploratory gimmick — they'd get our witnesses up in the box and swab them out. Belli put on a few police and asked a few questions; but he was so anxious to stert teaching us backwoods boys about psychiatry that he laid his whole case in our lap. Now we knew where to do our homework, and at the trial we were ready for him."

Belli, far from thinking he failed to use the bond hearing to explore the prosecution's case, seems to believe he *introduced* this ploy to Texas: "In California the prosecution has to reveal its case beforehand, but not in Texas, so we used the bond hearings for that purpose. Wade and those other guys didn't know what we were doing. If you were going to hide a secret message so that Wade and Alexander would never find it, all you would have to do is put it in the book of Texas penal law. But most of all, we used the bail hearings to educate the community, change its sentiment, acquaint it with our sophisticated defense." He admits this gave away certain things to the prosecution: "along the way this process would provide for the prosecution some of the discovery that we were seeking for ourselves. I believe in practicing what I preach." He was also supplying the thing he had relied on when accepting the case. "This was a big trial that could focus worldwide attention on mental health and its unsatisfactory, archaic relationship to the law. Dallas, I was confident, was a sophisticated city. I knew it had good medicine. I assumed it would have a district attorney who knew medicine." As he ventured out onto the minefield, he thought he was entering a classroom. "Mel thought we had to do something right away to get on top," Tonahill says. Like his client, he believes in "taking the play away."

Melvin Belli, legal cockatoo, operates out of the gildedest of cages — California Historical State Landmark No. 408, the Belli Building, second oldest structure in San Francisco, restored at a cost of half a million dollars. *Psittacus tortius,* with a thick white comb — hair of a snowiness his painted complexion (in the portrait hung over the mantel) easily matches or rivals: Belli theophanized looks sculpted from ice cream, then partially allowed to melt, given the angular angelical look of a confectionery El Greco. Alexander's bare white office looks like a consulting room in one of the newer hospitals. Belli's lair has 221B-Baker-Street touches of Science — bloated apothecary jars, rachitically grinning skeletons, richly bound medical volumes. Overhead is Belli's self-conferred coat of arms (*Rex Tortius*), lit by Liberace chandeliers; and, at the end of the room, a desk center-staged before the window — tourist buses pass, their entrails buzzing with his name, and he is glimpsed at work. The window is limned with gaslights — appropriate frame for this new Crummles. In Dallas, the Belli hotel room was not as efficiently on display, but its doors were open. Milling reporters, who clotted around him everywhere like Joe Btfsplk's mushroom cloud, thronged in and out of the suite; had a drink; traded quips, admired, wondered; applauded or panned the show, and left.

At ease in his office, Belli turns his memory acidulously, vaguely back toward Dallas. "I had the greatest doctors making this beautiful scientific demonstration — Guttmacher; that man from Yale . . . Schafer? Fisher [*he means Schafer*]; and the one from Houston [*he means Galveston*]." But he seemed most interested in the accompaniment and aftermath of the case — above all in its publicity. "Jack made Mark Lane a millionaire. That Kaplan in *The Saturday Evening Post* [*he means Edward Linn*] completely lost track of what we were doing. I'm suing *The Post.*" Why? "Because" (switch is thrown; heavy quantum of charm about to be discharged; brace yourself, here comes Belli as mischievous-cute-boy) "because they're solvent."

"And that book by Kaplan and Wirtz [*he means Kaplan and Waltz*] — those small-claims-court professors are completely wrong. They never tried a case." (Professor John Kaplan, of Stanford University, was Assistant U. S. Attorney in San Francisco before he went into teaching. Before that he had been in the Justice Department, after being an editor of the *Harvard Law Review*. Professor Jon R. Waltz, of Northwestern, was a trial lawyer for ten years before he began teaching; at Yale he was an editor of the *Law Journal*.) "They are getting paid as professors and by a foundation, and they write a book." (Mr. Belli, who is paid a great deal more than either professor, published a book on the Ruby trial — his twenty-ninth published volume.) "They took me on so I would carry their book and make it sell. Luckily, it didn't work. One of them even sent me a letter — I had never heard of him — wanting an invite to one of my parties."

The stories about Belli's entry into the case vary. Earl Ruby says the ghost-writer for Jack's newspaper story (William Woodfield) suggested Belli, saying his participation in the trial would help sell the story. Woodfield left word at Belli's office, then the lawyer called back while he was out and said to Mrs. Woodfield, "Get me that case — I want it so badly I can taste it." Joe Tonahill agrees with this version, which appears to be the correct one, and says he and Belli were to gain their $100,-000 fee from the sale of Woodfield's story. In his book, however, Belli says Jack Ruby himself sent out the plea for Belli's service; Earl Ruby stepped into a courtroom unknown to Belli and watched the man at work, then came up and offered him the job. Only later, with "Woodfield in tow," did Earl mention the plan of selling Jack's story to the papers — and Belli, revolted by the idea, walked out of the case. He does not write where he expected to get the $100,000, apart from the story; nor why he walked back *into* the case — the newspaper idea was never abandoned. When we asked him about his assumption of the case, he had still another version — that what he objected to was a plan to pay his fee from appeals sent out to various Jewish organizations: "I don't want this to be a *cause* instead of a case," he told Earl. Yet in his book he gives five reasons for representing Jack, and four of the five are causes: "to save Jack Ruby, to strengthen our law, to demonstrate the inadequacy of the archaic M'Naughten Rule on legal insanity, to wed more securely modern science to modern law, to help Dallas solve its problem."

He also gives inconcinnous versions of his exit from the case. In his book he says: "The Ruby family fired me." In a *Playboy* interview, he claims: "I was not fired. I bowed out of my own accord. I lost my objectivity that day in Dallas. Once I lose my objectivity, I've lost my value. . . ." Yet, on the subject of objectivity, he told us: "I try to be clinical, but I guess I'm at my best when somebody's kicking the shit out of some poor little Jew boy. Then I can take them all on."

The same confusion surrounds Belli's famous courtroom outburst when the jury returned a death penalty for Ruby. Joe Brown had at last got his camera into the courtroom, arguing that TV could not affect the verdict now. Belli, tieless, in a silk sport shirt, erupted vesuviusly under the cameramen's lights: "May I thank the jury for a victory for bigotry and injustice!" To *Playboy* he said, "It was a spontaneous outburst of horror. . . . I shouted long, vituperatively, and in tears." Yet earlier in his book, he said: "My outburst was not uncalculated. . . . It was a rational, detailed, and considered indictment of the injustice that had been perpetrated." We asked Joe Tonahill, who sat beside him at the moment, what he thought of the incident: "Well, Mel says he had it planned, but I didn't know about it. He looked surprised to me. You know, it's like the whore who gets pregnant: 'This isn't supposed to happen to *me!*'" Belli, of course, thought it shouldn't happen to America: "American justice had been raped — outraged — and, shouting and in tears, I was its spokesman there."

Mr. Belli, who is so critical of Mark Lane's and others' commercialism, bustled through Dallas trailed by a ghost-writer at times and by a camera team preparing records of the case. (Barney Weinstein tells us he tried to take movies of the Theatre Lounge act, planning to call it Jack's Carousel.) At the first interview with his client, Belli wanted a *Life* photographer present. Ruby did not mind: "He was impressed more than anything else with me. He said, 'Now the case is made.' It was like: The surgeon from Johns Hopkins walked into the operating room, the patient breathed easier. The other prisoners knew his lawyer was a great lady's man — that gave *him* masculinity. When it came to summoning the woman he dated for years, Jack asked me to go easy on her. He became a man protecting his girl — that lifted him up to me. He'd talk about my clothes, and feel them." Belli is acutely conscious of his sartorial impact. Sent to represent a man suing Errol Flynn, he met the movie star for the first time: "When I went down to Hollywood to question Errol and walked in wearing a white suit and a black Homburg, his eyes lit up." Flynn wanted to play him in a movie, Belli told us — but now that Errol is dead it will have to be Tony Curtis. "Jack had some doubts about my flamboyance. But I assured him that it amazes people to see me so scholarly and sedate in court after they've seen me in my red pants and vest. Jack liked the velvet briefcase." Class! This was even better than Jada's gold Cadillac with her name on it!

Ruby did not yet realize this iridescent counselor had come to protect a "poor little Jew boy." Bustled in and out of bond hearings in December and January, Jack veered as far off course as his escorts would allow him, toward serpenting microphones that swayed out at him in corridors and anteroom. He delivered rambling homilies against hate, assessed the crackpot literature being sent him, delivered garbled messages to "the right-thinking people of America." Buoyed up by the appearance of Belli in his corner, he in fantasy became another Belli — teacher, lecturer, man of the world ("*That lifted him up to me*"). Before he went out past the tangle of microphones, he would ask Tonahill, "How do I look, Joe? Is my hair straight? How are my clothes?" Though he had always preferred being seen without his glasses, now he aped Belli's professorial stage business — dangling his bifocals from their right hinge, chewing meditatively on one or other ear clasp.

If Jack did not know his hero's strategy was to make him an object of pity, not respect, he *certainly* did not realize the Belli plan involved an assault on Dallas. Belli told us: "I guess at the beginning he *did* feel that he had joined Texas. . . . I tried to persuade him not to trust the D.A., but he always felt that Alexander was his friend. Jack kept talking to his guards about the case until I convinced him they were taking advantage of him." Tonahill adds, "Some guy was even reading the Bible with him to soften him up, until we convinced him he was betraying him." Gradually, Jack began to give up old friends in the comforting dazzle of these new ones. If he could not be a Dallasite, if it had all been a terrible misunderstanding — well, all right. He could take on the world, with giants by his side like Mel Belli and Joe Tonahill. No matter how bad the disease might be, he could breathe easy. The Johns Hopkins surgeon was in the operating room.

"Belli may be a real curly wolf in San Francisco," Alexander says, "but he wasn't Ned-in-the-First-Reader in Dallas. We just played with him." For instance? "Well, on jury selection, we had file cards for all the prospective jurors, and we'd get together and shake our heads over people we really wanted — or Henry would pass one we didn't want without any real needling questions — and Belli would fall for it. He'd waste one of his challenges doing our work for us. Once Henry even told them a boy had a policeman for his father, and they spent a strike on him, though we knew the boy was a rebel against his father's ideas.

"Belli picked a perfect jury — perfect for us. He wanted people who could understand his fancy psychological talk, so he chose people who were educated, middle-class, never been to clubs like Jack's, couldn't sympathize with his world. Then Belli was out to beat Dallas, he tried to get people from outside the city limits. He didn't realize that some of the little towns around here are the really straitlaced fundamentalist areas. I can tell by a juror's accent what area he comes from, and when Belli started picking, I knew we had him. Belli's tone-deaf. From the first juror I knew Jack would get the death penalty."

Belli likes to lecture — even to those who have dropped in for an interview. He spells out words like a schoolmarm: "Jack had a ferret- (f-e-r-r-e-t) like quality." He also likes to use medical terms, and condescendingly defines even the simplest of them: "Then there is hyperventilating (overbreathing). . . .

Jack looked as if he had arteriosclerosis (high blood pressure [*sic*]) and had been drinking too much coffee." His subordinates obligingly call him The Doctor; he told Sam Bloom in Dallas that he knew more about medicine than his own experts. He gives lectures in his own field too — like this protreptic exercise on jury picking: "A juror who says he can vote death and keep his hands steady when he says it is a juror who can honestly make such a vote. If he twists his hands, that means he won't vote death. Take my word for it. This is the experience of thirty years as a lawyer and of many, many capital cases." For some reason, this reminds us of Paul Goodman's rules for dealing with people: "In sizing up a situation I always looked at a man's crotch or where a woman's fingertips were wandering." It also reminds us of Mr. Belli's self-assessment: "I'm wild, enthusiastic; I love people. I'm a Leo, you see, born July 29, 1907." He also likes to describe himself as "a Latin" (his is the generation of Valentino).

So far as we know, Belli did not cast any juror's horoscope. Instead, he had his inkblots all ready in the courtroom for repeated attempts (quashed each time by Judge Brown) to give prospective jurors the Rorschach test, thus (like The Shadow) exposing what he calls in his book "the feelings that lurked in the subconscious minds of the Dallas citizenry" — though earlier in the same book he deplored attempts to establish " 'scientific' selection of jurors."

Choice of jury dragged on for two weeks. Belli, still fighting for a change of venue, alienated those jurors who made it past his unremitting criticism of *any* Dallas panel. Ruby, still alert at the defense table, listened uneasily, whispered back and forth with Tonahill, passed Belli notes:

"Don't fight with them today, because I'm sure they have something up their sleeve."

"Don't make me more hated in Dallas than I am already."

Belli told us, in his office: "The whole jury panel looked like they came out of insurance companies. I decided if I couldn't

get warm people — waitresses, etc. — and I had to have cold
fish, at least I wanted to have *intelligent* cold fish. We got a
couple of people who should have been tolerant — some divor-
cées — but I guess there was no way in God's world to get to
these little mean insurance-company minds, especially with
such a sophisticated defense." In his book he gives a different
theory to account for the jury's strange immunity to the Belli
mesmerism. "In some fashion, as in that movie I had seen about
the man brainwashed by Moscow, the people in whatever
passes for the Kremlin of Dallas could figuratively press a but-
ton and, as if it had signaled transistors in their brains, direct
the thinking of this great city's people." (Actually, the oligarchy can function so easily because it does not, and does not
have to, mesh with the ordinary citizens.) At any rate, Belli got
his bright classroom of twelve students. Murray Kempton, re-
porting the trial for the *New Republic,* took it as a mark of
Belli's skill that Dallas "spared him [Ruby] a trial by a jury
composed entirely of his peers." Alexander, looking at the same
group, merely grinned — "a perfect jury."

As February went past, the confidence of the New Year was
daily seeping out of Ruby. At the jury selection, one note to
Belli read: "I will never have a real chance to prove myself."
Perhaps his two giants were not enough. After the second bail
hearing, he began to think better of the advice Joe Cavagnaro
and others had given him — maybe he should have Charley
Tessmer in the case. He asked his friend Tony Zoppi to see
Tessmer. But Tessmer recounts what happened: "When Zoppi
mentioned the fact to Belli that Ruby wanted him to contact
me, Belli blew his top. 'Hell no! Not another Texas lawyer. I'm
already saddled with three of them!' " (Tonahill; Tom Howard,
who had not yet been nudged out; and young Phil Burleson,
the "book man.") It was one of the last efforts Jack made, under Belli, to act on his own behalf. The busy Californian had
ignored the snowfall of notes fluttering down the table at him.
When Alexander, questioning Dr. Manfred Guttmacher, asked

him to comment on the fact that Ruby looked sane enough to help his lawyers with written instructions, Belli interrupted the cross-examination to the tell the courtroom, "That's assuming facts not in evidence, that he's assisting his attorneys. I represent he is not able to assist his attorneys." Later, the defendant would tell Chief Justice Warren, "Had Mr. Belli spent more time with me, he would have realized not to try to get me out completely free." Reporters noted that Jack grew visibly dimmer as the trial wore on, less involved, a distant figure. The foreground was Mel's. We told Belli that Judge Brown thought Ruby was neglected by everyone during the trial, including his own lawyers: "That's not so! I issued orders that someone should go to see him every day. We made Burleson do it, and it was at my orders." Ruby was not very often allowed to finger the rainbow clothes he so admired; rainbows are too high to touch. For an intoxicating moment he had touched one, but since that moment he had been inexplicably sinking. Even his skin sank and blanched, giving his quicksilvery eyes greater prominence. Alexander was watching him, deciding how he could use this physical change for his own purposes.

In his white office, Alexander's thoughts move tidily on to the trial: "Belli gave it to us by going for broke — all or nothing. He forced the jury, if it thought Jack had even a little bit of guilt, to give him the chair. He told them it was acquittal or nothing. You can't give a jury that kind of dare. And all he had going for him was some fancy doctors' talk and a few mildly abnormal squiggles on a piece of paper" (the electroencephalogram). "He came to town to sell a piece of paper. Now, if you just get a psychiatrist to put his views in everyday language, it will sound like damfoolishness to a jury. I have learned, for instance, that if you ask a psychiatrist whether he thinks sexual aberrition [sic] shows a man is mentally unbalanced, he'll say no. That doesn't go down with a jury.

"As for the squiggles, I got Dr. Gibbs, their main witness on them, to admit that electric impulses are given off by all sorts of things and can be registered on the E.E.G. paper. Then I walked over to the courtroom wall like this." He rises, pins in one shoulder, puts his corrugated face against the wall, his eyes those of one listening to an important phone call in the presence of others, eyes vainly semaphoring, trying to tell us how interesting the conversation is. " 'You know, doctor,' I said, 'if you went to the wall here and laid your ear against it, you could pick up a sixty-cycle hum that's in the building?' The bailiff told me that, at the recess, the whole jury went running over to the wall of their chamber and listened to the wall hum." So much for unexplained squiggles.

Alexander's cross-examination of Dr. Gibbs was not all gimmickery, however. He had been doing his homework on the E.E.G. since Belli tipped his hand at the bond hearing. "I took a copy of Jack's E.E.G. to Chicago and Madison [another was flown to Houston, New York, and Baltimore] to talk with the best specialists we could find. This was while the jury selection was on; just to keep them in the dark, we had Jim Bowie hint that Henry was mad at me and had taken me off the case. Belli still believes that in his book. He was like some poor Ay-rab standing in the desert by his camel — he don't know there are radio messages passing through the air above his head."

We asked Melvin Belli, back in his Victorian lair, about the charge that he went for broke. "What was I to do? I had to go with my doctors." Belli says he took the case in order to fight the M'Naughten Rule concerning legal insanity. Several people have wondered how, at that stage, Belli knew Ruby was insane. He had not talked to him or to any of his doctors. Luckily, the first interview with his client (the one to which he tried to bring a *Life* photographer) bore out Belli's premonition — he found Jack not only arteriosclerotic in appearance, and over-coffeed, but "too excited": "He was overcontrolling. It didn't reach the manic step, since I never saw the other side, the depressive. There was no swing. But there was something there, I could tell. I have had informal training in these matters, and most of my cases involve some neurology, some psychopathology, some physiology. But I didn't want to make a hasty diagnosis — that's where those small-claims-court professors are so wrong, thinking I made the diagnosis first. I said, 'You see something here, but Mel don't jump. Get the best there is in the United States on this thing. There's enough money in this case!' Then my doctors found psychomotor epilepsy, and everything they said is being proved right — look at the autopsy! They found tumors in Jack's brain" (cancer tumors). "Every day that goes by, we're proving more and more of our medical case. At the time, no one knew much about psychomotor variant. But in forty years, in twenty years, we will have left a monument!"

Belli was pleased when, a month after he had taken on this insanity case, Dr. Roy Schafer of Yale gave Ruby the Rorschach and other psychological tests: he diagnosed organic brain damage and said Ruby's "test responses are very similar in many respects to those obtained from patients who have psychomotor epileptic seizures." Belli was exuberant: "Organic damage is demonstrable — it is like four fingers or six." This was familiar territory to the dramatizer of personal injury in suits against insurance companies. He was especially impressed when Ruby was submitted to the E.E.G. machine and the results were sent to the eminent encephalographer Dr. Frederic A. Gibbs of Chicago. Just a month earlier, Dr. Gibbs had published a paper arguing for the existence of a "psychomotor variant" E.E.G. reading — i.e., abnormally slow brain waves emanating from a part of the brain different from the one that typically signals a psychomotor condition. He maintained that this pattern is only a variant of the classical one for psychomotor epileptics. After receiving Ruby's record, he wrote in a letter that this E.E.G. contained examples of the variant pattern. Now Belli, who likes courtroom props, was given something to handle, hold, and flourish — his "sheet of paper," six hundred feet of it accordioned into a green shoe box. He was unperturbed by the fact that this analysis was new and still disputed, that it was based on E.E.G. abnormalities capable of differing interpretations. He had made many an elusive injury obvious in court. And the man who loves medical tongue-twisters was given a new term that fairly clicked and buzzed computerlike across his tongue while he sang the glories of science. In his closing argument, he would refer to "the diagnosis of an epileptic psychic psychomotor epilepsy ('psychic' from the mind)." Psychomotor psittacism!

The burden of proof in a murder case is on the prosecution. But this was a strange trial — there could be no question that Ruby killed Oswald. Tom Howard would have forced the State to prove malice, which was difficult for two reasons. Split-second timing brought Jack into the basement, ruling out premeditation unless, like European conspiratorialists, one considers the whole Dallas police force in on the plot (which the prosecution could hardly argue). Second, Ruby's many comments to the police — that he did their job for them, and was glad he had — were of doubtful admissibility, since they were taken while he was in custody. Howard would not have tried to prove strict insanity, merely instability — enough to make Ruby, in an uncontrolled instinctive moment, murder Oswald "without malice." But Belli assumed a complex burden of demonstration. To make his case he would have to prove that:

(a) Jack Ruby was subject to psychomotor epilepsy fits; and

(b) his E.E.G. readings proved this; and

(c) not only was he a psychomotor epileptic, but he was in a fit at the precise moment when he shot Oswald; and — essential step in a "M'Naughten defense" —

(d) this fit made him incapable of knowing right from wrong at the time of the shooting.

To these absolutely necessary steps Belli added a fifth. If the jury accepted the police version of Ruby's comments after the crime, it would appear that he shot Oswald consciously and deliberately. Belli was, therefore, prepared to argue that Ruby had been in a "fugue state" of diminished consciousness during the epileptic seizure, one which caused amnesia in the immediate aftermath. Thus, Ruby's readiness to confess could be explained as a form of "confabulation" — that is, the anxiety to fill in a memory-gap by inferential reconstruction of one's acts performed in the fugue state. Belli's own premier expert on psychomotor epilepsy, Dr. Gibbs, would testify that a fugue condition is not necessary in this form of epilepsy — indeed, that "consciousness is commonly maintained right through the seizure." Nonetheless, Belli gratuitously undertook to prove his fifth point, that (e) Ruby was not only in a fit at the moment when he shot Oswald, but in a fugue state.

Ruby's lawyer had to prove (a) through (d) — *all* the steps — in order to establish his case; and he gave the impression that he had to prove (e) as well. Yet not one of the four defense experts testified to all five conditions — or even to the four essential ones. Dr. Schafer could not testify to (b) or (d). Drs. Towler, Guttmacher, and Bromberg would not testify to (c). The prosecution had no difficulty finding experts who would deny one or several of the essential links; they put eight doctors on the stand, and had more in reserve. All eight of them disputed the crucial point (b) — crucial because Belli organized everything else around Dr. Gibbs's verdict on the E.E.G. — and one of the experts, Dr. Holbrook, testified against all five of Belli's points.

To rear this elaborate structure of medical inference was difficult enough, even for one with Belli's virtuosity; but it was made even more difficult by several things — by Joe Brown's unpredictability, by a jury already alienated under the repeated assertion that they could not be fair, by a set of prosecutors Belli consistently underestimated. Just before Tom Howard left the case, he remarked that the ability of Wade's team had not yet soaked into Belli, "But I think it's about time it did." Tonahill remembers, "I couldn't convince Mel that Wade and Alexander are dangerous." No one has convinced him yet. In his office he still muses complacently that "They were about the easiest I ever met."

Furthermore, the National Epilepsy League, resenting any

public suggestion that epilepsy leads to murder, harassed Belli (who exasperatedly called their representative "the sandwich man for a convulsion league"), and supplied the State with expert testimony. Then Belli's main prop turned out to be a bore — the jury easily tired of the search, through four hundred and thirteen accordion-folds of inky spiderings, for ten of the slow-wave patterns. Jurors were assured they could have the green shoe box in their chamber during final deliberations; but there would be no stampede for "the piece of paper" during that short session — as there had been to hear the humming of the courthouse wall. Even Belli's melodically caressed vocabulary was not as impressive as it might have been — not, anyway, after Alexander asked the jury "if they got their psychomotor variant from the psychomotor pool" and Henry Wade played with the term "conflaberation." Wade called the defense counsel "Dr. Belli," and Alexander topped that with a reference to "Dr. Tonahill." Belli, who has a rather proprietary attitude toward medicine and its practitioners ("my doctors"), went out of his way to quote Wade's sardonic accolade and to tell us in his book that the great Gibbs called him "Dr. Belli." At the trial, he addressed the doctors as one of them, prefacing the statement of medical facts with "we have found that. . . ." Sometimes he spoke almost as teacher to pupil. When one of the experts said "I think you are going beyond my competency now," Belli graciously let him off the hook with these words: "Well, I was going to get you really in over your head then, because I was going to talk about Naffziger signs and the rest of these things." But this fraternal attitude toward experts led him into trouble. In his eagerness to "talk their language," he picked up the pleasantly rolling "bisynchronously" from Dr. Towler — and instantly misused it. Dr. Guttmacher contributed the idea of "islands of memory" in the post-seizure amnesia — which Belli adopted, but in the form "islands of amnesia."

To top all these disadvantages, the jury selection seems to

have drained all the energy from Belli. "By the end," says Tonahill, "I had to steer him out on the street to keep him from being run over by a cab. He was taking all those pills — to go to sleep, to wake up. He'd take out a handful and offer me some." Jack's sister told friends that Belli looked like a man who had just suffered a stroke. On the last full day of testimony, he was so groggy that he forgot the name of the Rorschach test and, while questioning a doctor (Mackay), could not recall the name of the one who had just preceded him on the stand (Forster).

Short men sometimes have an instinct for "seeking higher ground." Belli, a short man, calls those he admires "stand-up guys," praising their "stand-up qualities." He can be impressively energetic when allowed to prowl the courtroom. The prosecution therefore had the judge remind him, when he tried to rise, that in Dallas a lawyer must question witnesses from his chair. "They wore him down," Tonahill sighs. "If we made any mistake in the trial I think it was his wrangling back at them." Lawyers sometimes adopt the complementary roles of a two-man professional wrestling team — a "bad guy" who goes in and roughs up the adversary, followed by a "good guy" who simultaneously wins the crowd's sympathy and the victory. Alexander told us this is how he and Wade operate (with demonstrated effectiveness). Belli and Tonahill had planned to counter with the same strategy: "We agreed at the outset that I would be the rough-and-tumble Texan, and Mel would be the suave and polished one. But when we got to court, he started slugging as hard as I could." Despite all his assurances to Jack that in court he would become "sedate and scholarly," Belli tried this case at the top of his usually nuanced voice. "He and Tonahill tried to outdo each other," Alexander remembers, "we called them Flopsie and Mopsie."

Though Belli is learned and eloquent, he yearns to be "one of the boys." The association he seems proudest of is that with Errol Flynn. His language is studiedly coarse; he likes to recall

his days as a seaman; and he makes no secret of his attraction
to the ladies — "I believe in the Constitution, the Bill of Rights,
and sex, and not necessarily in that order." Cross-examining
policemen, he tried to use "cop talk," and left officers puzzled or
amused. "Do you know what 'Property' means? I'm using the
jargon as I thought the police department did. Don't you call it
'Property'?" Alexander, with his instinct for the jugular, knew
what he was doing when, at the trial's outset, he called newsmen's attention to the "fruit boots." In the courtroom, he called
his foe "Mr. Belly" until he was informed by Judge Brown that
the correct pronunciation is Bell-eye. "Well," he reflects now,
"he *is* a portly old gentleman. At the next lunch break, I went
up and asked the judge, in a loud voice, if he would like to join
me for a plate of spaghett-eye or raviol-eye." When Dr. Guttmacher described Ruby's exaggerated interest in his own appearance and clothes, the prosecution table turned its eyes, not
on the defendant, but on his lawyer. Too low for judge or court
reporter to catch it, they whispered mock encouragement:
"Atta boy, Melvin. Show 'em your muscle, Mel. Show 'em your
words. Show 'em your fruit boots." Did this disturb him? "Man,
he'd come un*wound*." Tonahill shakes his head sadly and says,
"They de-energized him."

All through the trial, Alexander took a blunt he-man approach toward the dandyisms of the defense lawyer and his
client and his witnesses. He called "Larry" Crafard, who had
been living in the back room of Jack's club, "the boy whose eyes
wiggled." When George Senator was on the stand, Alexander
asked about the arrangements in the apartment he shared with
Jack; then, in his last argument, he sneered a reference to "his
room-mate, or at least his apartment-mate." He addressed a
witness by her professional, stripper's name (not by the legal
one given from the stand). He dripped contempt for the whole
defense crew. Under this prodding, the "suave and polished
one" had to stand up and slug. "They made fun of my legal
Latin. They were prejudiced against me because I am a Latin."

As he grew more frustrated in court, he grew more vehement at the press conferences that occurred several times daily, he called reporters into his hotel room, grew more and more insistently "one of the boys," less and less "sedate and scholarly." Through glassy eyes Jack Ruby watched the metamorphosis. For a while, he had been in his own mind another Belli ("This gave him masculinity"), had mimicked him, almost mirrored him ("That lifted him up to me"). He too became a winner — the "great lady's man." Now he saw the original Belli weary and bedraggled; shouting and agitated; looking arteriosclerotic and over-coffeed; hyperventilating. He heard him say things like, "I am just too tired to respond to that one, Judge," and "I'm still tired from yesterday's beating." He saw Belli becoming Ruby.

For a few days of the trial, Ruby kept up surface appearances of liveliness and poise. But girder by girder the structure was giving. For three days the prosecution made its case — policeman after policeman remembering this damaging thing or that thing he had said. Sergeant Pat Dean, Ruby's friend, remembers how Jack looked at him without reproach while he gave evidence that after his arrest Jack told him he had thought of killing Oswald two days before. (After the trial, with incorrigible generosity, Jack gave Dean a copy of the Warren Report with a fond inscription in it, and tried to give him his watch and his gun.)

The police were against him. That didn't matter, now. He knew that. What ate at him those first days, jolt after jolt, was the *defense*. Belli tried to make each policeman admit that Ruby was a "character" (he meant an oddball, unaware that "character" means "police character," or criminal, in Dallas cops' jargon). Wasn't he like the village idiot — Belli phrased and rephrased the matter — who is tolerated till one of his weird pranks misfires?

Tonahill recalls Jack's squirming agony those days. " 'Why is he doing that, Joe?' he would ask me. Jack wanted to have his cake and eat it too. He knew we had to make an insanity case, but he wanted us to do that and leave him a great big hero. He kept saying he wanted to be dignified. 'Dignity' was one of his favorite words — but we had to show him for the nothing that he was." Bob Denson, the private investigator Belli hired in Dallas, watched inside the courtroom as "Belli lost his client" — as Jack shied away from him, from everyone, withdrew into himself, withering as the "village-idiot" theme recurred in every variation.

Alexander saw what was happening. "I always keep one eye on the defendant to see what rattles him. I want to know, in case he takes the stand. With Jack, I also had one of my men watching him all the time, to see how things registered." On the trial's fourth day, George Senator took the stand and described Jack's wild behavior on Saturday and Sunday. He was wearing Jack's suit. Alexander falsettoed questions at him insinuatingly before limp-wristing him away. Jack was wild-eyed. But whenever he is thinking, "It is just like looking into a crawfish's eyes, isn't it? That's right, isn't it?" Alexander drew everyone's attention to the broken man at the table: "Take a look at him . . . see if you don't agree." Ruby was being killed. He looked like one who could kill. The scant life left him now all glittered in his eyes. Their hurt cringe could be made to look like guilt. Alexander used those startled trapped eyes as he had used Candy Barr's impudently prominent "bosom," to indict their owner — to shame the man averting them, hiding from his judges.

Jack did not want attention now. On the day before Alexander's assault, the TV films of his crime were screened — run three times, the first times he had seen them. He tried to hide from the comparison of that celluloid thing up there to himself. "Sit nearer me, Joe," he said, crouching under Tonahill's friendly bulk. "Don't let them see me, Joe."

But there was no place to hide. Belli kept trying to introduce the family medical record to prove Jack congenitally insane.

Jack, the family protector, heard his brother's and sister's psy-chiatric care likened to his mother's final madness. Belli elicited from Dr. Towler the fact that Jack had contracted gonorrhea, though Towler himself said this had no relevance. ("Joe! why *that?* What has that to do with the case?") Belli was in full stride now. Dr. Guttmacher said Jack told him that he "fell for that man" Kennedy. Would you say (Belli pounced on the phrasing) this indicates a latent homosexuality? "I think that there are suggestions of it." Ruby's head gave a hooked marlin's turn in mid-air, mouth working (this small barbed anchor once infixed, he will not slither off). It was the final visible cringe, during the trial, of a man who had been described days earlier, by his psychologist, in these words: "His attraction to people in positions of prestige or class, was typically tied in with the idea of his acquiring some worth, or some feeling of esteem for him-self, since he depends very much on outside sources for feeling self-esteem." No respect left, no self-respect; and loss of that is death before death. Ruby was already sentenced; these were the throes of dignity's last going-off.

That was on the fifth day of trial. Alexander tells us what happened the next morning. "Four days before the verdict, the gerds had trouble getting him to dress. 'Why put on my clothes,' he said, 'just to go be sentenced to the chair?' Even when they got his other clothes on, he tried to go out without socks." Men going to the chair do not wear socks.

The trial reached its climax on the seventh and eighth days of testimony, the last ones, a Thursday and Friday. Judge Brown, who meant to get his jury home by the weekend, was determined to run through all the remaining witnesses on Thursday, no matter how long it took. But Dr. Gibbs, who had refused to appear earlier, was disturbed by the prosecution ex-perts who disputed his E.E.G. reading; late Thursday after-noon he telephoned that he was coming, and caught a plane that night. At first Joe Brown refused to give the defense an-other day — which elicited Belli's threat that he would turn Joe

Tonahill loose filibustering. The Judge allowed them to bring a last witness to the stand on Friday morning. It was understood by everybody that the next day would be the final one.

Gibbs's descent was announced dramatically; he seemed a *deus ex machina* sent to rescue an expiring defense effort. (The reporters' "ghoul pool" of wagers on the outcome had fallen into desuetude as fewer and fewer newsmen could be found to bet on an acquittal.) A Detroit *Free Press* man began by thinking Ruby would get a light sentence, "but then the State had about eight witnesses that changed my mind." Eight doctors — every one of them disagreeing with Gibbs. If anyone could pull the case out, it should be Gibbs, the *discoverer* of psychomotor variant. His testimony was climactically isolated from all others — sole witness brought forward, first thing in the morning, on this final day.

Furthermore, Belli had been hymning this man's virtues all through the trial. The lawyer, who semijocularly calls himself "the Great One," tends to think in Carlylean terms of people who dominate their field with a lonely eminence. In his eyes, medicine is like the law — it has *its* great ones, too, who tower above the rest. He asked expert medical witnesses this kind of question: "Who is the outstanding man in your area?" Scholars do not think in terms of top guns; the witness replied, "I can't answer that." But Belli's idea of the profession is pure Hollywood: "The surgeon from Johns Hopkins walked into the operating room, the patient breathed easier." It is a matter of knowing who "the stars" are — Belli has a little litany of names he recites: "Dandy of Hopkins, Cushing of Harvard, and our own great Naffziger of California." Dr. Gibbs, he had assured the jury in every way possible, belongs in that select company. He was incredulous when others dared to disagree with the great man, the George Washington of encephalography. In his book he attacks a medical opponent of Gibbs, mocks him for his insufficiently reverent attitude toward "scientists who happened to be more eminent than himself."

This exercise in hagiography was tactically sound. Gibbs's letter on Ruby's E.E.G. had been ruled inadmissible at the trial, so Belli used all his courtroom skills to signal its contents, over and over, to the jury; he kept the name "Gibbs" ringing, through the questioning of doctors, like a bell of victory. He was sure that Gibbs himself, who dislikes the ordeal of cross-examination, was not coming.

Till he came. There was no way a mere thing of flesh and blood could live up to this advance billing. The climactic air of his appearance made letdown inevitable and more drastic. For the plain truth was that eight men *had* disagreed with him. He could do nothing but deliver his own opinion again, one already conveyed to the jury over and over (if anything, in more certain and dramatic form than the uneasy witness could give it). Gibbs is an expert, but he is not infallible. The infallible Gibbs existed only in Belli's rhetoric. The witness' direct testimony lasted only half an hour.

Alexander sat there, that half hour, watching the fallible Gibbs, sensing his repugnance to the thought of any grilling, gauging to a centimeter the amount of push his "perfect" jury would allow him; would, at this late date, *cry* for from him, thirst for as a stimulant, something to interest them again. Yesterday's session had been long; the trial, with its continual slow coolings and quick flarings of emotion, had drained spectators as well as participants of their energy, made drama impossible, reduced everything to roaring sameness. Alexander saw a jury tired by the wrangles that had been whirled back before it again and again, bobbed up and bobbed down, technicality carousel — law's up-and-down, sublime-silly, now this one now that one, (now which is *which* one), sublime, sub-silly, sublilly, subliminal (jurors are sleeping now). Question (objection) and Answer, Q-wrangle-A, Q A, Q Q A, and on; pecking and screech of the *psittacus tortius*, Q (Belli), A (doctor), Q (rampant Tonahill, riding up-down, snort-snort), Q (Wade) A Q (drawling); background Brown diddling of melody; break, lightbulbs, *pop-pop-pop,* microphones; back Q A, on Q A, sneer A Q laugh, and bluster (puff) smoke in Brown's brown airless (fans) endless courtroom hum, on and on, endless and droning, and on. Alexander had all along been watching the rhythm of it, the old dull carousel he rides intently as the coolest-eyed gun in the posse. He measured the point in the rumbling machinery where he could, carefully, insert his spanner and crunch it to a stop.

With Dr. Guttmacher, an experienced man on the stand, he had moved warily, showing respect. But the letdown in the jury box told him he could move in hard on this man, with ridicule and sarcasm and vicarious punishment of the saint's acolyte. Alexander had handled the medical technicalities in the trial, showing an astonishing knowledge of the cases Guttmacher and others could cite of epileptic disorders. That had kept him busy. Now he could forget the cautious exploratory style of questioning he used on earlier defense experts. It was time for the "bad guy" to put in his appearance, with the sneer that wins no personal sympathy but hurts its target nonetheless. His taut Wichita Falls voice twanging with contempt, he painted Gibbs as a researcher buried so deep in his laboratory that for twenty-eight years he did not bother with a license for practicing medicine; a doctor who could not write a drugstore prescription; a man cobwebbed in inky zigs and zags. Twisting his tight grin out, Alexander played with the witness:

Q "Well now Doctor, as a matter of fact, you can soak a rag
   doll's head with salt and hook up those wires and get an
   E.E.G. reading, and if the elevator starts about the time you
   stert to read, you'll get a reading on the elevator, won't
   you?"
A "I won't get an electroencephalogram."
Q "You'll get a recording?"
A "Something that I would not recognize as an electroencephalogram."
Q "Or if you pack a clay doll's head with iodized gelatin,
   you'll get an E.E.G. reading off of it, won't you?"

A "Not what I call an E.E.G."

Q "Well, you'll get a tracing that's very similar to that?"

A "To your eyes perhaps, but not to an experienced electro-encephalographer."

Q "Now Doctor, if you went to the wall here, this wall, and laid your ear against it, you could pick up a sixty-cycle hum that's in the building. You know that, of course, being from Chicago where the buildings are tall and lots of steel in them, and the elevated goes by occasionally. You know you can pick that up, don't you sir?"

A "I certainly do."

Wichita Falls outsmarting the city slicker from Chicago "where the buildings are tall." The jury was awake. Adjourned at ten-thirty while the Judge prepared his charge to them, they went back to their chamber and clustered at the wall, alive with talk about the hum in it. Alexander had stolen the show from the star.

That last day dragged on. The jury was out all afternoon as Joe Brown heard defense complaints about his charge and talked to Sam Bloom's people on the looping of cables through windows to bring the voracious TV cameras, with their attendant lights, in at last upon their prey.

Last scene, that night, eight-thirty. The long series of arguments is opened by the prosecution. "Bad guy" first, hit hard before they tire. Off at the other end, six speakers later, the "good guy" will ride in, silver-haired, for the poised closing plea. Time enough then for a genteel emphasis on law, on civilization's order. This is the time for a gut appeal. Clicking the murder weapon, miming the killer's malice, Alexander burrowed his way down to basics — fear, revenge, hate. He made the jury view the scene entirely, twice, from two different angles — imagine oneself in Officer Leavelle's shoes, with Oswald braceleted to one's wrist. You move out — "as if I were moving toward the corner of this table." With Leavelle you *see* something: "We know that was Ruby. Ruby had the gun in his hand when Leavelle first saw him. He was moving —

Leavelle saw the gun, saw the face, heard the boom" [*click! click!*]. The man is moving toward *you,* gun booming [*click!*].

Then, starting upstairs again, come down with Officer Graves, holding Oswald with your right hand; move out and see Ruby strike, off (*just* off) to the side of you — a blur; a bullet easily deflected; *reach* for it, ward that gun away from you: "Graves was fortunate. To get Ruby's right hand, with the gun in it, get hold of Ruby's right hand, break that arm back around his leg. . . ." (Ah, he *got* him. *You* did. *Get* him. *Get Ruby.*) "And Officer Leavelle was fortunate that Graves didn't grab a half second faster than he did, because it would have been Leavelle that got shot instead of Oswald." A matter of seconds — of inches. "From the time of the entire event, the time of the shooting, from the time Jack Ruby moved out of that crowd and ducked his left shoulder, coming out" [*click! click!*] — "less than twenty seconds. Now, that's fast, folks."

He did it to show he has guts? "Now, don't tell me it takes guts to shoot a man that is manacled, it doesn't. . . . Don't talk about sporting; there is no sport in that. . . . Now, if Jack Ruby had wanted to cut somebody up, and shot it out with him, cut it out with him, standing toe to toe — that's something else." This was not a shoot-out. It was a gun-down, a gut-shot, a coward's act.

Alexander mines down and down, below dry arguments to the thing that will make men vote for another man's death, pointing the gun at them, Ruby's gun, sneering, shouting, making them *fear* the one who used this weapon. Belli condescendingly called the speech a revivalist's tirade. Sybille Bedford, sitting in the audience, wrote, "It was lurid and coarse, and hideously fascinating."

Having whetted their willingness to kill, Alexander ticked off, now, the abstract arguments for their decision. On one side, squiggles, read by a man with "a little play world all his own" of paper and ink: "I tell you there is a difference between a practicing doctor and one who hasn't. You might compare it to the theoretical physicist who can't even put tubes in his own

TV set without getting shocked." On the other side, eight *practicing* medical men — "You could have had a world congress on neurology and psychiatry right here" — who said the paper and ink did not prove Ruby an epileptic. *Epileptic?* When no earlier fits were known? "Don't you know that if Jack Ruby had been having any kind of epileptic fit . . . they would have had witness after witness, family after family in here telling you that he was crazy?" But he was not crazy. He was a thrill-killer — one to be killed. That's all, folks.

A good job. Not a suave and polished one. One that makes you squirm uneasily and want to get off the hook (one gets off by voting the death penalty). A good job — like the Candy trial. Could Belli top it? That *is* what everyone wanted to know. They had to wait three hours to find out — while the whole team on each side spoke up: competent jobs by Burleson for the defense, Watts and Bowie for the prosecution, with an hour of comic relief supplied by Tonahill. Joe had not thrown any pencils lately; but he had been getting in his licks all the same, so many of them that Judge Brown finally burst out at him, in the presence of the jury, "You have to bull your way through everything!" Not that Joe was lacking in the subtler touches, too — a Bible prominent on the table, a picture of President Kennedy visible there, and a shouted objection when Alexander moaned "Oh my God" during a heated exchange with Belli: "He took the Lord's name in vain!"

Now, late Friday, Tonahill assured the jury that their raised arms at the oath had been extended to shake hands with the Lord, whereas the prosecution wanted them to take *Oswald* by the hand! Joe's medical argument went slightly askew: "Dr. Frederic Gibbs. Now that is one for the book. Epilepsy stimulated him into developing the E.E.G. . . ." As for Ruby, "the only thing wrong with him, he had too much patriotism." Patriotic epilepsy.

When Belli rose to give his closing argument, it was late — nine minutes to midnight — and everyone was weary. The jury's attention was a commodity to be bargained for. He

freshened it with periodic returns to the most interesting subject he could think of. On the need for Faith he assured them, "I
once did a lecture on this." Concerning the M'Naughten Rule:
"I have been on a lot of programs pro and con." He enlivened
the science of encephalography by claiming that Dr. Gibbs in-
vented it "the year before I got out of law school — I gradu-
ated from Boalt Hall, University of California in 1933." Re-
minding them that posterity would direct its attention to their
verdict, he gave this warrant for that attention: "I have tried
cases in any number of courts and jurisdictions in this country
and abroad." He let them know that he frequently cites the
Bible, though he didn't plan to that night. Countering the
charge that Ruby executed lynch law on Oswald, he proved
this could not be so by saying: "My life has been dedicated to
the law. Perhaps except for the months that Howard Naffziger
wanted me to leave the law and go into his specialty of brain
surgery, other than for those few perhaps months I think I have
dedicated my whole academic life to my discipline, the discipline of the law." On the subject of compassion he admitted, "I
often say to myself, with this event that happened here, had I
been there, had I been so situated, there but for the grace of
God and a stronger constitution of mind could go I."

Belli told his *Playboy* interviewer: "I only wish I could take
him [Richard Nixon] and all the rest of them who believe in
gassing and 'frying' felons, through the agonizing ordeal of the
last days of waiting in the death house to be hanged or electro-
cuted, through the gut-wrenching last meal, through the writing of the last heartbreaking letter to one's wife or daughter.
Let me do just this, nothing more — and I'd be able to defeat
capital punishment single-handedly." Ironically, this reliving of
the condemned man's last moments was the high point of the
twenty-five arguments Tom Howard made successfully to Dallas juries. But Tom Howard was gone, and Belli did not mean
to ask for mercy in the Ruby trial.

His four experts had touched disconnectedly on the five key
points of his case — he emphasized their stature more than

what they had said in his last argument. Belli could plead for a light sentence, "beat the chair," or try to patch his medical case together again and "go for broke." He went for broke. "I guess," Tonahill muses, "Mel didn't want to spoil his record with a conviction." Belli said the jury could not "arrogate the right" to give his man a single year in prison: "If you put a felony of any kind on him, he won't be eligible for Veterans Administration. He is now, being an ex-serviceman. You men know that."

Why did he take this course? He tells us in his book: "Would it have been moral to take this sick man, this mental cripple and have him grovel, 'I'm just a Jew boy and I'm sorry. Please forgive me.' I can't agree that demeaning Ruby in that way would have been right, tactically any more than morally." He would not demean Jack. Why, "I marched this boy" (he argued to the jury) before doctors — "I got the best in the world" — to show that he had gonorrhea, latent homosexuality, psychomotor epilepsy, village-idiocy and "bad stock":

"In the old days we used to call them — what? The village clown? The village idiot? There's the chained wolf; there's the hunchback of Notre Dame; there's our own Emperor Norton out in San Francisco, the old humpty-dumpty who would bend over and allow people to hit him on the backside. . . . The man who is always around the police station, bringing the coffee, the man who brings the doughnuts, the sandwiches, the man who can be sent out for the cold beer. . . . The problem of the mother, the father, the sisters, the brother — who comes from the bad stock and has the personality problem plus the psychomotor epilepsy. . . ."

Tonahill wept at his colleague's eloquence. (This midnight he had a handkerchief.) Ruby sat there, not reacting — deadened, by now, to everything. Henry Wade rose, posed the law briefly, asked for his twenty-fifth death verdict — a handsome Southern gentleman, loose white locks parted in the Dallas manner, just off-center (like Alexander's, like Ruby's).

The verdict came fast, after two hours and nineteen minutes.

Men hesitate when asked to put a human being to death. But this jury had seen Ruby gradually exanimated before their eyes, turned into a thing; and things are easily disposed of. Jack heard the verdict without visible disturbance. Belli boiled over in front of the cameras, still a slugger, not the scholar; wearing an unexpected black sport shirt, buttoned at the neck, under his black jacket (Errol would have loved it). "Dallas is a city of shame!" — Jack's city, where he will live in shame for three more years while Belli flies away to write a book. Imprisoned in "his city" but exiled from it, a total outcast; inside a Dallas jail, living on the moon.

"A One Hundred Percent American Patriot"

i

Not much was left him by the trial—not even his name. The law found him guilty under a name—Jack Rubenstein—the law had removed from him seventeen years back. This was the reverse of an adoption process—the disowning of Jack Ruby.

In many ways he was now a displaced person. He no longer had even a cell to call his own. For his last years, he camped in a corridor—on a "mezzanine" level between the sixth and seventh floors (6-M) where the Chief Jailor, E. L. Holman, has his office. To reach Jack, authorized visitors first dipped into the county court's shallow basement (shadow of that city basement where Oswald died); parked there, took an elevator to 6-M. One steps into vestibule space before an office, a barred gate to one's right. This gate opens on a narrow hallway stretching left (visiting room across the way). Moving left down this strait runway you come to another gate, guarded outside and in by a four-man rotating team; on the other side of that gate, in an area extending to the right, is the outer little court of Chief Holman's office, and this is where Ruby bivouacs. A barred cubbyhole to the side, used as a holding cell when prisoners are brought to see Chief Holman, is now left open. It allows Ruby to escape the main thoroughfare, though not to privacy. A guard is stationed to see in there (where the toilet is). At the end of this entry-way Jack paces, a door leads onto iron stairs that corkscrew down over "tanks" (twelve to fourteen men per tank). Every day Ruby wound down these stairs to take his shower — an early trip, since the showers are scrubbed by trusties before 9:00 a.m. Jack must be out by then. It is the most pressing deadline of his daily schedule. (Several guards argue that Ruby, if he were serious about suicide, would have tried to jump from 6-M down to the "tank" level.) He lived under the constant scrutiny of Chief Holman (who met most visitors in the outer works of the jail, keeping his office moated behind Jack's campsite). Ruby, being Ruby, labored to please and impress "my Chief." He wanted one of the first reports on his polygraph test sent to Holman.

He had no moment to himself. Sleeping or awake, in bed or out, on the toilet stool, dressing, undressing, studying the thinned hairs, shaving that second time meticulously close into every fold of skin — later racked, over and over, with vomiting — he lived under the tired, skeptical gaze of men who resented their assignment, locked constantly in the bowels of this steaming jail with a man trying to "con," impress, or frighten them. They all got on each other's nerves in time.

We asked Sheriff Decker about these arrangements. Why the close watch — to prevent a suicide attempt? "No, Jack wasn't going to kill himself. Jack liked Jack pretty good. He rubbed his head against the wall once. We rushed him to Parkland for tests and X rays, and then gave him the treatment he needed — a little Merthiolate." Then why the twenty-four-hour watch? "Well, pahdnuh, I've got two hundred men in that jail; and there's probably another Jack Ruby among them — one who would take a crack at him to be a hero." Did he watch TV, or have a radio? "No, that jail has soft walls. With a noise to cover them, prisoners would cut it up like cheese." Why was his cancer not discovered earlier? Both eyes, the good one as coldly as the glass one, measure us; the Marshal kicks dust in the main street, ready for a stare-down. "I tell you. I'm not even going to write my *own* book, pahdnuh. I don't see why I should write yours." Indian stiffness of face, cold-shouldering us out.

Before his conviction, Ruby was not subject to imprisonment's full rigor. It was a time of examination (doing his Rorschach, his other tests with Dr. Schafer, driving across town for his E.E.G. at the Olinger Clinic, interviewed by Dr. Guttmacher and others); a time of exhilarating telegrams; of trips through newsmen in and out of court (bond hearings first, then change-of-venue hearing); of headlines, courtesies, comings and goings of lawyers; selling his memoirs, "reading his reviews." Finally, there were two weeks spent in choosing jurors — by now things were going sour for him — and nine draining days of trial. Excitement had kept him going; but now all other things calmed, and he was restless.

He was a night animal, prowling from The Carousel to The Vegas to Lucas' B and B; dropping in as the ads went to press at dawn for the afternoon papers; buying other stragglers ham and eggs, the before-bed breakfast of these men with inverted schedules. In jail, he had nowhere to prowl, no night spots, no money to treat the police with as they sat there every night; often he could not sleep, played solitaire, turned his back to escape the Argus-scrutiny of guards; was wakened early, prodded out of bed after nights of sleeplessness.

He was a man of jerky energies, perpetually on the move; able to have his way in little things — because no one cared enough to oppose him, because he could handle those few who did by using his fists. If he did not like the way his morning eggs were scrambled, at a diner, he went behind the counter and cooked his own. Now he was cooped up in a schedule of *day*life — up for his shower, regular meals, no quarreling with the chef. He tried to wheedle favors, an extra hour in bed, extra minutes on the telephone, one phone call beyond the quota, no shower that morning, more food kept in his hallway (he was given tea and coffee, kept sugar and salt in Dixie cups, got them mixed one day and threw a tantrum). He learned the little arts of survival that come with being in prison — how to get extra cream (collect it from leftovers when a lawyer is served coffee in the visiting room). He gossiped with trusties who came in to mop his corridor, but was not accepted in the prison "grapevine" — he was too haughty when he first came, putting himself above the other prisoners. Even after the conviction, Jack would say on occasion that he was not a common murderer like the other two men living under death sentence in that jail.

It was a life of perpetual little frustrations which he could not assuage by bitching at his girls, taking the mike from his M.C., greeting an important person, hitting a punk. There was no play to take from the men he lived with in a chafing proximity; he never hit a guard. He did swing at a lawyer once; but his few physical outbursts were senseless — hitting his head on the wall, breaking his glasses, throwing a spittoon at the light bulb, trying to stick his finger in a socket, tearing up his prison coveralls. The defense lawyers portrayed these as attempts at suicide, though Jack himself denied this. His guards thought he was putting on an act. Neither side seems to have realized that jungle animals must strike, occasionally, even at air. It was a kind of shadowboxing with his many nemeses.

Under this twenty-four-hour scrutiny, cocooned from outside things, without companionship of other prisoners, even the most stable personality would wobble somewhat. But this was a volatile, unconfined, violent man, gregarious, needing the limelight; nonexistent if he could not see approval of some sort mirrored at him in strangers' eyes. His narrow world began to fluctuate in odd ways as dark moods congested in him, undischargeable. Add to this the fact that prisoners just condemned to death customarily plunge into despondency, and cycle up again (if ever) very slowly. Add to this: the county jail is one of the few large establishments in this city that is not air-conditioned — prisoners regularly sulk in the summer, flare up easily with snarling edginess. Jack's trial ended in March and his spirits went down with the Texas summer's onset. He wore shower sandals without socks, and pulled the standard white coveralls off his shoulders in the stifling air. He had given up his exercises (maintained before the trial) and he went from 38 coveralls to a size 40. He was greedy for his pitchers of iced tea, which he turned into sweet lemonade with sucaryl and lemon slices, then gulped at in the Dallas heat.

Before the trial, not even defense psychiatrists claimed Ruby was psychotic. Soon after, even prosecution doctors (Stubblefield and Holbrook) thought he was paranoid and needed treatment, perhaps in the hospital. New doctors came and went diagnosing new things as Jack's mind darkened, cleared, dimmed, recovered, and dipped again. One of these doctors had performed LSD experiments on an elephant, and it suited Bill Alexander's grim humor to tell Jack the man was getting ready to give him elephant shots: "And you know what that elephant did? It trumpeted, lay down, defecated and died." Alexander told us: "Dr. Holbrook has been doing studies on the effects of imprisonment. He predicted Jack's swing down after the trial in March, and he predicted his swing up again in October. After that, he was pretty much on a plateau."

Jack's guards thought he was "playing crazy" when he raved that he would die, all Jews would die, for what he did. But Ruby worked hard to prove his sanity when psychiatrists were in his cell, and he resented anyone who told the press he was insane. He assured his brother he had never tried to kill himself. He grumbled to guards that his family and lawyers were trying to make him out a crazy man. And through all the hallucinatory cloudinesses — shower, sunburst, mist — runs a hard determination to tell his story. His lawyers, swept in and out of the case in a continual bickering stream, tried to make him hold his tongue until the new trial they were fighting for; but, as Alexander puts it, "there was no differential between his brain

and his mouth." Besides, he had listened to lawyers before the
first trial, and what good had it done? Tom Howard told him to
plead he was incited by Oswald's smirk; others asked him to
blame Harry Olsen, the policeman who told him Saturday
morning that Oswald should be "cut in little pieces." Then he
was told *not* to mention these things — they would indicate
prior motivation and intent. Plead this. That. Psychomotor.
Plead epilepsy. Don't take the stand.

Belli himself gives us this bit of dialogue with his client:

> With a weary gesture, Ruby slapped his hands down on the
> metal table between us and shook his head impatiently. "What
> are we doing, Mel, kidding ourselves?" he asked.
>
> I was tired, too. "What do you mean, Jack?" I snapped.
>
> "We know what happened," he said. "We know I did it for
> Jackie and the kids. I just went in and shot him. They've got us
> anyway. Maybe I ought to forget this silly story that I'm telling,
> and get on the stand and tell the truth."
>
> He was absolutely sincere. At that point, with his mental ex-
> aminations behind him and the outline of our defense clearly
> established, he was suddenly ready to admit that he had shot
> Lee Harvey Oswald deliberately and that our contention that
> the shooting had occurred during a blackout in which he was
> incompetent to know what he was doing was a fraud.

Belli, of course, says this was "confabulation" patching over the
psychomotor episode. Ruby was assured he would be acquitted
if he just shut up and let the lawyers fancy-dan before the jury.
He was not happy at this. Even before the trial proper began,
he had pangs of desire to give up all pretense and get his story
out. He scribbled notes to his exasperated lawyer: "I could
plead guilty and insist on polygraph." This urgency to tell his
story grew upon him as the chances for acquittal waned. What
if he had sacrificed his credibility to no purpose? Would anyone ever believe him when he admitted his defense had been a
sham? And, after all, conviction meant one thing: disaster for
the Jews. He had done it to prove that "Jews have balls." In his
telegram-induced euphoria, he was arrogant enough to think

his little deed had "redeemed" an ancient people. What, then, did it mean if he were discredited? What would that do to the Jews? He had worried for days about the impact of a Jewish name — Bernard Weissman — on the ad attacking Kennedy. What of the Jewish name — he was now Jack Rubenstein every day in court — that would be vilified everywhere when he was condemned? Pencil notes from the last days in February first sound this theme: "How about the repercussions our people?" It was beginning.

Then he was convicted. Condemned by his friends, by his own city Dallas — and for what? He hammered at that question day and night, in what his guards came to recognize as the "if-only" routine. If only Little Lynn had not called when she did, but a little later. . . . If he had not parked where he did, with that last-minute illegal swing across the street — he would have gone a block further down, then, and lost the crucial seconds. If only he had driven a different route; stopped at the wreaths; been behind two people instead of one at the Western Union office. The if's moved illogically back in time: *if* he had married Alice, stayed in Chicago with Earl, been a success in some other business. Or they jumped forward, after the act: *if* only Percy Foreman had defended, or Charley Tessmer. He retraced in disbelief the steps that brought him into this odd corner, trapped there by a hostile world of friends.

How could this possibly be? How did it happen? *Did* it happen? Or did deeper things happen that explain the surface craziness of these events? Jack Ruby condemned? For what: killing Oswald? He could not accept that as the truth. What was the crime? — he killed a rat (so what?), this would not turn dear friends on him, make him lose his city (even if they had to punish him in some way, surely they would not *hate* him too?). Why should America hate the man who killed the thing disgracing it? There must be something more.

That "something" he found in newspapers, pawing backward through them from the entertainment section (his regular starting-point, even in his lowest moods). There he caught echoes of the speculation on his role in the whole Dallas sequence — thoughts involving him with Oswald. With the creep! The thing he squashed had stuck to his hands, tarred him, left him tainted. Day and night he felt the uncleanness of it crawling on him. The thing he despised, threw out of his club, cast out of his life — the old thing he hated because he was its victim: the sleaziness and drabness, the cynical acceptance of one's failure, the raucous drunken home he ran from every day of his life. It had caught him at last.

In the person of Oswald. How absurd. But, crazily, logical. How much it would explain! It made sense of those otherwise inexplicable hatreds Jack felt laser-beaming at him through the very walls. Under all the surface formalities, they must think (Mayor Cabell, even Bill Decker and "my Chief," even Bill Alexander — how could they? but they *must*) that he belonged with Oswald, *was* an Oswald, a punk; a coward with no guts, no balls. Ruby would plead, soon, with Earl Warren: "At this moment, Lee Harvey Oswald isn't guilty of committing the crime of assassinating President Kennedy. Jack Ruby is. How can I fight that, Chief Justice Warren?"

He had been a hero those first days — the vigilante avenger, "the man who killed the man who killed Kennedy." But the jury treated him like any common murderer, "the man who *killed.*" Or had they? How could they forget the cause of all that weekend's tragedy? The singsong of it had to work in them, as in him: *the man who killed, the man who killed . . .* KENNEDY, *killed Kennedy, the man who killed Kennedy,* KILL THE MAN. Yes, he understood the hate, too well. It was his hatred of Oswald turned now on him, a blind instinctive hatred for the man who could erase all the promise of the Kennedy years. Jack was linked with that killing, smudged all over with it; and everything must be cleansed. He was suffocating now with hate — Jack Ruby's old old hate for Jacob Rubenstein. He knew there was some hidden ugly thing he carried out of that nightmare home. He had tried to kill it in himself, to kill everything that reminded him of it (the punks, the creeps, an endless supply of them, haunting his clubs, his life). Somehow the world had caught sight of that thing in him, saw Oswald and Ruby meet like a man hitting his own image in a mirror. Oswald is dead, why should Ruby live? Kill *all* the punks, all those who killed the President, *both* men who had killed Kennedy. Killing, on that weekend, was one thing: killing Kennedy. He had joined the orgy, out of hatred of Oswald. He was too like him — brothers in the killing; and the world found out.

Riding always, dizzied slow or fast, on this "man-who-killed-the" merry-go-round, his mind grew preternaturally clear regarding the circle, the consistent platform of linked theory, on which he spun. Clear as his little world, his oblong cube of moonscape (time capsule sealed in the Dallas jail, open it after the holocaust, feed on the prime victim last, who caused it all). Clear as the two guards always watching him, seen across the blink and turn of the intellect's merry-go-round, the two of them moving like ticket collectors from carousel horse to horse. It is only beyond the twirl of the merry-go-round's string-of-pearl blinked lights that the outside world grows dark, receding. That world ceases to exist as the circular thoughts float off, an insanely clear turning island of Jack's linked two thoughts, his serpent-carousel swallowing its tail: Rubenstein killed Kennedy? — *We* will kill the Jews! (How easily that *we* came to him, Ruby joining the hunt of Rubenstein.)

When Ruby's first lawyers heard of Jack's warm conversations with his night guard, a man named Stevenson, they expostulated with him. They said he was being pumped, was giving the cops ammunition they would use against him in the trial. But Jack had a hard time restraining himself. He wrote notes like this:

I was so confused one nite. Ive been for a week to find out about the four guns. Then before you told me I had spoken to Stevenson the guard about that, which was a mistake? I think

The lawyers were worried about more "confabulation" like his "Some one had to do it" phrase. Jack could not understand that. He had already shifted mental gears — considering harmful only those things that might link him to "that person" (even to use Oswald's name revolted him). He had been questioned at length about his trip to see McWillie in Cuba; he told them about the gun sent to Las Vegas and the four guns he asked Ray (of Ray's Hardware) to send "Mack" while he was still in Havana. What four guns? Just ask Ray.

But Ray said he knew nothing of this set of guns — only of the one he sent to Vegas, which was returned to him. Was he afraid of being involved in the shipment of guns abroad? Had Jack promised to place the order, then convinced himself he followed through? Had he called, been told Ray could not do that? Then the inconsequential call had slipped Ray's mind? These are the things he tried to puzzle out, December nights, while "Steve" was there.

It did not matter, of course, in terms of the prosecutors' case against him: the Dallas force wanted no talk of conspiracy around the trial. But "incrimination" to Jack meant anything that would make his cop pals hate him, not something that would give them legal arguments. Something, therefore, other than his shooting Oswald. (Buddy Walthers would not hate him for that — he shouted it to Buddy in his time of triumph: "I did it! He looked just like Corky Crawford!" Jack was the *foe* of punks, just like the good cops he admired.)

Cuba, then, was the thing to fear — a link with Communists, and so with Oswald, with the "Commie rat" (as Jack regularly called him). The phantom quartet of revolvers haunted him. If they could not believe him on this thing, they might doubt the rest of his story. If he were lying on this point, then he was linked with Cuba, with smirks and attacks on Kennedy and fair play for Castro's Cuba. Another Jew alongside that shaming Jewish name upon the ad, making them hate the Jew, Jack Rubenstein, hate all Jews. (Dr. Schafer, after giving ten psychological tests to Jack in December, wrote: "He feels generally damaged, impaired and repulsive.") The adulation he received after his act had stilled, for a moment, these doubts about himself, self-hate, the slide of his eyes on to that next group which was buzzing with the tale of his ridiculousness. Now it all came back redoubled, in crushing strength — that old friend-foe of his, Ruby-Rubenstein at war with himself, forever trying to kill the punk in him, the hidden Oswald.

Even at the trial, while his lawyers worked to save his life, Jack's mind was elsewhere:

I will never have a chance to prove myself.

There isnt any chance of taking a lie-detector test or truth syrum.

Don't fight with them today, because I'm sure they have something up their sleeve. When Wade made the crack about Cuba, and Alexander mentioned that I didn't have to take the stand. Don't make me more hated in Dallas then I have already.

I could plead guilty and insist on polygraph, Im worried how I can be miscast . . . Our people may suffer.

It had begun.

All that was back in February. After his conviction, Jack's terror of the Oswald-thing he had been tarred and pitched with grew; he felt the hatred for him mounting everywhere — in guards, resentful of confinement with him; in the hallway itself, so lacking in distractions; in Dallas, angry at Belli's continuing assault (UPI quoted the lawyer's claim that Ruby "might be put in a hole some place and killed with a shiv . . . that would be the way to prevent an appeal . . . another way for Dallas to dispose of him"); in America, dazed and incredulous still over the loss of Kennedy; in the rest of the world, certain there had been a plot, uncertain only which plot was the real one (*every* plot included Ruby).

Everything he had done backfired — the shooting, for Jackie; hiring Belli, for class; the psychomotor epilepsy stuff, for an acquittal; the cultivation of police; his trying to please Dallas. Nothing else had worked; then why not try the truth? But no one would believe him, anyway — not Ruby the liar (those damn four guns), the pretender (faked defense, not taking the witness stand), the coward (*Bill* said it — he shot a man wearing cuffs), the cowardly comical bald fat Jew Jack Ruby Rubenstein.

Wait a minute, though, one minute, what about — and why not? — take a lie-detector test or some truth serum! Then they would *have* to believe him. But there is no time. The hatred mounts too fast, and he is under it; turn the hourglass over, he is still buried in the sands when they start running back. They will never love him again, stop slaughtering him everywhere, stop killing Jews, all Jews, for Jack's sake.

These are the themes that weave, then ravel out, then weave, ravel, tangle, in the three-hour session Jack had, at last, with the Warren Commission. It was three months after his trial — three hot sinking months of increasing terror, isolation, desperate nights. By now he was shouting through a glass inclosure, uncertain whether anyone would hear, ringing insistently one bell that made no sound: *the truth* (what is truth?), *this* truth, this *is* the truth (or is it?), listen, see the truth (where is it?), *truth,* where did it go?

"I would like to be able to get a lie detector test or truth serum of what motivated me to do what I did at that particular time, and it seems as you get further into something, even though you know what you did, it operates against you somehow, brainwashes you, that you are weak in what you want to tell the truth about and what you want to say which is the truth."

Dr. Manfred Guttmacher found Ruby's memory of the assassination weekend already confused in December. He lost sequence and sense of time, fidgeted at details, departed along

entering strands of the story. Meanwhile, too many were remembering *for* him — Say you saw the smirk and went berserk
(*punk-smirk, berserk*); say that on the stand; — no, you didn't
see the smirk, you were blacked out; *don't* say that on the
stand; don't, in fact, *take* the stand, you'll louse things up, "con-
fabulate," you jerk (*smirk, berserk, punk Jack the jerk*). Then
policemen remembered, but *mis*remembered (no, Bill, not for
hate, not in cowardice, for Jackie; no, Pat, not *planned* for two
days, not planned at all). He sat up nights casting and recast-
ing timetables: Yes, he went here, *then* there. No. There then
here, here-there, here then, *then* what (so what?). Throw it
away, start over. No, don't throw it away (stop supplying them
with ammunition, Jack). Doodle it over, make it indecipher-
able (Jack the counteragent). Stop talking to the guards
(they're spies), stop talking to myself, the place is bugged. The
truth — but (shhhhh) softly. Ring the bell quietly; *someone*
will hear (but who?) — Ruby the jerky bell-ringer, smirking
berserk. The guards must not hear. Don't talk to them (but,
after hours and days of loneliness, at night, or half asleep, or
with a burst of the old Jack — "I demand respect, even in my
situation" — he always *would* talk; he always had).

From fiddling with the hours of his crucial three days, Jack
moved on back, reconstructing his whole life; ruminated his
promising doomed past, remasticating, gagging, regurgitating
all the bitternesses, failures — poor failed Jack, poor Rubenstein. His "spotty background," he said over and over, could be
"dirtied." No one would see, anymore, how he had tried to rise,
had risen in fact, come so far — only to slide back, far back
into a dirtiness the world abhors, an Oswald dirtiness. When he
moved ahead, past the three resisting days his memory tried to
cope with, things grew even hazier as he microscoped them
with a doodling pencil. He elaborated spoked cammed plots,
labyrinthine hatreds, repercussions, plots. "They" had done so
much to him, they *had* to do more. And to others. When Clayton Fowler, his lawyer, came to visit him, Jack would put his

fingers to his lips, gesture toward invisible "bugs" in various corners, and write dramatic warnings on the yellow legal pad: "Slaughtered . . . H L Hunt may [*sic*] behind . . . they have told their followers I killed the president." Fowler would try to discuss Jack's case, the appeal, the progress in reversing his conviction. But Jack merely scribbled more desperately at him: "The only thing you can do for me, is to try to get to the president for me to get a lie detector test, try and contact Abe Fortas in Washington and tell him what is happening here. They are torturing my people." Laboring at the bell, its noiseless beat that no one heeds. "Do you know that the newspapers are not printing the truth about *anything*." Then he would whisper that They were after him (Fowler) because he had testified for Jack at the change-of-venue hearing. Fowler must escape to Israel, live there; the last stronghold.

Now, before the Chief Justice and Senator Ford and their assistants, Jack had his chance. He could tell his story. For one full hour he did it, in detail: Friday. But after that first hour, his attention began to wander. Justice Warren tried to bring him back to his train of thought, over the next two hours — Move on to Sunday, to the killing. Jack pounced on that: leave out Saturday? did he think he had forgotten where he was? He still had to tell about Saturday. He never did. Things clouded. His doubts returned: who would believe? And once that acid begins its work, where does doubt end? What *is* the thing to be believed?

"As it started to trial — I don't know if you realize my reasoning, how I happened to be involved — I was carried away tremendously emotionally, and all the time I tried to ask Mr. Belli, I wanted to get up and say the truth regarding the steps that led me to do what I have got involved in, but since I have a spotty background. . . . Different things came up, flashed back into my mind, that it dirtied my background, that Mr. Belli and I decided — oh yes, when I went to say that I wanted to get on the stand and tell the truth what happened that morning, he

said, 'Jack, when they get you on the stand, you are actually speaking of a premeditated crime that you involved yourself in.' But I didn't care, because I wanted to tell the truth. He said, 'When the prosecution gets you on the stand, they will cut you to ribbons.' So naturally, I had to retract, and he fought his way to try to vindicate me out of this particular crime."

Mr. Rankin, of the Commission, asked Jack whether he was carrying a gun on Friday when he saw Oswald the first time: "I will be honest with you. I lied about it. It isn't so. I didn't have a gun. But in order to make my defense, more accurate, to save your life, that is the reason the statement was made." His lawyers argued repeatedly, during his trial, that if he had wanted to kill Oswald in his conscious moments, he would have done it Friday night, not Sunday in his epileptic fit. Jack felt that he had destroyed his chance of getting the truth out by allowing the defense to create useful impressions about him that made no contact with reality, by agreeing to stay off the stand lest his "spotty background" be brought up by Alexander to embarrass him. He had sat in court, incredulous himself, wondering how the jury would accept all this: Mr. Ruby does not use profanity; Mr. Ruby carried a gun on Friday; Mr. Ruby is an epileptic, a village idiot. How would they ever believe him now? They will think he is lying, about the four guns, about everything: "[Ray] denies I ever called. Evidently he feels, maybe he feels, it would be illegal to send guns out of the country. . . . I wanted someone to go to Ray Brantley. . . . This definitely would do more harm, because if I tell my story that I called Ray Brantley, and he denies that he ever got a call from me, definitely that looks like I am hiding something." But he has no hope except the truth now (cold hope), and he will not change his story to accommodate the obstacle that has arisen (Ray's embarrassment? bad memory?). He not only sticks to the tale, but worries it like a nagging tooth.

He is terrified at the idea of further lapses from truthfulness. Did he tell them about Harry Olsen, early Saturday morning?

If not, it was because he did not want to get Harry in trouble with his wife (he was in the car with one of Jack's strippers) — and — "May I read that, Joe? May I please?"

Joe Tonahill has written a note to show to Arlen Specter of the Commission. It reads: "This is the thing that started Jack in the shooting." Several of Jack's friends, and some of his family, think Officer Olsen's anger at Oswald put the idea of killing him in the back of Jack's mind, "planted the seed." Now Jack, suspicious that his lawyers will make him plead something false again, asks for the note — but cannot read it, his brother Sammy has not brought new glasses since he broke the others in a rage. Jack digs his nose at the letters, half makes them out: " 'This is the girl that' — what? — 'that started Jack off.' What is this other word? . . . That is untrue. That is what I wanted to read." Still not certain what the note says, Jack feels the protective glass cage being lowered around him again by his would-be defenders, leaving him isolated with his undiscerned true story, muffling the bell: "Gentlemen, unless you get me to Washington, you can't get a fair shake out of me." Finally, as Jack cools down a bit, Justice Warren loans him his glasses, and he makes out the first sentence. "You are lying, Joe Tonahill. . . . You are lying, because you know what motivated me. You want to make it that it was a premeditation." The murder-without-malice lawyers wanted Jack to plead for sympathy, say he was egged on by a Dallas policeman. The fugue-state lawyers tried to convince him this was part of his "confabulated" story, showing an intent, however hazy, to kill the man. Jack remembers what each lawyer said against the other lawyers. By now he only trusts them when they tell him to distrust. "You can't tell Joe [Tonahill] or Phil [Burleson]," he had scribbled on Fowler's pad. Feeling that all other lawyers had dishonored him, trapped him inside falsehoods, he smuggled a long note out to the first attorney he had talked to on that Sunday, Jim Martin: "Judge Brown, Phil Burleson, Joe Tonahill are all Nazi's." He had no one to defend him. Belli gave him an

inscribed copy of his book, *Dallas Justice,* when it appeared.
Jack angrily tore out the inscription.

*"I want you to question and requestion me on anything you
want, plus the fact I do want the tests when they are available.
. . . I am as innocent regarding any conspiracy as any of you
gentlemen in the room, and I don't want anything to be run
over lightly. I want you to dig into it with any biting, any question that might embarrass me, or anything that might bring up
my background which isn't so terribly spotted — I have never
been a criminal. . . ."*

As he sat there talking to them, the glass pane all about him
thickened. This would not do it. What would? "I have been
over this for the longest time to get the lie detector test. Somebody has been holding it back from me." Justice Warren promised he would let him take such a test; his counsel could arrange it. "I don't think I will get a fair representation with my
counsel, Joe Tonahill." They assured him that a polygraph machine could not register a whole story of the sort he wanted to
tell; but if he would tell them the story in sequence, they would
check key points later with the polygraph. "How do you know
if the facts I stated about everything I said, statements with
reference to, are the truth or not?" Who would believe *him,*
trust Oswald-Rubenstein? Justice Warren asked him if he had
known Oswald before the assassination: "That is why I want to
take the lie detector test. Just saying no isn't sufficient."

The very politeness of Earl Warren suggested he was just
"being nice," listening because he had to. As with his guards,
Jack tried the shock approach: "Gentlemen, my life is in danger here. Not with my guilty plea of execution." (Whenever
Jack wants to be impressive, he opens his sentence with "Gentlemen.") They were still too calm; ring the bell harder. "I am
being victimized as a part of a plot in the world's worst tragedy
and crime at this moment." They can no longer get him to follow a line of thought in his narrative. Bill Decker tries the stern

paternal treatment, tells him to be a man. Jack answers: "There is an organization here, Chief Justice Warren, if it takes my life at this moment to say it, and Bill Decker said be a man and say it, there is a John Birch Society right now in activity, and Edwin Walker is one of the top men of this organization — take it for what it is worth, Chief Justice Warren. Unfortunately for me, for me giving the people the opportunity to get in power, because of the act I committed, has put a lot of people in jeopardy with their lives. Don't register with you, does it?"

He is spinning his wheels. He begins to weep. "I must be a great actor, I tell you that." Decker had offered to leave and take his men with him. Jack said no: "That wouldn't prove any truth." Later he *does* want them out. Decker agrees; but Jack finds a new reason for hesitating: "If you are not going to have Joe leave. . . ." Decker says Jack's counsel should be there to protect his rights. "Bill, I am not accomplishing anything if they are here, and Joe Tonahill is here. You asked me anybody I wanted out." "Jack, this is your attorney. That is your lawyer." There is no deflecting him now; or rather, no directing his zigzags to any goal: "He is not my lawyer." The session is disintegrating as Jack's thought-span dwindles: "I bet you haven't had a witness like me in your whole investigation, is that correct?" He keeps circling back to the fear that no one will ever believe him: "How can I prove my authenticity of what I have stated here today?" The Chief Justice says he is under oath; is that not enough? "No; because I will say this. You don't know if there is anything to disprove, but at this moment, there is a certain organization in this area that has been indoctrinated, that I am the one that was in the plot to assassinate our President." Mr. Rankin asks what organization: "The John Birch Society." "Can you tell us what basis you have for that, Mr. Ruby?" "Just a feeling."

He told them his family was in danger. They asked why. For standing by a man the world holds guilty of the President's death: "Well, assuming that, as I stated before, some persons are accusing me falsely of being part of the plot — naturally, in all the time from over six months ago, my family has been so interested." Friends have been sympathetic, too, and put themselves in danger: "That sympathy isn't going to help me, because the people that have power here, they have a different verdict. They already have me as the accused assassin of our beloved President." If the world believes that, how can it fail to exterminate the Jews? And people were trying to convince President Johnson of this, so his power would be used to further the extermination. That is why Jack has to get to Washington and convince Johnson it is all lies. "And I know our wonderful President, Lyndon Johnson, as soon as he was the President of his country, he appointed you as head of this group. But through certain falsehoods that have been said about me to other people, the John Birch Society, I am as good as guilty as the accused assassin of President Kennedy. How can you remedy that, Mr. Warren? Do any of you men have any ways of remedying that?"

Maybe it is too late already. Perhaps the Birch Society has already convinced the President, and Johnson is helping them now: "I wish that our beloved President, Lyndon Johnson, would have delved deeper into the situation, hear me, not to accept just circumstantial facts about my guilt or innocence, and would have questioned to find out the truth about me before he relinquished certain powers to these certain people." Late as it is, though, he must pull at the bell-rope, move his silent bell: "All I know is maybe something can be saved. Because right now, I want to tell you this, I am used as a scapegoat, and there is no greater weapon that you can use to create some falsehood about some of the Jewish faith, especially at the terrible heinous crime such as the killing of President Kennedy. Now maybe something can be saved. It may not be too late, whatever happens, if our President, Lyndon Johnson, knew the truth from me. But if I am eliminated, there won't be any way of knowing. Right now, when I leave your presence now, I am the only one that can bring out the truth to our President, who believes in righteousness and justice." Telling Chief Justice Warren is not enough. The Birch Society is not afraid of him. It openly attacks him, on signs like the one Jack photographed: "You have a lost cause, Earl Warren. You don't stand a chance. They feel about you like they do about me, Chief Justice Warren."

Ruby wanted to prevent men from thinking he contributed in any way to the death of President Kennedy, and — as usually happened with Jack — his very efforts to forestall suspicion brought it upon him. His gesticulating mystifications to Earl Warren were attempts to fight a shadow-enemy, the reports that he was in on a conspiracy. Against these amorphous rumors he flails as wildly as a boxer in the ring with an invisible opponent. Conspiratorialists take certain of these wilder swings; arrange them with careful cutting, splicing, editing; and play back the picture of a Ruby shrewdly punching at fellow conspirators in their hiding place.

Mark Lane, for instance, devotes a whole chapter of his book, *Rush to Judgment,* to Ruby's session with Justice Warren. It is a surgical masterpiece. When Ruby tries to explain that he killed Oswald out of regard for President Kennedy, the transcript gives us this passage: "I never called the man [Oswald] by an obscene name, because as I stated earlier, there was no malice in me. He was insignificant, to my feelings for my love for Mrs. Kennedy and our beloved President. He was nothing comparable to them, so I can't explain it." This gets shortened, under Lane's scalpel, to "there was no malice in me." Aha! No malice? Then a cold plan — a conspiracy. Lane comments: "Would this not suggest the logical question — if he did not hate Oswald, why did he kill him? The Commission failed to ask it." *Failed to* because Jack said, in the very next sentence, why he did it — and had been saying this off and on throughout the session. Yet Mr. Lane's knife is so busy snipping and carving on every quotation he uses that it takes extraordinary persistency to piece the original statements together in their original context.

One cannot admire too much the ingenuity of Mr. Lane's labors. He can separate out a whole strand of thought, assembling nearly every word that touches on it, yet omit each concomitant thread that would rule out his inference from this one strand. He spends three pages collecting Ruby's requests that the Chief Justice take him to Washington for questioning (Strand A). Yet he artfully steers around all the places where Jack explains *why* he wants to go there (Strand B). Of course, sometimes Strand A is so interwoven with Strand B that Lane has to omit a relevant quotation entirely — for instance: "Take me back to Washington tonight *to give me a chance to prove to the President I am not guilty.*" Guilty of what? At least six times Jack returned to this important theme in his argument (Strand C) — that he was considered guilty of the President's death; and he was considered this because (Strand D) *"some persons are accusing me falsely of being part of the plot."* Not only does Mr. Lane neglect to mention strands B, C, and D in connection with Strand A. He actually interprets the latter in a sense contradictory to the other three. He quotes Ruby's pleas to go to Washington as veiled promises that he will *confess,* if only he is taken out of the hands of his menacing fellow-conspirators, the Dallas police force!

With Mr. Lane and his fellow theorists, there is no end of arguing. Lean on one part of their structure, and you are engulfed in collapsing fabrics of cobwebby surmise. They rely on the creation of cumulative doubts, each gaining strength from interdependence with the others — which means that their linked guesses have to make a kind of *corporate* sense. Any alternatives to the Warren Commission's judgment of Ruby must, to be convincing, be looked at in concatenation with the whole sequence of events. The conspiratorialists rarely put their sketchy alternatives to this test; but the logic of their position leads them to adopt most or all of *this* explanation, in sequence:

— that Ruby, who was in a conspiracy with Tippit and Bernard Weissman, not only exposed his connection with them, but did it shortly before the assassination, in a place (The Carousel) where everyone knew him, where they drifted automatically toward him, hovering as he talked, ready to put a word in;

— that, planning to attend the President's death, he nonetheless went to an office five blocks from the scene and allowed himself to be engaged in a conversation which was broken off by the other man only five minutes before Oswald's first shot;

— that Jack puff-puffed his way to Dealey Plaza and made some unimaginably swift contribution to the death of Kennedy;

— that, having run through streets where he was very familiar, he turned around and ran back, unrecognized; and thus

— that he spectacularly outraced John Newnam, who had started a three-block walk to the office *before* the President was shot, and who came upon a calmly seated and unwinded Ruby when he arrived at the *Morning News;*

— that, having made this extraordinary and unobserved dash to and from Dealey Plaza, Jack made just as rapid a pass at Parkland Hospital, motoring there, penetrating the confusion just long enough to draw attention to himself with a visiting reporter, then speeding off to The Carousel in a record time for this senseless track;

— that Ruby then drew attention to Weissman as energetically as possible, flourishing the ad he signed;

— that he further drew attention to himself, jumping up all over the place;

— that he labored to suggest there was a conspiracy, photographing the John Birch sign against Earl Warren and broadcasting the idea that this had something to do with the killing;

— that he drew attention as well to his link with Tippit, saying when he heard of his death that he knew the man;

— that he changed his story later (in captivity) to please his fellow conspirators (now his putative captors); yet the plot's

masterminds must not have been displeased with his original
blabbing on the subject, because the hypothesis demands, of
course,

— that Jack (who was talking everywhere of conspiracy)
was deputed to kill Oswald (who had said nothing so far) in
order that the former might *shut up* the latter;

— that, being so deputed, he let himself be sidetracked in
the critical period by one of his girls and, in order to send her
twenty-five dollars, put his timetable at the mercy of a Western
Union man dealing with another customer and then with Jack;

— that his collaborators at the jail also put their schedule at
the disposal of things beyond exact control (summoning the
armored car, hunting out its driver, finding him at Sunday
School, waiting for his arrival);

— that the conspirators at the jail brought Jack in by way of
a public door, at which they placed a guard where (barring
accident) he would seem to be conniving with Jack's entry;

— that they excluded everyone else from the jail basement
(thereby making Jack's entry anomalous), yet admitted newsmen by droves, thus making sure that any telltale look or gesture of recognition, any sign of timing, would be recorded;

— that when Oswald had already been brought down in the
elevator and Ruby was already on the ramp (both reaching
these points by routes strewn with accidental interruptions),
someone honked a car horn to bring the two together — a su-
perfluous exercise, since there was nowhere they could go by
this time (back up the elevator? back up the ramp?) except
toward the encounter with each other;

— that the conspirators sent out their own men (knowing or
unknowing — if the former, they have extraordinary control; if
the latter, there is danger of angry reaction when suspicion
turns on the police officials who sent the men out) pinned close
to Oswald, taking the chance that Jack would hit one of them
or (if they were not in on the scheme) that they would inter-
pose themselves, perhaps deflect Jack's shot;

— that these same conspirators, who had earlier handcuffed

Oswald's arms behind him, brought him out with one hand free
and one cuffed to the man beside him, so he could pull his arms
together and shield himself if he caught sight of Ruby advanc-
ing (the gesture he did make after he was shot);

— that the conspirators took the chance of letting Jack get
only one shot off, when Oswald could have been silenced for
sure by several quick shots;

— that they let all this be recorded on-camera, though the
possibilities of self-revelation (from the police who were sup-
posedly in on it) or of interference (if any were not) were
unlimited;

— that having quieted Oswald with a bullet, the conspirators
found they had a confessing Ruby on their hands in June of
1964; but

— that, instead of disposing of him as swiftly as they took
care of Oswald, they let him take a polygraph test a month
after his attempt to confess;

— that they let him live on for two and a half more years,
talking to a whole succession of reputable lawyers and psychiatrists called in by Ruby's family; indeed, let him testify at public hearings;

— and that this was not because Ruby lacked valuable information, since he *was* prevented from going to Washington;
besides, some of those who talked to him (Tom Howard, for
instance, and Dorothy Kilgallen) died in suspicious circum-
stances;

— that after a public trial and an attempted confession in
1964, and all kinds of opportunities to speak out in 1965 and
1966, Ruby was at a late date (1967) killed or allowed to die, a
new risk undertaken by the conspirators for no discernible
gain;

— that the Ruby family and their lawyers were either in on
the conspiracy and faked a deathbed recording or were allowed by the conspirators to tape and release a genuine deathbed statement.

Running through all Jack Ruby's ravings there was an improbable truth, no matter where it came from — an orphaned waif-truth. He repeatedly maintained, to anyone who would listen (and no one would for long), that his words were being distorted, the world would not believe him, he could not tell his story; that his life was being interpreted as unpatriotic, his personality merged with Oswald's, his actions tied to those of the men who had killed Kennedy; that this would cause widespread hostility, hurt his country, blacken his name. Again and again he said these things — wild things.

"And, poor booby, he was bang right."

ii

Jack's lightning-bug attention lit and dimmed now on one subject only: he wanted to clear himself — of his phantom crime, in the court of public opinion. He had lost all interest in his real crime and the courts of law. But the lawyers — shifting and clotting around him while he hardly noticed them — were interested.

Belli left the case as he had entered it, trumpeting *Don't worry Jack, I'll save you* and trying to get a photograph out of the prison to *Life* magazine. "Psychomotor epilepsy" left the case along with him.

Tonahill did not quite depart. He was wallowed over to the exit in the turmoil over Belli's leaving; but he stuck in the doorway of the case, an undislodgeable bulk pushed at, from time to time, by other lawyers as they entered or left.

The tall flamboyant Texas lawyer Percy Foreman, who defended "Candy" Mosler, looked briefly in, shuddered at what he called the intermeddling of a "civil lawyer from Detroit," and left.

Dr. Hubert Winston Smith of the University of Texas law school, an attorney and M.D. who had been Belli's medical adviser for the trial, launched with great fanfare "an exhaustive and scientific analysis of the Ruby case from cellar to garret" — then withdrew because his department frowned on this effort.

Meanwhile that "civil lawyer from Detroit" was exercising more and more control. He was Sol Dann, known before this as the man who waged a stockholders' war on Chrysler. When Dann started hiring and firing other counsels with Earl Ruby's sanction, the case ironically spiraled back to Dallas. Dann heard that Clayton Fowler, who testified at the change-of-venue hearing and had stayed on cordial terms with Belli, was head of the Dallas bar association. Actually, he was at the time president of a *criminal* bar association — of that easygoing unglamorous efficient crew of men who "outcon," when they can, their pals in the D.A.'s office. The case had come back to Tom Howard's world: Fowler shares an office with the very first lawyer of all, Jim Martin, and with C. A. Droby, who went on a much-discussed night trip to Ruby's apartment on the day he murdered Oswald. Martin and Droby, along with George Senator who took them there, are living inconveniences to those who think dark things were learned on that voyage, leading to the death of three participants — inconveniences compensated for by sending Tom Howard himself along on the trip, and explaining his death that way. (Unfortunately for the theory, Howard was not with them.)

It is ironic that Dann returned the case to this provenience, because he was about to make Belli look like a piker as the enemy of Dallas. He came to town, however, knowing even less about Dallas than Belli had, and at the very outset enlisted an integral part of it. Fowler is a tall, likable, soft-spoken Texan with a magnificent balding head. His carriage at first suggests that he takes pains to keep that large round red cherubic face correctly balanced; but it is only the result of his careful maneuvering upon a wooden leg. Fowler's arts are those of the original case — outpolite the prosecution; feel the community's pulse, flatter its vanity, coax out of it its magnanimity; win a murder-without-malice verdict. But to get back in a position to make this plea, Jack's lawyer must first win a reversal. Fowler needed an appellate lawyer, and he turned to a good one, slim bookish Emmett Colvin, an elegantly vested, buttoned, lapeled lawyer, with suits that seem to have come in matching sets with the volumes of his thorough law library.

But Mr. Dann, back in Detroit, did not want to attack Dallas from within, with Tom Howard tactics. He had entered the case because he felt certain that Jack Ruby was the victim of inflamed community anti-Semitism. In a memorandum meant to be the basis for the Ruby case's future conduct, he explained Jack's conviction this way:

Jury acted with malice and without cool meditation. . . . (Psychiatry may be unable to remove *their* suffering guilt feelings). . . . one wonders whether *the jury* (took off their hoods when they entered the jury box) or were in *their* right minds when they returned the *death* verdict. . . . The Jury, not unlike Ruby, felt the need to "right a wrong" and respond (K.K.K. style) with a verdict of death for Ruby, in keeping with "public sentiment" as expressed by the *prosecution* who *represented Texas justice.* But *what* demented Anti-Semitism in the jury's *personal* lives made them vulnerable to such needs and pleas? What hateful obsessions or connections with the K.K.K. or John Birch Society led *them* to "act on impulse" and make their hasty death verdict? . . . Texas has no monopoly on hate and prejudice, but vicious Anti-Semites like Rockwell and Gerald L. K. Smith are openly and primarily supported by such Birchites as the Murchesons [*sic*] and Mr. Hunt, one of the wealthiest oil men in Texas. (Such men *too often* exert their influence even over *courts*). . . . Not unlike Ruby, the jury had no freedom of will, no cool freedom of choice. The jury became slaves of the *will of the prosecution* who expressed the desires of "The State of Texas" for the death penalty. . . . Any juror who concealed or failed to reveal his personal prejudices or whose family had connections with organized Anti-Semitic groups, like the K.K.K. or Birch Society and was not impartial, and did not qualify as a juror. The jury tried Jacob Rubenstein —*the Jew*. (This name was used by some reporters.) They punished Ruby as though he killed their *hero*. (Was Oswald one of their kind?) It is frightening to think what a Texas mob would have done to Ruby and other Jews if *he* killed *the President*. What would this jury have done "for" an Oswald, if he killed a Jew or Negroe [*sic*] strongly suspected of assassinating the President? Both the Court's and Prosecutor's possible personal prejudices or those of any member of his family who had any connections with any organized Anti-Semitic groups should be investigated. . . . I have great respect for the Courts of Texas, but as one reviews the proceedings in this case, one wonders whether this trial took place in America — or was it held in Nazi Germany or Russia? . . . But all will learn, (as Hitler and others did) that they defeated *themselves* and condemned *their* goal in life, by using Anti-Semitism.

Mr. Dann saw the whole case in terms of anti-Semitism, which tortured Jack Ruby in his youth, made him start a life pattern of fighting because he hit kids who insulted him as a Jew, made him want a father he could be proud of, made him adopt Kennedy as the father of all Jews, made him train to kill the anti-Semitic Nazis in the war, made him murder Oswald as the killer of the Jews' father; and made him suffer an unfair trial, defended by an anti-Semitic Texas lawyer before anti-Semites on the bench and in the jury box and at the prosecution table. Mr. Dann even discovers anti-Semitism in those Jews who take a different view of the case from his, not casting everything in terms of anti-Semitism: "This type is against raising the Anti-Semitic problem lest it disturb their (false sense of) security. Even now, they prefer Ruby's quiet extermination rather than have it exposed to prevent a 'miscarriage of justice.' "

Emmett Colvin knew an appeal court has no authority to investigate the family connections of Judge Brown and the

D.A.'s staff, that a plea for jurors to confess their membership in the Klan would not be grounds for reversing the court's decision, and that attacks on the jurors (as insane, beyond the ministrations of psychiatry, or guilty by association — "Was Oswald one of their kind?") would only hurt the appeal effort. Clayton Fowler, who was looking forward to a new trial after the reversal, wanted to build up sympathy for Ruby; he knew he could not do it if Dann launched a running attack on Dallas, on Texas, on the trial's conduct, on Tonahill, on all his other targets. Very soon, Dann fired Fowler, and Fowler fired Dann (firing each other was to be one of the primary functions of the Ruby lawyers). Then Eva Grant sent Judge Brown a letter asking that all nine lawyers employed "of record" to this point be dismissed, leaving only Phil Burleson formally connected with the case. (Fowler told us he checked and found the letter came from Burleson's typewriter, but that Burleson denied all knowledge of it.)

Burleson had been eclipsed, during the trial, by polyphloisboisterous Belli and Tonahill. "Belli and Joe just barely let Phil in the courtroom," Alexander told us; "his main job was carrying Belli's briefcase." This turned out to his advantage: his dim receded role in the trial saved him from the resentments Belli left behind. He rode the storm, exercising an instinct for survival unique among the Ruby lawyers. Though Jack called him a Nazi and blamed him (along with Tonahill and Belli) for his conviction, Burleson stayed with the case. It was difficult at times: one day, when Tonahill came out of an interview with Jack, his pants were torn — "Jack started to take a swing at Phil. When I jumped up and grabbed him, I tore my pants on the table."

Sol Dann was still directing things from afar; and though he had decided to retain Phil Burleson, he thought him more a spear-carrier than a general. He was looking for other lawyers, preferably from out of state (his experience with Fowler and Colvin made him wary of Texans). In July of 1964, a week after his and Fowler's firing of each other, Dann brought George Woods, a skilled appellate lawyer from Detroit, down to work with Burleson on formal bills of exception. They met early in the evening, at Burleson's office in the L-T-V sky-scraper. But just then an outraged roar from the case's entry-way reminded them Joe Tonahill was still lodged there. Tona-hill, energetically fired by everybody else, took a Coriolanus view of the matter, and exiled Rome. He had been hired by a sane Jack Ruby. Psychiatrists now said Jack was psychotic, in-capable of forming new obligations; so his original agreement with Tonahill remained in force — all the newcomers were interloping. For a full year Judge Brown upheld Tonahill's right to remain in the case; but the Jasper lawyer was reduced to the status of *amicus* after Joe Brown recused himself.

Tonahill's intelligence system was very good — he had heard about this meeting of Dann, Burleson, and a new lawyer. He called reporters and told them to be on hand, took Clayton Fowler with him to Phil's office, entered, and erupted. The re-porters, kept outside, caught scraps of the argument, angry shouts, the shrapnel drifted off from Joe's explosion.

Tonahill's version of the meeting appeared in motions he later filed to get rid of Dann: "Sol Dann and his financial ex-ploiters of Jack Ruby wouldn't tolerate us because they could not exploit Jack Ruby and sell the suit he was wearing the day Oswald was shot to a wax museum. . . . Sol Dann wanted to degrade Jack Ruby's public image and jeopardize his appeal through a commercialization program in that Sol Dann wanted to incorporate Jack Ruby, Sol Dann was to become Chairman of the Board of Directors, and Sol Dann wanted to employ a public relation [*sic*] officer to handle Jack Ruby's appeal and Sol Dann was negotiating for a Jack Ruby book by the Michi-gan author of "Anatomy of a Murder.". . . Sol Dann, the business lawyer of the Ruby family, is well aware that if Jack Ruby is executed in the electric chair at Huntsville, that Jack Ruby will be the first Jew in Texas history ever executed; that such a fact will be utilized by Sol Dann for commercialization exploitation." Tonahill presents himself as the only one who can check "the moving grasping hand of Sol Dann and his fellow Ghouls . . . the creeping injustice Sol Dann is wroughting [sic] against him."

But Tonahill, in full cry, had met a man who is as quick with a typewriter as he is. Dann was blazing away on his side, with this complaint to the American Trial Lawyers Association:

That complainant and one George Woods, a fellow member of the Michigan Bar, arrived at the Dallas, Texas, law offices of one Phil Burleson about 7:00 P.M., July 22, 1964 and immediately began to confer with the said Phil Burleson and Emmit [sic] Colvin concerning certain legal matters.

That a conference was being held in an orderly dignified manner when suddenly and without previous notice, the said Joe Tonahill entered the library of the offices of Phil Burleson where the conference was taking place and without any introduction or further discussion began to berate, insult and threaten your petitioner with the following language:

"This is a Sol A. Dann exposé . . . We are in Texas now and you better listen . . . You Yid carpetbagger and interloper . . . Yiddish system of Sol Dann . . . A Yiddish program — we will move you out . . . You white nigger . . . Texas is an unhealthy climate for a Jew, . . . You typical kike . . . Better get out of Texas if you want to stay healthy . . . You won't stay alive until tomorrow if you don't get out of Texas tonight . . . We called you a God-damned liar — why don't you fight back? Are you afraid to fight? . . . You're nothing but a God-damned Jew-bastard . . ."

That the assault upon complainant was interrupted only because of the appearance of representatives of the press and television.

That petitioner has reason to believe and does believe that but for said interruption, Joe Tonahill would have carried his threats to physically attack your petitioner.

Dann had the Ruby family on his side (he and Earl met in Detroit through their children; Dann's daughter taught in the school the young Rubys attended). Now Eva joined the scrimmage, with a letter of complaint sent to the Grievance Committee of the State Bar of Texas on February 23, 1965. In this letter she claimed that Tonahill neglected his duties and obligations to her brother, undermined the effectiveness of Belli, and turned the trial into a circus. Tonahill had earlier told Eva and Sol Dann that Belli somehow went "berserk" during the trial. Eva now accepted Tonahill's word for this, but blamed the disaster on Belli's having kept such bad company (namely, Joe). She hoped the bar association would do something to remove Tonahill from the case; but they evidently thought this beyond their jurisdiction, and nothing came of her letter but increased tensions. All sides were manning their artillery now, and the noise was deafening. It was hard to see how they would ever find time, there among the howitzers, for anything but salvos. Each new effort undertaken for Jack was a new cause for dispute among Jack's lawyers.

There seemed, at this point, no way for the defense effort to go but down. Mr. Woods backed off after his violent first taste of the affair. Joe Tonahill was still latrant and immovable in the entry-way. Sol Dann was gargoyling along the affair's increasingly surrealist machicolations. Charles Bellows of Chicago made a brave effort at putting the pieces together, but dropped out very soon, a casualty of the escalating war between Tonahill and Dann.

Then, when things seemed hopelessly entangled, the defense team underwent a helpful population explosion. Dann took the Ruby case to his friend Ernie Mazey, a director of the American Civil Liberties Union in Detroit, who referred it to the ACLU in New York, where William Kunstler, the famous civil rights lawyer, became interested in it. Through these men, Sam Houston Clinton of the Texas ACLU entered the case. Meanwhile, in Chicago, the Ruby family had approached Elmer Gertz, an attorney familiar with freedom-of-the-press cases, to discuss a possible suit against Melvin Belli, who had criticized the family in his book. Mr. Gertz, whose most famous case was the paroling of Nathan Leopold, advised against any legal action that would cut across the main one — Jack's appeal. Soon, he was helping prepare that appeal. Tied together by telephone lines, this five-man team — Dann in Detroit, Gertz in Chicago, Kunstler in New York, Clinton in Austin, Burleson in Dallas — groped in darkening thickets of the case. All their names appear on the brief that went to the appeals court — and they won their reversal.

But things were so mired in several courts by the time they took over that reversal was not won until October 5, 1966 — two and a half years after the trial, three months before Jack's death. In those years the case grew, coiled, exfoliated, sent roots down, met obstacles in Texas, veined its way around them, ramified all over the country. The reason for this proliferation of motions and appeals — and for mounting white pillars of thick legal documents — was the simple problem: who represented Ruby? It was the raising of this question by Tonahill that made the Texas criminal appeals court send the case back to Judge Brown for a sanity hearing. Was Ruby competent and therefore able to direct his own defense? Judge Brown, given a whole new stage of the case to write about, sent his happy letter to Holt, Rinehart and Winston. But Dann tried to take the case into another court, to have a temporary guardian appointed. When he heard that the District Attorney's office would be a party to what he thought a pure probate motion, he gave up that effort to escape Brown's supervision of the case. Meanwhile, a journalist had tipped off the legal team about Brown's book, and they were taking depositions in New York from the publisher. Now they tried to get a stay of the sanity hearing by taking Ruby to the *Federal* court of appeals in Dallas, where Jack explained to the bench that he wanted Tonahill out of the case ("I never had any defense in court") and that Henry Wade and Melvin Belli had framed him for the murder of Kennedy. The court decided it could not grant a stay and sent the case back to the state court.

This decision was appealed to the Fifth Circuit Court, sitting in Florida — where the Dallas District Attorney's office found itself arguing alongside a strange ally, Joe Tonahill. Ruby's lawyers were told that they should first exhaust the resources of the original court (of criminal appeals in Texas) — which was soon done. That court would not even let the team file its motion. Back to Florida. Rebuffed again. Meanwhile, Ruby's lawyers had collected the evidence on Judge Brown's book. In March of 1965 the Judge himself asked that the case be reassigned, and in June he reaccused himself.

Judge Louis T. Holland now held a hearing to decide who Ruby's representatives were. Jack took the stand and recited his own theories. The Judge decided that, since the sanity hearing had not yet been held, Jack was legally sane and could fire Tonahill. The Texas Senate solaced Joe by voting him its congratulations for having "demonstrated more courage, loyalty and stability in the current Jack Ruby battle than anybody has ever shown in his generation." They do not do things halfway in Texas.

The defense now took the position that Judge Brown's disqualification invalidated the whole of the proceedings he had presided over — including Ruby's conviction. At a hearing, Jack's lawyers brought Brown to the stand and confronted him with his letter. The strategy did not work. The lawyers were also pushing along their old front — the attempt to stay the sanity hearing. They took a motion to the Supreme Court, where it was denied by Justice Black. They had Eva Grant withdraw her original request for a sanity hearing (filed right after the conviction), and maintained that this should end the matter. But it was the court of criminal appeals that had requested the sanity hearing (to determine which lawyers were responsible for Jack's case) — so Judge Holland finally held the hearing, a year after it was first scheduled, in June of 1966, before a jury. The defense lawyers stood mute, on the grounds that the whole sequence was invalid. (Sol Dann told us, "Having Jack declared insane would play right into the hands of

Tonahill.") The prosecution brought to the stand some guards who had observed Jack and said he acted sane — no crazy man could cheat at cards so well.

Ruby was still legally sane, then; Tonahill was allowed to file an *amicus* brief with the appeals court, but he could not argue the case as counsel of record. After two years of effort in half a dozen courts — with subsidiary battles over procedure, over proper filings, over the disposal of records — the five-man team had cleared the field and could argue for reversal.

The complications of the Ruby case were not only a matter of abrasive personal contacts — a musical-chairs game of mutual recriminations. Nor was it all a matter of legal maneuver and technicalities. All these things were present — along with something more important in the aftermath of the case: all the lawyers were unearthing plots and counterplots around them.

Tom Howard left the case stung by whispers he was leaking information to the District Attorney. Bill Alexander told reporters the defense squabbles were arranged so that an appeal could be made on the grounds that Jack did not have continuing and competent representation. He also said that Jack's delusions were rehearsed with psychiatrists, who were coaching him to "look crazy." Tonahill did not not think much of Alexander's plots; he responded, in a motion he filed to remain Ruby's counselor, by calling the Assistant D.A. "a tarantula-eyed one hundred percent pure liar." He renewed, in this document, his triumphant charge in the courtroom: "This same Alexander openly shouted the Lord's name in vain in open court."

Mr. Tonahill had his own plots to suggest: "Does Henry Wade want Joe H. Tonahill out of Jack Ruby's case because he wants to render ineffective the probability of Jack Ruby's receiving a reversal of his death verdict. . . . He might possibly be spared the devastating political embarrassment and disgrace as a prosecutor, lawyer, and citizen if Joe H. Tonahill is removed from the case. . . . . Could the persecutory conspiracy of the Jews have been planted in Jack Ruby's mind deliberately by someone bent upon eliminating the knowledgeable 'of the entire trial proceedings' Joe H. Tonahill from Jack Ruby's staff by building him up for the subsequent suggestion to his deluded mind that Joe H. Tonahill was not to be trusted and was a part of that conspiracy, as well as the doctors? . . . What was their motive in planting the seed of derision in his mind against his attorneys? To make that derision and antipathy against his attorneys and the engendering of extraordinary confidence in the prosecutors who seek his death, did they likewise, on their visits to his cell implant the delusional seeds that for what he did in killing the Communist Oswald he had caused a worldwide slaughtering of Jews, his family, and his attorney, and Chief Justice Earl Warren? . . . Is a reversal of this case because of the myriad of reversible errors injected throughout the long, long trial ordeal that *reach* the unbelievable number of assigned errors for appeal, and the consequent disgrace to the improvident and foolhardy reversible error tactics of the prosecution so great that the prosecution must at all costs eliminate by the defendant Jack Ruby, if they could do so by engendering his loss of confidence in counsel?"

These prosecution machinations worked smoothly in concert with the new defense lawyers' attempts to "throw" the case: "Sol Dann, Madam Eva Grant and Earl Ruby know that if Jack Ruby is executed, he will become the first Jew in Texas to be put to death legally. Has their conduct been consistent with persons who are interested in Jack Ruby's staying alive and not being legally executed? Or has their conduct been consistent with the thought of financial exploitation in the event Jack Ruby is the first Jew ever to be legally executed in Texas?"

The defense plot had two ingredients — the expulsion of patriot Tonahill and the bringing in of "Commie" lawyers who would discredit Jack (Mr. Kunstler had defended the Rosenbergs and taken many civil rights cases): "Some of the other out-of-state lawyers that Sol Dann was trying to saddle Jack Ruby with were lawyers for Communists and were connected with Communist causes."

Tonahill's version of interacting Dann-Wade plots to "railroad" Jack was not the most ornate conspiracy traced by a lawyer. Dann's conspiracy is even wider-spread and closer-woven; and at the center of the web, spinning shrewdly away, is that unlikely spider, Joe H. Tonahill. Dann explained to us that Tonahill a) brought Belli into the case; then b) drove Tom Howard out of the case; so that c) he could make Belli adopt the psychomotor epilepsy defense; insuring d) the effort of Dallas to destroy Ruby: "Now what connection Tonahill has with the Murchisons and the Hunts, I don't know. Except this: when Warren interviewed Jack Ruby, who was under sodium pentothal [sic], Tonahill passed Ruby a note, and the note reads, 'Tell Justice Warren you thought about it for two days' [sic]. . . . It is remarkable Ruby had sufficient awareness under sodium pentothal to resist Tonahill." We remarked that the record doesn't show any administration of that drug to Jack during the Warren interview: "He may have thought he was not under it, but it was definitely given."

Dann's plot is a bit confusing: while Tonahill is saving Dallas by bringing Belli in, a millionaire tries to rescue the city with a bribe to keep him out. Bad coordination in the conspiracy — which is not surprising, when one considers how far back in time and far out in space the plotting goes. Dann's memorandum touches some high spots: "Senator Towers [sic] of Texas, a follower of Birch Society program, urged the State Department to help Oswald return to the U.S. from Russia. . . . A few days [sic] before Kennedy arrived in Dallas, articles [sic] appeared in the paper and on billboards [sic] criticizing the Kennedy Administration signed by a Jewish name. . . . Anti-Semites have already used this case to plant and spread rumors that Ruby was connected with Communists and conspired with

Oswald to kill the President, and that Ruby killed Oswald to seal his lips. (Even the staid New York Times repeated these unfounded rumors). But as Tom Paine or Emil [*sic*] Zola would say — 'Truth is on the march.' There is no clear secular record of what happened 2,000 years ago, but the record in this case can be made clear for anyone to read by a new trial, so that the jury's determination of the facts in *this* case will not be distorted and added to an already sordid 1900 year old record of distortions, imaginations, conjectures and theories based on what one wishes to believe."

To go from lawyer to lawyer in the Ruby defense is a dizzying experience. You need an Ariadne to thread you back out. Yet this whole beehive is one stratum only of the buzz over conspiracy. At the core of the affair, Jack himself was hallucinating up conspiracies on a worldwide scale. Then, out on the edges of the case, dilettante investigators busily cloaked him and put daggers in his hand, raising those suspicions that fed his own nightmares — type and anti-type. It is a basic gambit in this game to reverse plot A and retain it as anti-A. When Tonahill announced the plot to introduce "Commies" in the case, Ruby told the press, at one of his public hearings, that Tonahill was saying this in order that he (Tonahill) might connect Ruby with Communists, and so destroy him. Most of the theories work either way.

The lawyers' hunt for conspirators grades in toward Jack's delusions in the center, out toward Mark Lane theories at the perimeter of the case. Tonahill explains Jack's nightmares as a madness deliberately sown in his mind by the prosecution. Dann links theories like Mark Lane's and the Dallas trial in this fashion: the anti-Semitic Murchison put Joe Brown up to publishing a book in order to discredit Jack and bring hatred on the Jews. Murchison used Holt, Rinehart and Winston to accomplish his foul purpose. The same firm published Lane's book, which ties Jack in with a worldwide conspiracy and therefore, through Jack, hurts the Jews. Falling suddenly down the rabbit hole, we called back up to him: do you think Lane an anti-Semite? "No, but he may be being used. It's too much of a coincidence" — (the regular prelude for a conspiratorial rondo) — "that the billboards attacking Warren, the advertisements in the paper contributed to by the Hunts or the Murchisons, and then the book by Brown, the offer to Belli, and now Mark Lane's book — there's too much of a tie-in with the Murchisons and the Hunts." Or, as he put it in the memorandum: "How much, and how long would the blood of Jews . . . be shed if *Oswald* were a 'Jew'? (Some indirectly try to connect him thru Ruby)." It is amusing to see Mr. Lane blown to the moon, riding on his own petard; but we decided it was time for a retreat. One step further, and not Ariadne herself could rescue us. This plot defies cartography.

The legal maneuverers pincered in, at last, upon their goal. On October 5, 1966, the conviction of Jack Ruby was reversed. When he died three months later, Phil Burleson told newsmen that he had at least this comfort, that he died innocent before the law, which had not yet proved him guilty. The reversal was on two counts — that Judge Brown should have granted a change of venue; and that Jack's statements to police, after the killing, should have been ruled inadmissible. Both these matters were treated in the winning brief, and in Belli's *amicus curiae* brief, and in another *amicus* brief filed by Tonahill and Emmett Colvin.

Burleson crowed when news of the decision reached him at his office. His secretary came running and saw him shout at the telephone like a happy child. He ran the news over to Jack, who was not interested in it. His mind was elsewhere. Besides, he had started vomiting.

. . .
iii

The polygraph test had taken place July 18, 1964. Arlen Specter, of the Warren Commission, brought F.B.I. polygraph operators and Judge Sarah Hughes's Federal court reporter to the Dallas jail. They used the same room (7-M, one floor up from Jack) the Chief Justice had used for interviewing Ruby.

They arrived in the morning. Jack had been told when he woke up that he must not take any medicine, nor any coffee after breakfast. All morning he paced the hall, restless and excited, hoping he would at last be vindicated. But on the floor above him, there was elaborate fencing over preliminaries. Sheriff Decker had called in his own polygraph operator (Allen Sweatt) to observe the test, and Bill Alexander was coming over from the D.A.'s office. The F.B.I. had been notified by Sol Dann that Ruby was not to take the test if representatives of the prosecution or police were present. He relayed the instructions of Earl Ruby — that no one should attend except Sol Dann and the Detroit psychiatrist Dann had brought to see Jack, Emanuel Tanay. Mr. Specter, however, knew that Ruby was still legally sane; that he had begged Earl Warren for the test; that the Chief Justice gave him a personal promise it would be made available to him.

Sheriff Decker thought he should at least let Ruby lawyers in on the test. Joe Tonahill — his intelligence service as good as ever — showed up on his own. Then, around 11:00 a.m., Decker called Clayton Fowler. It was Saturday and Fowler was out, that morning, mowing his lawn. The minute he heard what was up, he changed clothes, went to his office for Dann's correspondence with the F.B.I., and arrived at the jail by 11:30.

A police reporter saw the big phlegmatic man hop-skip-jump the few blocks from his office to the jail, and knew something was up. Other reporters were soon washing around the base of the jail; Decker poked his head in at 7-M and said, "Jim Kerr caught you making a fifty-yard dash and they are circling around downstairs and Jim Kerr is just going in circles wanting to know what Clayton Fowler is doing up in the jail."

For half an hour Fowler argued with Specter, flourishing the Dann letters, saying Jack should not be tested, especially with men from the Sheriff's and the D.A.'s office present. Specter agreed that Ruby did not have to take the test if he did not want to. But if he did, the Chief Justice was committed. So Fowler went down to argue with Jack. The session was a hot one. Fowler left, defeated, after 12:00, and Jack was taken to eat his lunch and get some rest. When he returned to 7-M, Fowler admitted Jack was adamant. Joe Tonahill chimed in, "If he wouldn't take it now. . . ." Fowler picked up the line of thought: "Well, I won't want to go back there, then." Tonahill: "If he ever gets his hands on you, they'll let him have it." Later, Fowler added to Tonahill: "You and I have done all we can do on it. I am not going to physically manhandle Jack Ruby!" (Clayton towered over Jack, but Jack had two good legs. Besides, as Fowler told us, "He was a tough little guy.")

Tonahill, who still had one foot in the case, did not agree with Dann and Fowler about the test. He knew Jack would not rest until he took it, and thought his willingness would earn sympathy in the appeal and retrial; it might even quiet some of the doubts and rumors about conspiracy. But on one thing Fowler and Tonahill closed ranks: they both wanted Bill Alexander out of the room. Specter said he would ask Alexander to leave during the actual graphing of Ruby's responses, but he could remain during the prior explanation of questions to be asked. Round one, tied. Then they tried to get rid of Sweatt, the county polygraph man. Specter agreed to this (round two, victory), but Decker insisted that one of his men must be there for the prisoner's security: it was decided that Chief Jailor Holman could stay, but he must sit by the door, at an angle where he could not read the graph. Round three, a draw.

These skirmishes, protests, disavowals for the record, counterarguments, and touchy final agreements all took time. One floor below, Ruby worried that his lawyers would once again snatch away this chance to tell his story. Two hours went by; then, at 2:23 p.m., he was taken upstairs — and the first thing he did was shatter the fragile agreements worked out in the morning and early afternoon: "And how soon will the answers be released, as soon as possible? . . . I want to get a copy to the Chief as soon as I can, Chief Holman over there." Assured of his rights by Specter, he pleaded: "I will answer without reluctance. There's no punches to be pulled. I want to answer anything and everything." Then he turned to Alexander: "In fact, Bill, you can stay here if you want to." Fowler argued with him, said the results should not be released to the police; but Jack wanted them sent at once to Henry Wade. "I want it to be released immediately to all parties concerned." At least, said Fowler, make Alexander leave? No: "I don't mind everyone remaining here." Clayton kept at it. Jack was getting angry again: "No, Fowler. . . . Now I've got the monkey on my back here." The two went to a corner of the room to settle it, Fowler pleading the family's wishes. When Jack came back to his chair, he said uncertainly, "Well, whatever my attorney suggests, I guess I will have to follow through." So Alexander, having been in, then out, then in again, was now out.

The formal papers of consent were explained to Ruby. He leaned forward to sign them, then — as they were being countersigned by witnesses—said to Tonahill:

"Did you get your pants sewed up, Joe?"

"It went through to my leg."

"That was a pretty rough brawl we had, wasn't it, Joe?"

"Yes."

"Joe, I'd appreciate it if you weren't in the room. Can I ask you to leave, Joe?"

"I'll be glad to leave, if you want me to, Jack."

"As a matter of fact, I prefer Bill Alexander to you, you're supposed to be my friend."

Alexander, officially out, was halfway back in.

Mr. Specter had told Jack, when he listed the people who would be present, that the psychiatrist William Robert Beavers, from Parkland Hospital, would be among them. Even then Ruby made an exception to his policy of letting anyone be present: he protested he would rather be served by counsel than by doctors. Now Bell P. Herndon, the polygraph operator, asked some routine questions about Jack's health, and told him again that a doctor would be in attendance. Jack flickered a suspicious look: "What is the preference of the doctor being here? Is he supposed to be my doctor, I mean Dr. Beavers?" Specter explained he was there at Tonahill's request. The subject nagged at Ruby. After some more questions, he broke out: "The reason why I say this, there was some newspaper items recently that brought up the fact that I was of unsound mind. Do I sound that way to you, at the present time?" Dr. Beavers was one of those who had said the polygraph examination would not be valid because of Ruby's psychotic condition. Jack did not want him around, influencing the "jury" he meant to convince. But after another private conference with Fowler, he capitulated.

Now Herndon showed Jack the (Stoelting) polygraph chair, and explained its purpose. He was ready to explain the first series of questions when the dance of protocol began again. Herndon told Ruby he did not have to answer the questions when they were first posed; this "dry run" was meant to explain the questions to him, so there could be no doubt or hesitation about their exact sense. But Jack preferred to answer right away. Fowler objected: Alexander would still be in the room during this preliminary run. "Please, let me do it, will you? . . . Fowler, I hate to dispute with you, but let me do it this way?" Fowler said his answers might be detrimental to him. Jack bristled at that: "They can't be."

"I'm talking about from a legal standpoint. Now, morally, I know how you feel and you want to do the best you can for the Commission."

"I will. . . . It's unfortunate that my attorney, Mr. Fowler, don't see as I do. I would like to give every cooperation without the slightest fraction of interference. That's why I requested that. You won't let me do it that way, huh, Fowler?"

It was a useless effort on the lawyer's part. After restraining himself for a few questions, Jack eagerly responded most of the time, in the trial run as in the test sessions. Herndon explained that questions would be asked in short sets, eight or nine per series. Then he attached Jack to the machine: pneumatic tube around his chest (he had to empty his coverall pocket, stuffed with odds and ends as his suit pockets had been), cardiograph cuff on his left arm, tapes on his fingers ("I notice you have one finger cut off on that hand. . . . Your hands are very good. They are not sweating a bit").

Ready. Alexander was asked to leave; as he went to the door, Jack, whose back was to the door, arched more objections over his head: "If Tonahill is going to be here — I don't believe he's — I know Bill Alexander is my friend, so he can stay, but Joe is supposed to be my friend." Fowler says that Tonahill can go, too; but Alexander *must* leave. Jack sighs: "Now, Bill, don't say I didn't request you, now." In the doorway: "I know it, Jack."

More fiddling with the apparatus. Jack and Fowler whisper together. Herndon tells Ruby more about the equipment and does some professional soothing. "Very fine, Mr. Ruby. You have been very cooperative. I don't think we will have any problem." Jack eyes the graph lovingly — his god from the machine: is it *sure* to work? "You can see the differences of nature — if certain things are wrong or right, can't you?" He turns around, trying to see Holman: "I want my Chief to understand this here and see that." Herndon purrs on, calming the subject, asking if he is comfortable. "Yes, I'm very much relaxed because I have nothing — I'm not sparring with it, so I must be relaxed." Ready? Herndon tells him he should consider no other questions, only the nine they have run through. A catch of dismay: "You mean that's all?" "Oh no; this is just series one, Mr. Ruby. We're going to cover many questions." "All right." The questions will be asked slowly. Jack does not like that; he wants to cover ground: "Believe me, I know the answers, so you can ask me as fast as you like." Herndon says he should look at the wall and ignore those seated behind or beside him. Jack, in his readiness to make it a perfect test, closes his eyes, and keeps them closed during each test series. Herndon later testified under oath: "It appeared to me that Mr. Ruby divorced the presence of these people from his mind during his responses to the questions." Make it undoubtable by anyone; perfect; infallible — so, just before the test began in earnest, out he burst again: "Fowler, I beg you to get Bill Alexander and Joe Tonahill back in here. I tell you. Will you do it, please?" The harassed Fowler just ignored him.

Each series would mix questions relevant to the assassination with unrelated queries, personal or factual, to make for a full range of response. The relevant questions in series one were "Did you know Oswald before November 22, 1963?" and "Did you assist Oswald in the assassination?" The first test ran from 3:10 to 3:12. The machine registered some confusion at two points — laughter over the middle name he sometimes used, sometimes did not; and embarrassment over his former arrests. On the relevant questions, Herndon later testified, no deception was indicated. That was true of the relevant questions in every series.

Alexander and Tonahill reenter after the graph has been marked. Herndon recites the next series: "Are you now a member of the Communist party?" *Shouted:* "NO!" A bit startled, Herndon reminds Ruby he need not answer now. "O.K." Jack responds. Then: "Have you ever been a member of the Communist party?" "NO!" More assurances, more agreement from Jack. "Are you now a member of any group that advocates the

violent overthrow of the United States government?" "NO!"
Herndon explains the scope of the question. Does Jack understand it? "Yes; and my answer is NO — no collaborating."

The cuckoo-clock routine: Alexander, Tonahill, out, in, second test 3:25-3:27, four relevant questions this time, no deception. When the third series is explained, there is a long discussion on number nine, "Did you tell anyone that you were thinking of shooting Oswald before you did it?" Jack wants to say
yes — he told George Senator the man should be killed Sunday
morning — but in such a way that "the time element" is made
clear: he had not thought about doing it for days. The question
is framed and reframed. Alexander offers a formulation, over
Fowler's objections. Alexander is sent out while Jack goes on
explaining what he said to Senator. Fowler warns him this
could be used against him in another trial. Jack does not care:
"I'm here to tell the truth. . . . Can I overrule you, Clayton,
where you won't be too angry if I overrule you?"

"Well, I have no — I'm not going to put a cob in your mouth,
Jack."

"Can I ask one more favor of you?"

"Sure."

"Will you let those two gentlemen back in the room, at your
request?"

"Not at my request; no sir."

"Please, Clayton?"

"If you leave that up to me, I say, No."

"All right, I'm going to answer your question. . . . So,
would you mind calling Alexander in?"

"Listen, Jack, will you please listen to me? This man got up
down there and asked the jury to send you to the electric
chair."

"I know it."

"He has not changed his opinion yet, and he will again ask it
at some later date. Now, is this the kind of man you want to
pussyfoot around in here with and let listen to these questions?
Just 'Yes' or 'No' — if it is — we'll bring him back in."

"Yes; I want him in here, and I want you to ask him to come in, please."

"I won't ask him to come in."

Jack turns to Tonahill, until now his foe. "Joe, ask him to come in." No. Holman? "Chief —" (a shake of the head) "I know." Specter, who wants to move on before Jack tires, says he will ask him back. Fowler: "Why do you want Mr. Alexander here?" "I feel I don't want him to think I'm hiding out on anything."

Jack switches tactics now, as he had with Warren; mutters dark predictions, what will happen to Fowler. Clayton, who has never believed in Jack's hallucinations, cuts off what he feels is nonsense: "Jack, I'm not worried, I'm not concerned about anybody trying to do away with me. This is the least of my worries." As he did whenever guards made fun of his apocalyptic fears, Jack retreats, all meekness now: "I want harmony, that's what I want."

Back to the question that had caused this circumlocutory fuss. Did Jack ever say he would shoot Oswald? Yes, but only on Sunday morning. "I said, 'If something happened to this person, that then Mrs. Kennedy won't have to come back for the trial.' That's all I said." Did you say *you* would do it? "No; I just made the statement. . . . In the flippant way I said it, I doubt if he'd even — you know — the poor guy may not even have remembered it." The question is at last formulated: "Aside from anything you said to George Senator, did you ever tell anyone else that you intended to shoot Oswald?" "NO." The rest of the series can, at last, be explained to him. "Did you shoot Oswald in order to silence him?" "No." Alexander's pen is flickering, Fowler grimacing. Jack is uneasy about his being in jail before. He says that his "thirty days" in Chicago could not really be called "serving time," but "That thirty days embarrasses me. . . ." Herndon: "I don't mean to embarrass you, Mr. Ruby. . . ." During the actual test, Jack does not answer this question; a simple yes or no would be impossible. It is his first nonresponse — on a nonrelevant question, for the reasons he explained. The third test began at 3:59 p.m. The needles traced emotional response to question four: "Are you married?" After the cuff is relaxed and the graph stops its scratching, Jack explains that he was thinking of Alice Nichols. If he had married her, "I would have been living in another part of the city, and I wouldn't have been involved in this." *If only.*

There was also a reaction to question seven, "While in service did you receive any disciplinary action?" "No," Jack said — but admitted after the test that he was thinking of the time when he was called up by an officer for brawling. The machine had indicated deception. This pleased Jack: "Evidently, you're getting a pretty good reading? . . . I wish you would prove to my Chief here, over there, how I stand with you." Herndon asks if Jack would like a break. "Oh, I want to go on completely."

It is now after 4:00. Dr. Beavers notes signs of fatigue in Jack. Specter asks the jailor when he normally eats dinner — 4:30. They suggest a break, but Jack resists. He is on good terms again with Tonahill — at least *he* wants him to take the test — and the two of them chat while Specter and Herndon make up their minds about series four. The series is given him, at 4:36. It includes a question on his entry of the ramp on Sunday. After the test, Jack wants to be questioned further: "Aren't you going to ask me as to whether or not he was going to come down, or anything like that?"

Time for a break; for dinner, and a rest. "I'm not hungry, jailor." At least lie down? He gives in, reluctantly: "We have only a twenty-minute break. That's all." The recess lasted an hour and forty minutes. This gave Fowler a chance to call Jack's sister, Eva, and tell her what was happening. He will regret making that call. Eva got on the phone to her brother Earl, in Detroit. Sol Dann, who was at Earl's house, angrily called the jail. When Sheriff Decker got Fowler on the line, Dann asked why Clayton had not prevented the test, and ordered him to have it stopped. Fowler tried to explain that his hands were tied; Dann fired him (whereupon Fowler fired *him*). Later that night, Fowler warned everyone present that Mr. Dann had threatened them with legal action: "I was informed by Mr. Dann at that time that it was his intention to immediately contact the Warren Commission in Washington and file a criminal case, a case of assault and battery, against all parties conducting this hearing, including myself and Mr. Tonahill."

When the test was resumed, Jack wanted to know if the reporters would be told about the test. "Now, with reference to hedging on questions and so on, don't you think some comment should be made that I wasn't reluctant in answering any of the questions that were put to me?" Specter said that seems a fair comment — passing the question, with a look, to Alexander, who agrees: "He was cooperative." Ruby: "I wanted to be more specific. That I *wanted* to be asked." Specter says that of course he will mention the test was given at Ruby's request. Jack wants, somehow, more — that words be more adequate, express his desperation for the truth: "But the point I wanted to bring out was that I wanted to specify that I also wanted to be asked any and all questions, regardless of what might be — subversive, or whatever thoughts might be in your mind." In fact — he turns to Alexander — "Bill, I think you can give these people certain questions and more potent ones than they know, because you probably know a lot of things that you have in your own mind and that you'd like to have answered too?" The customary flurry of protests from Fowler. Ruby prods Alexander nonetheless; with mounting excitement, he senses a breakthrough into the tough questions, like that old one eating at him, the problem of the disappearing guns.

"Jack, I can't really think of anything that I'd like to ask."

"Well, let me get this clear. I notice that the pictures brought out the fact that there are two sets of private boxes, close together in the post office. Did you gentlemen know this? Which is quite an insinuation."

"Jack, let's ask the question, 'Did you meet Oswald at the post office at any time, as far as you know, until the last day?'"

"Yes — and also they had a statement in there that I used the box for purpose of mail orders and to do business with Mexico and Cuba. That's incorrect because I never did business with Mexico or Cuba. Now, these are things that you gentlemen don't want to ask me, but Mr. Alexander would know what to tell you about that."

"There is one question that ought to be asked."

"I want that, Bill."

" 'Did any Cuban or foreign influence cause you to do any act?' "

"Very good — very good."

"Because there has been some question about maybe Jack was motivated from Cuba, and we ought to eliminate that and ask him a question to give him a chance to eliminate it."

"Also I want to get the gun situation straightened out. You know what I'm talking about — the Ray Brantley call."

"Yes."

Specter tried to break off this time-consuming search into new questions. That could wait till the prepared ones had been asked, those based on Ruby's testimony with Earl Warren. But Jack is not satisfied with the leisurely, spot-check, on-again-off-again, tense-lax methods of the polygraph operator. He wants cross-examination. He wants Alexander. Bill explains Jack's special concern about the guns, and Jack nods his agreement: "All I did was relay the phone message to Ray Brantley, and he said 'Oh, I know Mr. McWillie very well,' and following that I never followed up or seen him. Now, this is incriminating for me because all I did — like a tool — got myself involved by relating a message that somebody else wanted. . . . There was no conspiracy — but you'll go into that."

Specter: "You covered that also in your testimony before the Commission."

Ruby: "Yes; but that doesn't prove anything."

Alexander: "Let me suggest one question there to ask him?"

Specter: "Yes sir."

Alexander: "Did any telephone call you made have any connection, however remote, with your shooting of Oswald?"

Ruby: "NO."

Alexander: "That will cover it."

Tonahill: "How about asking him if he didn't tell the Warren Commission the truth several weeks ago in answering every question they asked him?"

Ruby: "I didn't elaborate enough with them and we didn't go into it enough, because I was telling a complete story. Yes; I'll answer that — certainly."

Specter: "Fine; that will be asked you."

Herndon: "That will be somewhat all-inclusive."

Specter: "We'll have that for the very next series."

Alexander: "Did you have any telephone conversation which related in any way with the shooting of Oswald?"

Ruby: "Also, ask me whether the phone calls were in reference to the union trying to get somebody to help me with my club."

Alexander: "Let's make another question about that. 'Did any union or underworld connection have anything to do with the shooting of Oswald?' "

Ruby: "Very good!"

Specter: "Yes; I will add those in and cover them to the maximum extent possible, and I add that reservation because there are a great many additional questions to be asked which we have already mapped out."

Herndon: "Do you want me to proceed with the usual preliminaries?"

Ruby: "You don't have to proceed with them. Why don't you just call them out to me and I'll answer them. You want to go through a formality — a previous thing."

Alexander: "Jack, he's got to have a record."

Herndon: "I want to make sure you understand the question involved."

Ruby: "I'm sure I do."

Herndon: "I feel in fairness to both of us, we have to do this."

Ruby: "Believe me — believe me, you don't have to go through that formality, if you want to save yourself a lot of time, and I think you'll like it better."

Alexander: "Jack, he has to have a written question that's keyed to this tape."

Ruby: "Yes; I follow that, but he doesn't have to go through the preliminary explaining to me this because I'll answer anything you want 'off the hook.' "

Specter: "Mr. Ruby, we appreciate your willingness to do that and we'll take you up on that to the fullest extent possible, but Mr. Herndon has to do some preliminary questioning which is indispensable to his evaluation."

Ruby: "All right, get him to minimize if he can." Herndon says that if they dispense with the preliminary run, then Alexander and Tonahill will not know what questions have been covered.

Alexander: "I don't think Jack has any objection to us staying here at this time, do you, Jack?"

Ruby: "No; I certainly don't."

Fowler: "Well, of course, I still have the same objection, and respectfully request again, Jack, that we're not trying to hide anything — don't misunderstand me."

Ruby: "Just a minute — let me tell you something. I want to straighten up some things. Whether he leaves the room or not, Mr. Alexander is going to know everything that went on here, so please concede to it. . . . The only reason I want Mr. Alexander here, I want him to know my effectiveness when I answer the questions."

Fowler: "Jack, that's very well, and I don't think he has any doubt that you're trying to hide it and all of that."

Specter: "Then, let us proceed as we have before, with Mr. Herndon announcing the questions in advance but going through a minimum amount of preliminaries so that he is satisfied that he can evaluate the results."

Ruby: "Yes."

Specter: "And we will proceed on that basis."

Ruby: "You can run through them a lot faster and I'll grasp them."

The fifth series touched again on the armored car and Jack's entry via the ramp — and asked, as well, "Did you ever hit anyone with any kind of weapon?" Jack explains why, in his business, he had to hit some people: "These boys are real bad boys, and they all have records, and they're pretty tough guys." He looks to Bill for confirmation, and Alexander nods, "That's right." Why, one man threatened to pull a gun on Jack: "Once

they get you cowered to that extent, then you're doomed. . . ."
(Take the play, don't let him get the jump.) ". . . and there's a
funny feeling when I was with him, that you have with them"
(with the punks). "So, I got my pistol and I cornered him. . . .
Finally he said 'I was only kidding,' and there's a certain reaction you have and I can't explain it." (Don't ever stop him, he
needs his jungle-instinct, for survival.)

The letdown was already beginning. The whole thing was
not working. Jack still felt truth like a clumsy big stone in his
chest; these polite, widely interspersed questions — with only a
shallow Yes, bare No allowed him — could not dislodge a thing
so weighty. The god from the Stoelting machine, he began to
fear, would fail him, as his earlier saviors had (Mel and Joe, for
instance, and Earl Warren):

Ruby: "Have I been evading any of your questions?"
Herndon: "You have been most cooperative — thus far no
problems."
Ruby: "But you can't tell how I stand, can you?"
Herndon: "Mr. Ruby, I will want to take a considerable
amount of time to review these charts very thoroughly before I
come to any conclusion."
Ruby: "How long would it take — how long will it take?"
Herndon: "Well, I can't answer that question with a definite
answer. It depends on what I may run into when I study these
very carefully back in Washington."
Ruby: "Bill, will I still be around when the answers come
back?"
Alexander: "Yes."
Ruby: "Raise your right hand and give him your word."
Alexander: "That's right."
Ruby: "Chief, you heard him, did you not, Chief? You and I
should live so long."

The fifth series — a long one, five minutes, began at 6:45.
After it, Specter left the room briefly, and Herndon offered to
take the equipment off; but Jack was against this. "You're not
going to ask any more questions? Do you want to go through

that stuff there?" He eyes the prepared questions greedily; Herndon says they should wait for Specter. Then Jack asks Alexander to interrogate him some more, about Cuba and other things. They continue along this line after Specter's return:

Ruby: "The most important question — you haven't asked me yet — why did I shoot Oswald?"

Alexander: "Jack, they can't ask that kind of question for this machine. They can only ask you — was it for a certain purpose. It has to be a 'Yes' or 'No' answer."

Ruby: "The point is — if I was carried away emotionally, and because I felt that, it sounds so unbelievable. Why shouldn't I be asked a question, Why? — What motivated me to do it?"

Specter: "Mr. Ruby, answer now the question, 'Why did you shoot Oswald?' and then we will turn that around into a question to ask you for a 'Yes' or 'No' answer."

Ruby: "At the particular moment, after watching television, all that —"

Fowler: "Jack let me interject right now, again, as your attorney — I advise you not to answer this question."

Ruby: "Clayton, I'm sorry, I've got to answer it. I've got to, because, believe me, it means an awful lot to me. I didn't want — I felt so carried away — that at that particular time of the great tragedy I felt somehow in my little bit of a way I could save Mrs. Kennedy the ordeal of coming back for trial here."

Series six: 7:08-7:10 p.m. Did he know anything about a *Wall Street Journal* found in his car? Did he ever overcharge a customer? "Are they important — those questions?" (Are they playing with him? Cat and mouse, with Jack the mouse?) "I know more important ones than that." (Are they fooling him? But, if they are, could it be to make the test work better? He can do nothing but play along.) "Of course — I'm kidding."

Series seven, explained. Did he have a gun Friday night? (no). Series seven, given. May we tighten the chest tube? "Make it as tight as you want it. I want to get it right." Series eight, explained; given. A twenty-minute break. Series nine: did Jack ever meet Oswald at the post office? "Pardon me —

why don't you say, 'Did you ever meet him at the post office or at the club?' Wouldn't that be good too? . . . Or, 'How many times did he come up to the club?' — that's something else. Also, somebody said that they saw Tippit, I — this Mr. Lane stated that he saw Tippit, myself, and Oswald at the club — so go ahead, I don't want to throw you off."

Series nine. Is Jack still alert? "Don't worry about me. I'm in good shape. The point is — I want to get as much in as we can. I don't want you to miss anything, because there's a lot of pertinent stuff." Series nine given. Then series nine-A: did he kill Oswald to spare Mrs. Kennedy? (yes), did he know the Tippit who was killed? (no). Series ten (8:27 p.m.). A desperation like that which made Jack cling to Earl Warren, loath to let him go, dominates the last half hour of the test. Jack wants to wipe away all doubts. How can he make people *believe* him, *understand?* "Whether or not I am of criminal background or whether I'm an honest and sincere person, because all those things came out and suspicions came out that Jack Ruby was involved in this and that and leaves a lot of suspicion as to my background and my character. That's very vague, but that's what I'm trying to bring out."

Alexander: "How would this question be? 'Are you a police character?' "
Ruby: "NO."
Tonahill: "Are you a one hundred percent patriotic American citizen?"
Alexander: "Are you a law-abiding citizen?"
Ruby: "That's better — that's the question!"
Alexander: "Are you a law-abiding patriotic citizen?"
Ruby: "Yes."
Tonahill: "Are you a one hundred percent American patriotic citizen?"
Ruby: "Yes."
Herndon: "That can be asked."
Ruby: "That's very good — shall I elaborate on this?"
Specter: "Yes."
Ruby: "I became closely attached to our beloved President

when we had our problem in Cuba at that time. That was a very tremendous speech and then I followed him on television and in magazines where he went — to Ireland and different places. Now, Joe asked a very good question. In other words, either you are American or you're half-and-half or you're indifferent to the way you feel about your country and how much you love it. . . . I'm very lax in certain details and things, and yet for the emotional feeling and the feeling for giving my life and for loving this country is so great, that I think when you asked me that question, 'Are you a one hundred percent American' and if I answered the truth, it will greater effect than any other way you can ask me. . . . This is the ironic part of it, that wouldn't it be a tremendous hoax, or certain people would probably believe it that way, that here's a fellow that didn't vote for the President, closes his clubs for three days, made a trip to Cuba, relayed a message from a person — from Ray Brantley — look at circumstantially how guilty I am. If you want to pull all these things together? Then, I happen to be down there, which is a million and one shot, that I should happen to be down there at that particular second when this man comes out of whatever it was — an elevator or whatever it was — all these things — plus the fact of the post office box and other rumors that they saw us together at the club — how can we give the clearance that the ads I put in were authentic, my sincerity, my feeling of emotionalism were sincere; that that Sunday morning I got carried away after reading the article, a letter addressed to Caroline and then this little article that stated Mrs. Kennedy might be requested to come back and face the ordeal of the trial? Also if there was a conspiracy, then this little girl that called me on the phone in Fort Worth then is a part of the conspiracy. Do you follow me?"

He strains and strains, but it is no use. The stone will not budge. No one will know. No one knows me; I am Jack Rubenstein.

They ran a final series (number eleven, 8:55-8:59 p.m.), just to please Jack:

Herndon: "Do you consider yourself to be a one hundred percent American patriot?"
Ruby: "Yes."

A long day (morning negotiations, afternoon wrangles, afternoon and evening tests) — but it ended with Jack still saying he was fresh, still begging to be questioned; still coughing ineffectually while the stone grew heavier and would not come up.

His worst fears were realized. The polygraph examination raised little interest. Back in his corridor, Jack fell to new depths of puzzled helplessness, catching at crumbling ledges as he fell — at newspapers (no vindication), at his Chief's responses (nothing there), at lawyers, at the doctors who came in. The defense team took the position that the test could not be valid, since Jack was insane. Others said it was too prolonged to have any force (responses dull after a while). Conspiratorialists must of necessity ignore it (as Mark Lane does) or attack it — as Harold Weisberg does: "The lie-dectector test borders on the ridiculous. . . . The brief transcript, slightly more than three pages, clearly reveals the purpose for which the 'test' was conducted by the Commission and included in the Report (pp. 809-13). Ruby was restricted to 'yes' and 'no'. . . . The entire performance was a gruesome farce. Even then, however, the obvious and necessary questions were not asked. The Commission restricted itself to what was only self-serving. This did not prevent the Report from invoking the word of a madman in support of its theory, that Ruby, too, was a loner."

How does one deal with wild stuff of this sort? First, the transcript of the test does not run three pages; it covers sixty-six pages, with thirty more pages of testimony on the session from Dr. Beavers and Bell Herndon. Weisberg is referring to the Report's summary of answers obtained from the questioning. Second, Ruby was not restricted to Yes or No answers except when the needles were moving. He explained himself before and after the actual test question; when he answered for the graph, exigencies of the technique made one-word replies necessary for sound interpretation. Third, the Commission asked in every way whether Ruby was involved in conspiracy. Jack's answers are enough to rule out Weisberg's theory — which is why he must treat them as a madman's. Fourth, the Report did not "invoke the word of a madman in support of its theory." It quoted J. Edgar Hoover's evaluation, "In view of the serious question raised as to Ruby's mental condition, no significance should be placed on the polygraph examination," and added: "The Commission did not rely on the results of this examination in reaching the conclusions stated in this report." But conspiratorialists are beyond correction.

The test *was* too long to serve as an ideal model — the latter part of it was conducted more for Jack's consolation than to obtain results. But some of the key questions were asked early in the session, while Jack was fresh — e.g., did he know Oswald before, did he assist Oswald in the assassination, questions asked in the very first series — and his answer to these key items at the outset are enough to dispose of most conspiratorial theories about him. Dr. Beavers, a defense psychiatrist who opposed the test — on whose diagnosis, in fact, F.B.I. Director Hoover based his refusal to count the tests as decisive — complimented Bell Herndon on his skill in pacing the test in such a way as to keep Ruby relaxed: "I think he held up rather remarkably well. At least, this is my opinion. I haven't been present with polygraph interrogations, but he certainly did not show undue stress, either physical or emotional, and handled the questions better than I thought he would. It did seem like he was getting, in a sense, his day in court, which was by reasons of his, as I understand it, trial procedure and presumed defense tactics not allowed him in the first trial. This to me is what he kept coming back to during the course of the examination, that he wanted to get his story out, and during the times I have seen him . . . I was impressed with the skill of the man giving the test. I felt the breaks were fairly well spaced. He didn't show an excessive amount of fatigue, in my view, except before the first break. He seemed to show more fatigue then than he did later on."

On Jack's mental state during the test, Dr. Beavers had this to say: "I felt that so far as my ability to evaluate this man in responding to questions, that any delusional state did not interfere with awareness of the past, with the presence of seemingly adequate memory, with the presence of an apparently reasonable appreciation of reality in reference to his whereabouts and his behavior in the critical time that was under discussion. In short, he seemed to behave like a man with a well-fixed delusional system in which whole areas of his thinking and his behavior is not strongly interfered by the delusion."

Conspiratorialists who ignore this session nonetheless draw extensively on the meeting, a month earlier, with Justice Warren, where Jack hinted darkly that the truth could not be known until he took the test. Those hints of what he *would* say at the test cannot be interpreted in isolation from what he *did* say at it. He was not promising to tell a new story, but begging for new *proof* of his sincerity.

The estimate formed by the man who actually gave the test is the most important one. Dr. Beavers testified to Herndon's skill. The subject was cooperative. The equipment was good. So were the conditions — Herndon was pleased that the jail lights are not fluorescent, they sometimes interfere with a good reading. (Alexander did not ask whether he allowed for any hum in the jail's wall.) Mr. Herndon, as befits him, kept evaluation of the test results within his province. He could not pronounce on Ruby's mental condition. But *if* Ruby was competent, then the charts would indicate that "There was no area of deception present with regard to his response to the relevant questions."

It did no good. When next Jack moved through newsmen at a public hearing, he shouted that "the plot" was suppressing results of his polygraph session, so the excuse for killing the Jews would not be removed. He shouted it, expecting nothing. The shout would do no good. Nothing would. The test had not.

After the test, he was broken. Several months later, he rose to

his "plateau" of listlessness and stayed there (with only brief
flashes of light or dark through predominating gray) for two
years — fall of '64 to fall of '65 (Joe Brown disqualified, lawyers varied and shaken down to the final team of five), fall of
'65 to fall of '66 (sanity hearing, appeal briefs and arguments,
reversal).

Two months after the reversal, and two months before Jack's
second trial was to begin, Bill Decker went to see him. The
Sheriff had not seen him for some time — he had been in the
hospital himself, being treated for emphysema — but he had to
go to the jail on December 9, to introduce Jack to the Sheriff
from Wichita Falls. The case had been assigned for retrial in
Bill Alexander's home town; Decker would soon (he thought)
be surrendering the prisoner to new custody. Those who
watched Jack daily had not noticed the swiftness of his decline;
his growing nausea, vomiting, "tight chest" seemed to have no
explanation — nerves, perhaps, and a cold. He was often sick
and grumbling now, and the guards had steeled themselves
against his whimpering self-pity. Eva brought Jack stomach
medicines. In November, Diana (of the bow-and-arrow huntress act) brought him some Pepto-Bismol — she would be at
Parkland herself when he arrived, recovering from her suicide
attempt.

The prison doctor had been treating him for a cold during
the last week. But Decker took one look at him and knew it was
more serious than that. He called in the County Health Officer,
who said Ruby should be rushed to the hospital for tests. That
first night, they called it pneumonia; his lungs were full of fluid.
But the next day, they cut a node out of his neck and tested it.
Cancer. Jack thought, for a while, it had been injected in him,
but the doctors convinced his lawyers this could not be, and
they convinced Jack. He had regained some of his interest in
life. He was the center of attention once more. He was in a
room again, with a window. He could sleep in the dark, away
from that constant corridor light. He had a television set in his

room, for the first time since the Sunday morning whcn he watched commentators struggle with their grief. He knew he was seriously ill. He asked for another lie-detector test: perhaps someone would believe him *now*, on what may be his death-bed. The doctors said they could not suspend medication to get him into the undrugged condition needed for a polygraph ex-amination. But an enterprising fellow had already arranged, before his transfer to the hospital, to record an interview with him. That interview became more important to Jack now, and more difficult to get. Earl Ruby and Elmer Gertz experimented with one tape recorder; found it would not work; got another one that fit into a briefcase. Earl carried it into the hospital room and put it on the bed, Gertz spread legal papers on it while Jack's sisters, Eva and Eileen, distracted the guard with conversation. Earl told his brother what was going on in the "code" of their childhood home, in Yiddish (which Jack had taken to speaking again, in interviews and on the phone, to baffle the constant eavesdropping of guards). Earl questioned Jack for a while, but soon dried up. Elmer Gertz took over:

"Had you ever known Oswald, Jack?"

"No."

"Ever know Oswald before?"

"Never had known him or seen him before."

Jack slid, as ever, toward his obsession with those guns.

"Is there any truth at all to the stories that Oswald had been in your club?"

"None whatsoever, it's just a fabrication — in one particular incident that has never been enlightened to the public, I be-lieve, is that a friend of mine, Mr. McWillie who invited me down to Havana, Cuba. I didn't come down, but he finally sent me plane tickets to come down as a good friendly gesture. So I accepted the invitation. I stayed with him for eight days, and then I left, and I had lived constantly with him the eight days, but then right after that he called me from Havana, Cuba, and said 'Jack, I want you to call Ray Brantley at Ray's Hardware store in Singleton Avenue and tell him to send me four Cobras — a Cobra is a little revolver. So, I did call him and gave him the address. When I called him he answered and said, 'Oh, I know Mr. McWillie very well' so that left it out of my hands. All I had to do was relay the message, but that is the only extent I ever had of any association with anything, business dealings out of the United States and that was only a message to relay."

And there was more "if-onlying": "The ironic part of this is had not I made an illegal turn behind the bus to the parking lot, had I gone the way I was supposed to go straight down Main Street, I would have never met this fate because the difference in meeting this fate was thirty seconds one way or the other."

The interview ran fourteen and a half minutes; an excerpt running just under four minutes was sold to Capitol records and incorporated in an album that hit the market just as Ruby's death was announced (the proceeds to the Ruby family paid for Jack's funeral). We were carrying another phonograph record when we dashed to Parkland Hospital the morning that Jack died — a record of local news coverage on the weekend of the assassination — and we were almost mobbed by reporters who thought it might be *the* record.

Jack's reaction after this recorded interview was much like his letdown after the polygraph examination. He hoped, by a final statement, to make the world see the truth. But nothing had happened. His family kept the tape recording secret. Something, Jack was sure, had gone wrong; or would go wrong. It inevitably had. He was thoroughly convinced, at the end, of what he had suspected all his life — that he was not convincing. No one would ever believe poor Rubenstein.

He lay there, cancered; and drugged to ease the cancer; with blood clotting, and no remedy because of the cancer; reticulated with the needles and tubes of medical desperation. Before him the meaningless patterns of television, that murky window on an outside world too far outside for him to reach again; ghettoed away from it once more; from the football games, the Christmas shows, the New Year, "Auld Lang Syne," cheerful blur cheerlessly watched, dwindling from him — quick linear shrink and last eye of light when the TV cord is pulled, a dizzying contracted cube of moonlight clarity yielding to the dark. On January 3, 1967, he ceased to care. To give a damn. To live.

iv

Jack Ruby, were he alive, would not have missed it. It was his kind of affair — newsmen, wisecracks, milling, evasiveness. TV cameras spreading their roots in weird tangles over the floor. Edgy officials, pushy bystanders. He would have been there, giving away sandwiches, introducing someone to everyone, passing out cards to The Carousel. But he could hardly be there. This was his affair in a different sense.

Phil Burleson put Ruby's brother and two sisters in a car outside Parkland Memorial and turned back toward the press conference room. He paused at the hospital steps to look at the car, which was breaking slowly through a surf of reporters; and as he stood there an old nurse said, next to him, "If you ask me, we are well off to be rid of him."

There was to be a press conference at 1:00 p.m. with the doctors. Some foreign reporters were there. The conspiratorial hum had gone up in volume. Did they give him a cancer pill? He said he would never leave the jail alive! Sevareid spanked Dallas, and Dallas cried. Bill Decker made the canonical comparison when they asked whether Jack caught his pneumonia (or whatever) from the draftiness of a prison corridor: "It is not a barn, not an open pasture. It was built to maintain and keep prisoners the same as they do in New York." The city breathed a sigh of relief when it was announced that Jack would not be buried there, but in Chicago: perhaps that would siphon off some of the arriving journalists.

Ruby had not been given much of the respect he craved for in his life. He received a modicum of it in death. Dr. Earl Rose, who conducted the autopsy, announced to chatting witnesses before he began: "Gentlemen, this is a morgue, a place of serious business. The deceased will be referred to as Mr. Ruby. I want no profanity or levity." The witnesses included men from the D.A.'s office and the Sheriff's department — Texans with cactus tongues. But for four hours they whispered their way politely around the customary four-letter words.

Four hours. The medical press conference scheduled for 1:00 was delayed until 3:00. Dr. Rose is famous for his thoroughness. His protocols are lengthy documents, yet done with the utmost compression. Dr. Rose has served in several states — including a period as Deputy Chief Medical Examiner in Virginia. He is not a parochial Texan, but he does believe in the exact performance of his duty. That is why he would not let President Kennedy's body be removed from Parkland Hospital without an autopsy. That is the law. He was pushed aside, in a scene made famous by William Manchester. If he had not been overruled, we would have one of those famous, finicky protocols for John F. Kennedy — one taken in the presence of the first men who treated the President, before he was transported in a roughly handled coffin (which had to be pulled free of the hearse-floor by presidential aides who did not know how to unfasten it). It would then be part of the public record — unlike the elusive Washington autopsy.

Dr. Rose is almost the only man involved in the Ruby case who commanded the respect of both sides — the prosecution and the defense. He not only awed the D.A.'s men; he won the gratitude of the Ruby family by his concern for them and his careful cooperation in checking into all the details of Jack's death.

He performs his autopsies speaking into a tape recorder, switching it on and off with his foot. After the customary photographs and external inspections, he removed, weighed, and microphotographed each organ. There had been a great deal of speculation among the doctors on the source of the cancer. Most of them favored the pancreas, but Dr. Rose thought not; and inspection bore him out. The pancreas was clear — the heaviest cluster of cancer cells was in the right lung. Death, however, had traveled up the femoral artery, which was mud instead of river down the whole right leg. Coagulations, drifting up from this mass clot, had sludged suffocatingly against the lungs. The brain, whose state had been so thoroughly debated, was sent to the laboratory for sectioning and microscopic tests. It revealed no organic disorder except some of the white cancer tumors coursing through his body.

Ruby was the seventh man to die at Parkland in the new year of 1967. That meant his code number was M67-007. (Oswald had been M63-356.) This code number was shortened on jars into which cells and tissues were placed for later examination. Ruby wanted, all his life, to be one of the boys, a big shot, a boss. He would have been happy, had he known: he was in the end, improbably, "007."

"The Communists or the John Birch Society or Both"

i

Most of those who spin hypotheses about The Plot that engineered Kennedy's death find a place in their spidery web for Jack Ruby. He would be at home in these men's company. He was one of the first conspiratorialists. He positively buzzed, that whole first weekend, with clues, hints, "scoops," and bloodhound persistency on the trail of "them."

It began, on Friday, even before the President's death — early Friday morning, in fact, before Jack went to bed. He had closed The Carousel, and told Bill Willis he would see the parade if he got his ad drafted in time (weekend ads are the most important ones). Then he drove to The Vegas to close it up. His sister Eva usually runs The Vegas, but she is still in bed recovering from an operation, and Laverne Crafard (Larry) is filling in. Jack picks Crafard up, gives him breakfast at Lucas' B and B, and drives him back to The Carousel, where Larry sleeps. This was at 3:30 a.m. The early edition of the *Morning*

News was out by then. Ruby always bought the papers as they hit the stand — to see if his ads had been correctly placed; to know what his friends, the important people of Dallas, were doing; to feed the brushfires of his superficial conversation with anyone still moving through the lonely hours before dawn.

He could not miss the full-page ad in that Friday's paper — a huge WELCOME MR. KENNEDY, then (in smaller but still heavy blocks) TO DALLAS. Jack liked that: the merger of two things dear to him, his President and his city. Down at the bottom — his eyes flit and skim, too restless to read the long printed list, each item headed with a heavy WHY — was a name, the chairman of the sponsoring group, Bernard Weissman. Merger of *three* things — Kennedy, Dallas, and a Jew.

But why the black border? Jack has sent enough cards of condolence (to the widow of that cop who had been killed, Officer Mullenix, for instance) to know that black stands for death. He has observed the mourning symbols of the synagogue. A welcome to the President should be framed in something cheerful; Jack sure could teach that Weissman about drawing up an ad. Then he read some of those why's: "WHY have you ordered or permitted your brother Bobby, the Attorney General, to go soft on Communists?" A rift in the merger — things at the center of Jack's life falling apart: a Jew attacking the President! And this President! And in the name of Dallas! What could dislodge these fixed stars of his life, set them in collision orbits? It was a thing outside of nature — therefore concerted by man's ingenuity. A *plot* to make the Jews look bad on this happy day!

When he woke up, before the Kennedy parade, Jack called Eva around 11:00 a.m. and asked if she had read the ad. She had glanced at it, without noticing what it was really about. He tells her to read it again and hangs up. After the call, he sets out for the *Daily News* to draw up his own ad for Saturday morning's paper.

First, he must see Tony Zoppi about the brochure he gave

him on Billy DeMar, his new M.C. He had hoped Tony would write a column on him, but Zoppi said he could not; Jack went to the entertainment office and got his brochure to use in the ad. Then, in the advertising department, he chatted for half an hour with Don Campbell. When Don went out, Jack doodled his ad into shape. He will tell Justice Warren, in the account of his actions on Friday, "I have ways of making my ads up where they have a way of selling the product I am producing or putting on on the show."

At 12:40, the ad man he normally works with, John Newnam, comes in from watching the President pass Austin Street, three blocks away from Dealey Plaza. "Hi, Jack" — Jack immediately asks why the *News* ran such insulting words about the President. Minutes later, reports come to the second-floor department — the President is shot, and some secret service men, and the Governor. After everyone's brief struggle with disbelief, in a flurry of confirmation and corrections, Newnam receives quick cancellations of some local ads. There will be no business this weekend. (Jack is torn: no business, then, for him? Of course not! Who wants to watch girls strip when mourning a father's death? Still, weekends are worth more than all other days put together; and they *are* behind; and the Weinsteins probably *will* stay open. On the other hand, he would score a moral victory if he closed and they did not. And he has a way of making moral victories into advertising that has a way of selling his show. The three-runway club, the *only* club with strip acts that stayed closed in honor of the President!)

Jack will vacillate all the next two days — asking whether he should, trumpeting he *must*, demanding why others do not, hoping they will; but hoping they will not, telling Larry to draw a "Closed" sign but not to put it out front until it is too late for the Weinsteins to see it and imitate him; telling others he has scooped the Weinsteins by running a "Closed" notice before they did — yet sincerely hurt by places that stayed open for business as usual in this catastrophe (he pleaded with friends like Ralph Paul and Joe Cavagnaro to close restaurants and hotels, he walked into diners and asked why they were open). He needs two things, irreconcilable — *publicity* for his grand gesture (call Don Safran, an item for his column) and, on the other hand, *secrecy*, so others will not follow his lead and take all the credit (men never see what a good heart he has — tell Don not to consult other club owners, he does not care what they are doing).

For some time he is ashen and subdued, brokenhearted, calculating, as the susurrus of disaster goes in and out of the newspaper offices and phones ring regularly. He will not commit himself yet; he must talk to Ralph and to Eva before he makes such a big decision. He is struck, already, by those other canceled ads. Is it only that business will be slow, or promotion out of place, these days? Or are others outraged by the paper that ran Weissman's ad — black for death? Has Eva heard yet? And did she read the ad again? He calls her to ask both questions. They hysterically tell each other not to be hysterical. Jack asks Newnam to calm her, *he* can't — this will prove what a good heart these Jews have; not like Weissman. Jack later explained his action to the Chief Justice: "I know it is a funny reaction you have, you want other people to feel that you feel emotionally disturbed the same way as other people, so I let John listen to the phone that my sister was crying hysterically." He takes the phone back. Has she read the Weissman ad yet? No. Well, they are canceling ads like crazy down here — which is what comes of being money-hungry enough to print things like that attack on President Kennedy.

Jack goes to the club. No matter what else he does, he must close it tonight; tell Andrew to telephone the band and the girls. Andrew Armstrong remembers he came in so disturbed that, when he threw his hat on the table and it fell off, he did not bother to pick it up. This was unusual for fastidious Ruby, who took good care of the hat that covered his baldness, a hat

he wore everywhere, at diner tables and delicatessen coun-
ters. (The hat is now in Bill Alexander's file cabinet, one of the
few items left in the "estate" that rivals contend for.) Jack is
elated and despondent; lonely and in need of someone to talk
to — he calls Alice Nichols, the girl who was "too good for
him." She is out, so he leaves a number — for the pay phone in
the booth "because I didn't want to keep the business phone
tied up." He is tense with the size of the decision he must make
— closed tonight, of course; but what about the next night, or
even Sunday? Should he risk the whole weekend? It is too
much for him. He calls his sister in Chicago, Eileen, and says
he has to leave Dallas. He will come up to her. It is an instinctive, halted gesture many were making — with some, indeed,
not halted. Breck Wall got up Saturday and felt he had to leave
Dallas: he drove to Galveston with his friend Joe Peterson.
Jack's dancers felt that way; one decides she will quit, though it
is against union rules, and go to California. A jeweler, Joe Bellochio, is telling friends the city should be abandoned. President Kennedy's "Irish mafia," bottled-up in Parkland Hospital,
felt the same irrational urge (as of one suffocating, toward the
air) to get out of Dallas.

Eileen calms Jack. Eva cannot move around yet, after her
operation. She needs someone to look after her. Jack has to
stay in town. Right. Jack hangs up and calls Eva. Has she read
the ad? Yes. But she is out of food, will he bring some over? —
and not from Phil's, she prefers the Ritz Delicatessen. He says
"Right away," but keeps returning to the dial and receiver, a
telephone addict, wanting other people to feel that he feels
emotionally disturbed the same way as other people — people
all over the country: friends, family, old acquaintances. Eva
will testify to the Commission: "His 'right over' came, I would
say it was, after four o'clock. Maybe a quarter of five. Maybe it
was five. Maybe it was even five-fifteen."

When he comes, he weeps as they watch the television.
"What a creep," he says of Oswald. "That lousy commie," she

answers, "don't worry, the commie, we will get him." He asks her again about the Weissman ad. What a thing to say about the President — Welcome Mr. Kennedy! The least it could have said was Welcome Honorable President. (The President of the United States is always "our beloved President" in Jack's dignified moods, or in formal things like newspaper ads.) What a sonvabitch that Weissman must be — if he's really a Jew. Maybe, though, he is a gentile, just using the name to discredit us. General Walker may be behind it all. Shadowily, in the back of his mind, the plot is taking shape.

But a more immediate problem cuts across the job of tracking down conspiracy: he asks Eva if they dare close both clubs through the whole weekend. Don Safran, entertainment columnist for the *Times Herald,* called earlier, he wants to know what the clubs will do. Jack told him he would call back. Now he and Eva decide to go ahead and close. Jack calls Don, tells him he does not care what the other owners do (which strikes Safran as uncharacteristic); calls advertisement departments of both papers, cancels the ad he was completing just when Kennedy was shot.

Still jerky with contradicting impulses, he moves from the telephone to the kitchen (can't eat), to Eva's bed (can't sleep). He calls Rabbi Silverman. Will there be services? Calls Hy (his brother Hyman in Chicago). Nibbles. Finally he leaves, to shower at his apartment and dress for the service. He reaches the synagogue late; thanks Rabbi Silverman, on his way out, for visiting Eva in the hospital. Afterward, as he drives along, he checks the clubs and restaurants: Bali-Hai, open; Gay Nineties, closed; Lucas', open. "In my mind suddenly it mulled over me," Jack would tell Earl Warren, "that the police department was working overtime." How could he help? — Sandwiches. At Phil's Delicatessen, he asks for eight "real good sandwiches" and goes to the phone. A friend of his answers, Dick Sims of Homicide. Sims tells him not to bother, they have all gone out to eat, in shifts. What to do with the sandwiches now?

The radio is on — Gordon's station, KLIF. Jack calls McLendon, who is not at home, and asks his daughter for the station's "hot line" — to reach the studio where men are up throughout the night, broadcasting. The only number she gives him does not work. That's all right, he'll get in somehow. He tells the man at the counter: "These are going to KLIF, and I want you to make them real good. They are still up working on this case." Jack drifts over to a table where SMU students are talking with two coeds, snatches up their paper, shakes it out and folds it to his ads for today — too late to change these. The clerk takes sandwiches and some bottles of pop out to the car — and receives Jack's customary tip, a pass to The Carousel.

Back in his car, Jack decides the quickest way to get KLIF's "hot line" is at the police station, where all the newsmen are. (He used to have that unlisted number, when he called Russ Knight to change his radio ads.) An odd exhilaration is tingling in him now. He makes his way up to the third floor (Homicide) between two reporters — fidgeting his pencil, as he moves along, on a card from his bulging pockets, the very picture of a busy shrewd reporter noting down details. His entry was possible, he would tell Earl Warren, because "Evidently I took a little domineering part about me, and I was able to be admitted." He tells one policeman he is covering the case for the Israeli press, and moves into the clotted hallway through which Oswald has been wrung, back and forth, all afternoon and evening (taken to the elevator, down for identification, back up, back into the crunch of shoulders and elbows, through the molasses-flow of men in this tight legal funnel). Now Oswald is brought out again, for the cameras to view him. Wade says they need more space, take him down to the show-up room, let the cameras view him in front of the one-way-vision screen — lay the rumors of mistreatment, let TV crews record the single injury given him in the struggle of his capture. (Dr. Earl Rose will write, in the Oswald autopsy, "There is a left periorbital hematoma which is purple in the central portion fading at the margins to a faint lemon-yellow. Total diameter of this is 1 and 3/4 by 1 and 1/4 inch.") They squeeze their prisoner back into the office, just in front of Ruby, Oswald passes not two feet away from him. The press conference, to be held in the line-up room, is announced; Jack's spirits soar. He explained his feelings to Dr. Manfred Guttmacher this way: "Everybody says, 'Hello, Jack.' It took away the tragic feeling. Everything was so bustling, so crude. I was in this swarm of people and suddenly Oswald comes. The reporters asked me who was this one and who was that one. I was in a complete change of mental reaction, already I am with the deal. They are going to take him to the big assembly room. History is being made."

Reporters and newscasters jostle four floors down, a shuffling turn of the human tide, and the soft pounding of this surf throws Jack Ruby up, high and dry, on a table at the far end of the room, up where the scan of cameras inevitably snags on him. He puts on his most serious expression, poises his pencil importantly. He even takes his hat off. He told Dr. Guttmacher, "I am standing on the table above everybody and people are asking me 'Who is that?' I even passed out some of my cards to these newspapermen from all over the world. I just had my cards printed with the Petty girl on them and I am proud of them." The journalists are warned not to interview Oswald; he is brought down. In a wash and tilt of white hats (the one group that wears Stetsons, of various gallonage, in Dallas is the city police), his face bobs defiantly, boyish, lightly whiskered, calm, almost smug, wearing his black eye like a badge — it gives his brows a sullen heaviness, and Jack thinks, "He looks like Paul Newman." (Dr. Rose again, in his autopsy protocol: "The hair is brown, slightly wavy. . . . Slight frontal balding." Over Ruby's body, the same man will dictate into his recorder: "The hair is brunette and there is greying, there is dandruff. It is thinning, more marked over the crown of the head but also bilaterally of the frontal regions. . . . The hair measures up to approximately six inches over the frontal and crown, and along the lateral aspect it measures up to one and one half inches.")

Chief Curry's admonition is ignored: medusa-clots of microphones snap forward at Oswald. Men shout questions, relay his answers, ask each other what was that, drown each other out. It was all history, and Jack was above it all — his pencil, too, moving purposefully. Curry takes his prisoner back out, up to the three maximum security cells on floor five (where Ruby will sleep Sunday night). Henry Wade remains behind to answer questions — a question, for instance, on what he calls the "Free Cuba Committee." Jack knows better; he heard it on Gordon's station. "Fair Play for Cuba Committee!" Score one for Jack.

Follow it up — back down into the toss of surf, swim energetically toward Wade as the D.A. leaves the platform and men swirl in on him. Jack reaches his hand out over other hands and arms: "Hi Henry!" (he knows everyone — the names of people, of committees, all kinds of important things). "Don't you know me?" (Jack Ruby, *you* know; I just helped you with that name.) "I know all these fellows" (cops, reporters, everyone with class). Hat firmly anchored again, he slides toward David Johnston, who was wedged forward, off the platform, with Wade, and stands beside him. Johnston is the J.P. who rode a squad car with Bill Alexander out to search Oswald's room. Several hours ago, he arraigned the man for Tippit's murder; he is now carrying the document that will charge him with Kennedy's murder — he must get him down, now, from the fifth floor to serve it. Jack does not know the Judge himself; when he hears the title, he does a gregarious double take, gives him a Carousel pass. Things are looking up.

Decidedly up. His eyes, searchlighting for a man to give him KLIF's number, pick out Sam Pate — not from KLIF, but one of the newscasters, he must know the number. He does; now Jack does, and he dials it — "On my way over with sandwiches." Ike Pappas of New York is at another phone signaling toward Wade to get an interview. Jack has already given Pappas one of his cards. What else can he do for him? He sees him gesturing and moves in (Pappas later testified, "My immediate impression of him was that he was a detective"): "Henry, you're wanted on the phone." Wade thinks it is his office calling, and takes the receiver. It had worked! Jack will tell Justice Warren, "I felt that I was deputized as a reporter momentarily, you might say."

It worked once. Why not twice? Back to the dial, K-L-I-F, hello KLIF? Do you want a scoop, an interview with Henry Wade? They want it. "Henry!" Twice. Try for three? Adrift in the crowd, disc jockey Russ Knight (known as the Weird Beard) has vague antennae out for something usable on his tape recorder. He is more at home behind the turntable, but this weekend has brought total mobilization to KLIF, and he was sent over, when his shift ended at midnight, to get an interview with Wade. Jack is on the first floor, on his way to the station, when he sees Knight's trademark pushing toward him. (At Jack's trial, Knight told Phil Burleson, who asked him on the stand why he is called Weird Beard: "Well, I think that's obvious. I use the name on radio, so it's advantageous to my personal image, if I may be so bold as to speak, to have a beard in person.") Jack greets him helpfully: want an interview with Henry Wade? Nothing is strange anymore; Knight, sent for just this purpose, merely nods and asks where does he go. Jack takes him back into the basement and introduces him.

While the weird one beards the District Attorney, Jack hovers benevolently. Scoop safely on the reel, he tags along with Knight, back toward the station. Care for a ride? Knight can walk the few blocks faster than a car would make it; but Jack must take his car, the sandwiches are there. At least he is sure of getting in now, he has helped them twice. Preceded by Knight, Jack enters triumphantly, distributes his largess, then waits in the studio to hear the tape. It is readied, played, introduced on the air (by Knight): "If I can say it with any believability, I have just returned from a trip to the Dallas Courthouse on a tip from Jack Ruby, local night club owner. . . ." It is very believable to Jack.

After the news spot, they walk out of the station together — Knight weary after his impressment into roving reportage (it is Saturday now, just after 2:00 a.m.); Jack nearing the peak of his day, excited at his new eminence. What more can he and Russ do on the case? His mind slips ahead to the untidy files that litter his car — a crime computer blinking, sorting, signaling, *yes!* The pamphlet!

A few weeks ago, he displayed his twistboard at the Texas Products show. Tammi demonstrated its (and her) motion and got her picture in the paper; after that, Jack went out every night and sold the boards, demonstrating them himself. A friend of his, Edward Pullman, was running a booth that displayed the boards (he used to drop in on Pullman and his wife at their home: "He wouldn't do anything, but he was looking for friends — he was looking for friends. He would come in on a Sunday with sweet rolls and spend an hour or two, with his dogs. . . ."). One night at the products show, Jack came upon Pullman with a load of spoils from the "Life Line" booth, H. L. Hunt's right-wing radio series. The spoils included pamphlets critical of the Administration. "I'm going to send this stuff to Kennedy," he told Pullman. Insults to authority were treason in Jack's eyes. "Nobody has any right to talk like this about our government." Pullman assured him they know all about such things in Washington. "Maybe they don't. I'm going to send it in." But Jack's investigation of these loyalty risks had guttered, like all his flax-fire ardors; the pamphlets are still in his car, unsent — he will never send them to Kennedy. But *providentially* there! What if they have something to do with the case? He and Russ could follow up this lead, perhaps beat the others out. One sort of treason leads to another — criticizing Kennedy may lead to *killing* Kennedy. Wait here!

He rummages in that Oldsmobile wastebasket, finds one pamphlet only, a radio talk on Heroism ("The hero, or the man who aspires to heroism, is first and last an individualist . . . making his own opportunities instead of being shaped by the people around him and the familiar ways of doing things"). What does Russ think of that?

Russ is tired, in no mood for detective work; he cannot follow Jack's leapfrogging logic. He rambles off, and takes Jack's "evidence" with him. Well, there are other leads to follow; and when he needs key information, he will call on Russ again — tomorrow. Jack twirls off toward light and movement, night moth beckoned by his goal. He must find other newsmen — they will be working on ads at the *Times Herald* — so many ads to be changed, they'll probably keep the evening shift over into the morning "lobster shift." He drives down Jackson, stops for the red light at Field. Harry Olsen and Kathy Kaye (Jack's stripper) are visiting with Johnny, a friend who runs the parking lot next to Abe's. They see him from the car where they are sitting, call out; Jack pulls over and joins them (it is cold now, and their talk leaves vapor trails, like Dallas jets).

Kathy is from England; some girls think she puts on airs, telling them that things are better in her native land — "Then why not take the next plane back?" they ask her snippily. Jack listens to her now — in England they would string an Oswald up. Harry is a policeman, off-duty this whole weekend with a broken leg. Jack does not know his divorce is final, thinks Harry wants his dates with Kathy secret. (Olsen will be asked to leave the force next month; he and Kathy marry and move to California.) Ruby tells them he has seen Oswald, who looks just like a rat. Harry thinks such a man should be cut in pieces. Jack keeps returning to the thought of Mrs. Kennedy "and the kids." For almost an hour he warms himself in darkness with these angers, fighting off the little ices of despondency that form on him when he stops moving; he returns, therefore, undaunted to his car and drives it on down Jackson. White Oldsmobile-moth making for *Times Herald* light. He has to give Gadash that twistboard he has been promising him — ever since Gadash set an ad for it and asked what *is* this thing? Jack takes the employees' elevator up to the composing room. The night watchman at the door knows him; he is often up there to see how his ads look in print, suggest changes, angle for better placing on the page of his little masterpieces ("Stripper Turns Teacher"); overseeing the creative process — inspiration, execution, correction, final polishing. He told Dr. Guttmacher, "The semantics of words — everybody says I am better than anyone at putting words together."

Gadash is there. How does this thing work? Jack always demonstrates. He and Pullman found that boards were not bought if they were left stacked lifeless on the counter of the booth; but every night, when Jack put on his demonstration, sales were made. He is expert by now; he spastically surfboarded these little platforms on his stage, told his audience the President advises exercise; he showed off, twisting, by the swimming pool at his apartment. The ball bearings work smoothly; so does Jack. Now one of the proofreaders, a woman, attempts it, clumsily at first, a novice; and some of the printers laugh for the first time that day (their afternoon-to-sunrise "day").

Jack tells Gadash he knows *his* paper would not take an ad like the one in the *Morning News* — Bernard Weissman's. He is sniffing plots again: "The sonvabitch is trying to put the frame on the Jews." But he will make up for it with his respectful ads — put black borders around *them* too (he tells Gadash, who makes it a twelve-point frame). One Jew shames Dallas with an ad; another will restore the city's honor.

Jack talks to other employees of the paper, asks Arthur Watherwax if he likes the idea of changing ads to mourning notices ("He was always asking somebody's opinion on something," Watherwax remarks of the exchange). Jack boasts of the "interview" he just had with Oswald and Henry Wade: *he* helped Henry with some of the facts in the case. Arthur drives a cab in his spare time (Jack wants him to suggest his club to out-of-towners). Does he think this will hurt convention business? Both men agree it will. What does Arthur think of the Weissman ad? Jack thinks it General Walker's idea — to make the Jews look bad.

Roy Pryor comes over; he has known Jack for years. Before he went into the printing business, Roy played sax and was an M.C. at The Silver Spur. In 1951, Jack used some blistering language on Roy, and got a black eye in return: "There was a wash stand in the back of the Spur there, and he was washing his face and I walked over to him and told him, I said, 'Jack, I'm sorry I'm fighting in your place here and working for you like this, but don't never call me a name like that because I just don't appreciate it,' and so he turned around and pop! he hit me right in the eye, you see, and boy! the sparks just flew . . . so both of us had a big ol' shiner, and of course, the guys in the band were up on the bandstand and were looking through the curtain. They heard the commotion and they were just rolling."

Typical ending to the story: "There was a grocery store down on the corner . . . he goes down and buys two great big steaks and both of us are walking around with these steaks on our eyes. I mean — that's the type of person, though, that Jack was." They are good friends now. Jack had Christmas dinner with Roy and his wife in 1960 ("We had a lot of yard and his dogs got out and run and it just seemed to be relaxation for him, and we enjoyed having him").

Jack runs through his repertoire again with Roy: "Poor Jackie and the kids." How he helped Wade: "You see, I'm in good with the District Attorney." How he saw Oswald: "He's a little weasel of a guy." How he went to "the line-up" through his "contacts." (Pryor's own opinion: "Jack was real impulsive and he happened to be there and they happened to be going in and that seemed like the thing to do. I mean — knowing Jack, if there was any kind of excitement or activity — and he had a tendency to 'big shot.'") Most of all, his ads: "The fact that it was in memoriam, a memorial, to President Kennedy, was primary, but secondary then was the fact he had scooped his competitors, and that was the word he used, 'scooped.'"

Yes, he had assisted Henry. No reason to stop helping him now. All bristle and self-importance, he tells "Grif" Griffith, "I have been doing favors for the people at City Hall — even though I was not supposed to be there. We are trying to find out who the man really is that placed the ad signed by Bernard Weissman. It is probably someone posing as a Jew."

He moves off on his mission, the big assignment "we are working on." How surprised Henry will be if Jack breaks the case. To do it, he must track down that imposter, "Bernard Weissman" — do it *tonight*, before he goes to bed.

Weissman knows he is being hunted. He has gone to ground. Ruby is wrong about his name. They *had* asked him to change it, all right, to please some right-wing bigots; but that was too much to ask of him. He was not ashamed of his name. He made damn sure it was on the ad — it would be dangerous to let Larrie get all that notoriety. Let them know Bernie Weissman was a power in the movement.

The movement. It looked discredited now. Weissman is hiding and will have to leave Dallas. Ruby is right; there was a plot behind that ad. Big plot.

It started in 1962, in a German beer hall; in Munich, as a matter of fact, just miles from the beer hall where another man's rise to power began. Five young GI's who used to drink there and talk about their country's need for more conservatism finally did something about it. In September, they took a private oath to defend their country and make some money. The former goal was to be accomplished through CUSA (Conservatism, USA), the latter through AMBUS (American Businesses, Inc.). In a prospectus drawn up by the leader of the group, Larrie Schmidt, CUSA is compared to the Ford Foundation and AMBUS to the Ford Motor Company. Later on in the same document, Ford (both Inc. and Foundation) is dwarfed by more ambitious comparisons: AMBUS becomes a business to rival General Electric, and CUSA is a third party strong enough to challenge the Democrats and the Republicans.

Schmidt, twenty-two at the time of The Oath, does not believe in thinking small. He was ringleader to these five boys, to a band of followers he called, with his taste for organizational acronyms, the EIC (Executive Inner Council); their job was the disposing to maximum advantage of the EIC — which never came into existence. Schmidt, unlike his fellows, had already done one stretch in the army, from age eighteen to twenty. After his discharge, he tried his hand at editing for a while, then re-enlisted — he liked the concept of military discipline. But he had plans for recruiting an army within the army: he liked to be on the ordering end, not the obeying one.

It was slow work. Not many were worthy (worthiness consisting of a passionate belief in capitalism and in Larrie Schmidt). But several disciples gathered around him in 1961, swayed by his rhetoric of conquest and patriotism and profit: "I, for one, despise anonymity, nothingness. I choose greatness — immortality — wealth — power, and influence. And, Bernie, so help me god, I am going to have these things. Whether I go down in history books as a great and noble man — or a tyrant — I am determined to at least be recorded in the history of our times. . . . I am well aware of my talents of persuasion. I was not able to get two-dozen followers for being a man of small stature. No man — not larry jones, not jimmy moseley, not norman baker, not bernie weissman, not ken glazbrooks, not bob weiss, not charlie altman, not herb starr, not bill burley, not hank tanaro, not richard harsch, not sheila mcdonald, not even my own brother and wife could resist my power of persuasion. I sold an idea, a dream, a hope, a plan for the future, a goal endless."

The plan was to defend capitalism by exemplifying its op-portunities. The right-wing moneybags should be happy to pay for such ardent young defenders of their privilege. Of course, other organizations compete for this ideological money; it would take time to establish credentials on a par, say, with the John Birch Society. The scheming GI's in Munich were too im-patient to spend precious years on slow growth and accept-ance. They yearned, over off-duty beers, for the chances of ci-vilian life — combined, of course, with the bracing army disci-pline, its drumroll of acronyms. They decided on a short cut, which Weissman explains this way: "In order to accomplish our goals, to try to do it from scratch would be almost impossi-ble, because it would be years before we could even get the funds to develop a powerful organization. So we had planned to infiltrate various right-wing organizations and by our own efforts become involved in the hierarchy of these various organ-izations and eventually get ourselves elected or appointed to various higher offices in these organizations, and by doing this to bring in some of our own people, and eventually to take over the leadership of these organizations, and at that time having our people in these various organizations, we would then, you might say, call a conference and have them unite, and while no one knew of the existence of CUSA aside from us, we would then bring them all together, unite them, and arrange to have it called CUSA. . . . We felt that after we had accomplished our goal — this is assuming we would accomplish our goal — any treasury that they had through membership dues or what have you would then be a common treasury, a CUSA treasury."

So Jack Ruby was right: the ad was the result of a plot. He was even right when he connected it, somehow, with General Walker and H. L. Hunt and the John Birch Society. He was wrong, however, in thinking Dallas had no responsibility for the ad. Dallas shone with promise for these men, casting its light as far as Munich; this city, they decided, would be the beachhead for their operation, it was clearly a magnet for conservative organizations and money. Larrie Schmidt, the first one to be mustered out, went straight for Dallas. (As soon as he touched American soil, the one-man SB, or Stateside Branch, sprang into existence; he had left Larry Jones in charge of the OB, or Overseas Branch.) Schmidt got a job selling insurance; he was about to be married. Yet he lost no time in launching the plan. He arrived in Dallas late at night on a Sunday. Early Monday morning he was at the office of the National Indignation Committee, the first group he planned to infiltrate. The results he scribbled happily off to the OB, with TOP SECRET blazoned across the top of each page, DESTROY across the bottom: "Well, gentlemen, we have arrived! Remember, when I said my first correspondence from Dallas would be on NIC letterhead?" Actually, he wrote on five letterheads, which seems to have been his total supply at the moment; pages six and seven are on regular stationery. He had gone to the top floor of the Corrigan Towers Building — he liked that, he was above them all — and met an official of the NIC, Jim Byers, age twenty-seven. He told Byers that he was the leader of a powerful organization, and gave him the description of it modeled for use on outsiders. He proposed a merger of CUSA under a new title — CUSA. The response, he wrote his fellows, was very gratifying: "In other words, they need and want me badly . . . I'm calling the shots — and I've painted a lovely picture — best con-job yet. The old 'something for nothing' — 'everything to gain, nothing to lose' bit . . . All is well with me. I have bought black raincoat, black fifth Avenue high crown Fedora and briefcase: best dressed young man on streets of Dallas, believe me."

But these actual conquests do not give Larrie the feeling of personal dominance he had while plotting world conquest with the devoted ones who were under his sway and in on his plans. He begs them to try for early release from the service. "Christ, I would give my left nut to have the EIC in this room right now!"

That same week, Schmidt spent four hours at the home of NIC's chief officer, Frank McGeeHee. They negotiated the merger: "McGehee [*sic*] is our type of man" even though "*he* expects to use *us.*"

The merger will place certain burdens on CUSA, however, a group which has been strong on discipline and weak on ideology. The group stands for capitalism and against Communism; but some of the boys are rather "liberal" about things like welfare legislation and civil rights. Bernie even voted for Kennedy in 1960! None of this worried Schmidt before; but now such deviations are dangerous, and must be stamped out: "One bad thing, though, Frank gives me the impression of being rather Anti-Semitic. He's Catholic. Suggest Bernie 'convert' to Christianity — and I mean it." He drills them on the importance of calling all Negroes "niggers." Vistas are opening. He has made plans for meeting "C. L. Hunt" (*sic*), and he has met the top editors of the Dallas *Morning News,* "the country's most conservative newspaper."

Weissman began to suspect that things were not as rosy as they had been painted when Schmidt, who was claiming great success in his insurance sales and boasting of money given him by NIC, added a request that his friends send him $25 a month expense money.

Schmidt's elaborate "take-over" activities did not keep him from the typewriter for very long, his only link with the true nucleus of his army. When he was not writing long missives to Larry Jones or Bernie Weissman, or shorter notes to "light a fire" under each member, he drew up complex organizational stemmata, estimating funds, marshaling the future legions, endlessly jingling down chains of command from his high perch. In fact, this is what he was best at. He divided and subdivided nonexistent armies: CUSA trifurcated into the Political Analysis Division, the Recruitment and Fund Solicitation Division (this was his favorite), and the Foreign Affairs Division. AMBUS had to settle for two parts, the Business

Management Division and the Public Relations Division. The country was parceled into six regions, each with a major city for its headquarters (all responsible, of course, to Dallas). Mr. Schmidt could not omit any of these far-flung details, since he was at the time the only member of CUSA residing in America. There were no subordinates to take care of minor matters for him. Besides, he liked articulating his Frankenstein all the way out to its toe-bone-connected-to-the-foot-bone. And when he tired of his responsibilities as leader of CUSA, he could tinkertoy AMBUS all the way up to his apartment ceiling: "Ambus will be a holding corporation for the following four corporations — Images, Inc.; Services, Inc.; Investment, Inc.; and Timesaver, Inc. . . ."

He composed a ten-page "Introduction to Conservatism, USA" for the use of new members. This included a "Code of Conduct" descending to minutest points of dress and etiquette. He urges his followers to avoid sartorial flashiness, boyish exuberance, and anything that will make a member look like a "nut." They must walk "in a straight manner" and take steps "deliberately." They must shake hands each time they meet, no matter how recently they have seen each other. They must *never* blow kisses at people in a public establishment. Though a demanding leader, Mr. Schmidt did not want to become puritanical: "If a young man must sow wild oats, let him do it discreetly, and not brag of his conquests or of his lust in public or to friends . . . If at times, our burdens seem great and we have a desire to 'throw a good one' and get plastered, do it in private, not in public."

His typing goes on and on, an exercise in self-hypnosis, faster and faster (too fast to pause for the shift lever — Damn the capitals, full speed ahead!). The ghostly armies form, march, fight, win, all at his command. Heels click, cash registers ring whenever he starts typing; he cannot stop, or those jingling sounds in his own mind might fade. What if the Supreme Leader should give in himself, succumb to doubt? So what if the start is small? The founders are great men, able to rely on one another, ready to come to a brother's need, and never deserting.

Even as he wrote it, the desertions were beginning. Meetings back in Munich were now attended by three men. There was bickering; the vision had faded; Larrie was not there to fan the coals. Schmidt heard of this and ordered purges. When the purged ignore him, he arranges a putsch — Larry out, Bernie in. He warned them they could all be replaced by other "bright, aggressive, ambitious and unscrupulous young men." He is sending them more organizational charts. He is getting desperate. The whole group is falling apart without him to inspire them. Who knows, they might not even be stepping deliberately. Perhaps even blowing kisses!

The new OB leader was even more rebellious than the first one. Bernie had refused to become a Christian or change his name. He didn't read the Ayn Rand books assigned him. He was skeptical of financial claims made by "Precusa" (President of CUSA). He aimed at a modest operation in Munich: "These men, you know who they are, are basically cowards, who were attracted not so much because of their personal politics, but more because of your personal persuasion. You momentarily convinced them, and yourself, that they were some sort of 'Supermen.' " Schmidt should dismiss Bernie. But what would be left he if he did?

He turns his eyes, perforce, from the OB to the SB. Nothing has come, yet, of the "merger" with NIC. He decides to infiltrate another organization, Young Americans for Freedom. He attends a meeting of right-wingers at the home of Dr. Robert Morris, finding there a "Clyde Moore . . . former PR man for T. L. Hunt [*he is getting colder*], multi-millionaire oilman," and lectures those assembled on their duties. The decision is made to absorb YAF, and Larrie writes ecstatically to Munich. As usual, he outlined the salaries future officers of his YAF branch would receive. And, as usual, he ended with a request for money, sixty dollars from each follower, to put them among the branch's Founding Fifty.

But his letters were no longer being answered. Members of the original group, their tour of duty finished, were quietly returning to the States, getting jobs, and steering carefully around Dallas. Larrie yearned for them, however, pursued them by telephone and mail, said they would have good jobs in Dallas, promised great things in the offing. Finally, one man joined him, Larry Jones. Schmidt has convinced him that they can move into the private club business, and suggests they start by getting Arthur Murray dance instructors to act as club "hostesses." Meanwhile, he has met Warren Carroll, a scriptwriter for the radio shows of "H. L. Hunt" (at last! he has it right). He begs Bernie to get in on a good thing, to come right away—plans are already being made for the big events of the right-wing season: Adlai Stevenson's visit, and President Kennedy's.

Bernie stayed in New York, impervious; unmoved by the lavish promises he does not believe. Schmidt must produce some tangible results if he means to stir the old faith of his followers. Just then, the "US Day" speech of General Walker gave Schmidt a "victory" he could lay claim to, rally his army to. He takes credit for the violent reception Stevenson was given. The movement is now prominent, thanks to the demonstration he organized. *Now* will they join him? The letter arrives opportunely. Bill Burley has come up from Baltimore to help Bernie welcome their old friend from Germany, Elsa Silbernagel, who is immigrating to America. Both young men are restless, not readjusting to civilian life, having marital problems, not happy with their jobs. At least Larrie is accomplishing *some*thing — which is more than they are doing. On November 2, Bernie and Bill and Elsa began the long trip to Dallas, Bernie driving his '57 Ford. It took them two days.

As Bernie half expected, the talk about jobs, about owning clubs, was all exaggerated. He and Bill had to answer the want ads; they became carpet salesmen, with only the one car between them. "This was one of the big disappointments. We had been promised by Larrie we wouldn't have any trouble making a living, that he had jobs and everything set up for us. That is one of the reasons I chucked my job in New York. I figured we would be able to survive down there. We got to the DuCharme Club, after a day or two, and it was a miserable hole in the wall that you could not really do anything with." It was the same with the Lavender Lounge, Larrie's only other "big possibility."

The grand talk of infiltration and influence was just as empty: "And the only thing I ever heard from Larrie about his brother was good: and when he mentioned that his brother had joined the Walker organization, I figured this is another step in the right direction. . . . So when I got to Dallas, I found that Larrie's brother . . . didn't have any sense at all. He was very happy with $35 a week and room and board that General Walker was giving him as his chauffeur and general aide. And so I tossed that out the window that we would never get into the Walker organization this way."

Schmidt had even taken false credit for the Stevenson coup: "Larrie led me to believe that he had organized the whole thing. And it transpired when I got to Dallas that I found that he had led a group of eleven University of Dallas students in quiet picketing near the entrance to the auditorium, and didn't engage in any physical violence of any sort." What a letdown!

Bernie and Bill could not make a single carpet sale. Bernie was living on the two hundred dollars he brought with him from his job in New York, husbanding gas for calls on prospective customers, extending negotiations with the DuCharme Club and the Lavender Lounge just so he and Bill can stop by for free beers. The "infiltrations" seemed a foolish game. Nothing at all had come of the NIC or YAF or Walker or Hunt connections. The notoriety that pleased Schmidt after the Stevenson incident also led to threats on his life and made him have second thoughts about fame. One connection still held promise — the only one that seemed willing to back words with cash — their connection with Joe Grinnan, an official of the John Birch Society.

Conservative forces in Dallas had planned two big fall demonstrations — one for Stevenson's visit, one for Kennedy's. But the Stevenson outbreak had them frightened. If a Kennedy protest was undertaken and violence occurred, the sponsoring groups would be vilified. On the other hand, if no protest at all were made, the zealots would grow restless (and tightfisted) with their spokesmen. Perhaps an amateur would steal the thunder of professional right-wing groups. It was a tightrope situation. What, though, if the professionals used their power — i.e., their money — to back the amateurs? If anything untoward happened, the John Birch Society would not have its name on the offensive material. But if it came off, they could take credit for arranging and financing the protest.

About a week after Bernie and Bill arrived in Dallas, Larrie came to them and said Joe Grinnan would get the money — about fifteen hundred dollars — for a full-page ad in the *Morning News* if CUSA would draw it up and sign it. They debated the matter, decided they must go along if they were to keep channels open for further money from this source. (The great infiltrators and conned "con men" are that easily turned into cat's-paws.) They do not want to use CUSA's name, so they decide to make up an "ad hoc" committee title, The American Fact-Finding Committee. Schmidt will not sign the ad; he has been stung by the publicity he courted; too many know where he lives, and one of those who sent him a threatening letter might act on it after this new provocation. Besides, he wheedles Bernie, Grinnan would like to have a Jewish name on the ad, to prove Conservatives are not anti-Semitic.

Bernie knows all about this game, as he knew the other one: first they wanted him to change his name, now they want to exploit it. But he is sure that he and Bill must go *around* Larrie to the Dallas men with money. He calculates the risk, and takes it: "We felt if this guy got any stronger, he would be able to move us out, or control us." Plot and counterplot, the CUSA "brotherhood." "So when the idea for the ad came up I said, 'Okay, I will put my name to it,' because I felt any recognition that came would then be in my favor, and if we took advantage of this, and because these organizations would have to back me personally as representing them, I could then denounce the anti-Semitism, the anti-Catholic, anti-Negro, and they would have to back me up, or else I would just tell the whole story about this thing."

On November 14, Larrie and Bernie and Bill pore over a list of questions aimed at embarrassing the Kennedy Administration (Larrie has extracted it from his growing file of right-wing pamphlets and manifestos). They carefully choose ten of the questions. Bernie makes up an original one of his own. When they show the list to Grinnan, he insists on the addition of another one (no question, no money). They are ready. On November 18 Bernie takes the ad to the paper. The advertising department says it will check with its legal staff; next day, agrees to run the thing. When Bernie goes to pick up money on the 20th Grinnan says he has collected only a thousand dollars so far, but he will have the rest tomorrow. Bernie relays that message (and the money) to the paper, and on the following day completes the transaction with $463 that Grinnan gives him. That is the eve of Kennedy's visit.

Another of the Munich gang, Ken Glazbrook, is coming in for the weekend, on his way across country; he will arrive just in time for the fireworks, late Friday afternoon. CUSA is on the brink of something big. Bernie and Bill go to a sales meeting at the carpet firm Friday morning — he is already being asked if he is *the* Bernard Weissman of that morning's paper. When the two finally get away for lunch, they turn on the car radio, and find out.

They were supposed to meet Grinnan and Schmidt at the DuCharme Club, to analyze response to the ad, but Grinnan does not show up. "He had heard this thing and took off. I guess he wanted to hide or something." Larrie is waiting outside the bar; they move to another one, strange territory, not wanting to be traced. Larric thinks they should scuttle underground. He is afraid to go back to his apartment. Stanley Marcus, they all agree, will use the assassination to crush the right wing: "They had us on the run and they were going to keep it that way."

When the news came out that Oswald was a Marxist, Bernie felt relieved, but not much. If the Left would kill a Kennedy, what would they do to a man who soared far off to the right of Kennedy, who proclaimed this in an ad? He lurked in his apartment, afraid to go out. Luckily, he had only been there two weeks; he was not in the phone book, not in the city directory. (Ruby knows; he has checked both of them.)

By Sunday Bernie has worked up nerve to look in the post office box he took out in the Fact-Finding Committee's name. Ken Glazbrook, who had arrived late Friday to join their obscurity and gloom, not their moment of triumph, accompanied him into the post office; Bill kept the Ford ready outside. The box was stuffed — had already been stuffed a morning before this, when Ruby looked into it. As Bernie took the mail, a Stetsoned man moved toward him. Ken gave the alert, and both men ran to the car. They watched the cowboy hat dwindle — a welcome omen. Three days later, all three men left Dallas, happy to be gone. All the letters postmarked after the assassination were hostile — some of them anti-Semitic. Ruby was right. Weissman's name was being used against the Jews.

This is the man Jack Ruby hunted that breathless Friday and Saturday, heaving at the rock under which, he was sure, verminous plotters were wriggling — Bernard Weissman; a schemer indeed, a conqueror of the world, lieutenant to "Precusa" himself; a patriot who came to Dallas to make quick money and fame by playing up to the establishment, by promotion and "contacts," by his deliberate step, his class, by buying clubs, by myriad small business endeavors ("Images, Inc."). Everything had backfired. He was hunted now, hunted for the name he would not change — and by a man who had changed his. Both men wanted to show conservative Dallas that Jews are "all right."

"CUSA" — black coat and briefcase and "class"; special men with a gift for advertisement, self-advertisement in particular; men born, they believe, for wheeler-dealer fast-buck lives, for adroit houdini-ing of "image" money. And where use these skills but in Dallas? Here was the plot Ruby was trying to uncover, Ruby the slayer of punks.

What is there about Jack Ruby that makes him stalk others, and be stalked himself, in what seems a house of mirrors where men flit from ambush to ambush upon themselves?

ii

Ruby was not the only one who was out on the Dallas streets playing detective after midnight on November 23. About the time Jack reached City Hall, climbed to the third floor ("Already I was with the deal"), Bill Alexander was coming down, pursuing a lead of his own, something that had been on his mind ever since he searched Oswald's room and found the Communist material: "I got busy with another deal. There was a Mexican fellah who had contacts with Communist friends and organizations; I knew about him from a murder case back in 1956. So we got a search warrant and went out to his house about two o'clock in the morning. We had called ahead, they were waiting for us; they did not demand we use the warrant, but invited us in. We shook the place down for about two hours, but it was just one of those cold trails that look so hot at the time — this fellah worked at the School Book Depository."

Alexander went to bed near dawn — like Ruby, for once. But Jack still could not rest. When he left KLIF, around four in the morning, he was determined to trace Weissman by his box number. It is in the ad, in his car (he took Eva's copy of the paper, too): Box 1792. Then he remembers seeing another box number, on something unpatriotic — he thought of sending it to Washington along with the "Life Line" stuff. It is on a sign in downtown Dallas, meant to be seen from the North Central Expressway: Impeach Earl Warren. Jack drives over that way, fishes an envelope up into the dim light, copies the box number. It is 1757, not the same as Weissman's after all. Still, the numbers are too close for coincidence! (This is the battle cry of conspiratorialists, who mock "the coincidence view of history.") Besides, aren't these Revolutionary dates? The spirit of seventeen something or other? He was on to *something;* he had two clues, and they were converging.

Well, he had one clue, the ad. He did not actually have the sign, he could not carry it with him — unless he had a *picture* of it. He turns his dragonflying car back to the west, toward Oak Cliff. Wake George, he'll be a witness as Jack collects the evidence (You observe the box numbers, Dr. Watson?). Call Larry at the club; he'll load the Polaroid. It is Jack's camera, used to photograph men on the stage with a stripper; but he never learned to load the pack, and it will be running out of film.

Dawn is coming, but there is no time to lose — bring the flash bulbs. The three men photograph the sign, three times. Jack copies name and address of the Massachusetts sponsor of the ad, and mutters importantly to George, "This is the work of the John Birch Society or the Communist Party or maybe a combination of both." Then Holmes and his two Watsons drive to the post office, check both boxes to see if there is any connection. The Weissman box is full of letters. Jack rings for the night clerk, asks what addresses were given for each box. The clerk cannot give out this information.

Even *Jack's* mental Geiger counter is running down now — he buys George and Larry breakfast — but it still beeps slowly in the presence of so many clues. 1792. 1757. Turn the numbers around a bit; two looks like seven. A code? Symbols: black border. Welcome Mr. President (no title, not Honorable or anything). Impeach Earl Warren (no title — come to think of it, just what *is* his title?). Spirit of seventeen something. Communists? Birchers? "Weissmans"? At any rate, not patriots. Not like Jack, the Jewish patriot, Jack says to himself, consoling himself, as he lapses, finally, into sleep.

For two hours. He told Larry, when he dropped him off at the club for the second time this morning, he would not be able to sleep (too many clues to ponder); told him they would have to buy dog food in the morning. Larry calls at eight to find out what kind of dog food. Half awake, Mr. Ruby (*pace* his trial lawyers) "uses profanity" — so energetically, in fact, that Larry, weary and disgusted after that camera hunt by moonlight, decides to move on again.

Like everyone else even half awake that morning, Jack gravitates toward television, gets initiated once more into darkness; it *did* happen. Long twilit morning struggle back to life. Shower, hair workout, and dress. Eva described her brother this way: "He is a very slow dresser. Anybody that probably can get dressed like in the Army, how they ever tolerated him, because it is hustle bustle, eager beaver — it could take him three hours to shave and dress, the way he wants to look like, because he stops and makes a phone call, but he was very slow." The television has picked up services from Central Synagogue in New York, the memorial address of Rabbi Seligson: "He had faced dangerous challenges before, in war and in peace; but they were dangers in which a man of courage had a fighting chance. What happened to him yesterday — this bloody, dastardly act — was so insane, so unimaginably vile, that it is hard to grasp." Jack listens, in tears.

Fully awake at last, Jack starts after noon toward The Carousel; but he is drawn today, as he will be tomorrow, to "the wreaths" in Dealey Plaza, where (this time) he parks and asks

Officer Jim Chaney which window Oswald shot from. Wes Wise is over in a sound truck for KLRD — a fellow newsman. Wes covers the prize fights, and Jack always saw him there. He knocks on the window, asks how the reports are going. Wes describes the presents he saw, at the Trade Mart, intended for the Kennedy children — two Western saddles. He congratulates Jack on his work for KLIF last night. (He heard it!) Jack is not partial, though. Even though Wes works for a rival station, he will give *him* a scoop, too — see those men over there looking at the wreaths? Yes. Well, they are Captain Fritz and Curry. Wes breaks out his camera; Jack joins him, uses the last plate in his Polaroid camera, left in the car last night (Larry did not have to change the film after all, and there is one shot left).

Which reminds Jack: he left the three pictures at his apartment! He must drive back for them. Back there, he decides to call McLendon, give him a scoop on those box numbers; he has misplaced Gordon's own number now. Luckily, he still has the station's "hot line" number from last night. Maybe they'll give him Gordon's unlisted phone. But no luck. Ken Dowe answers, another disk jockey pressed into news service — a newcomer who does not know Gordon's number. "Well, this is Jack Ruby. I'm a friend of Gordon's, I'll find the number."

At last, to the club. But a new idea strikes him on the way to it — he does not even go up and unlock the door to his own phone, but asks to use the one in the parking lot office. As he dials, he tells the lot manager, standing right beside him in the office, that he is acting as a reporter today. That is why he is calling — KLIF, Ken Dowe answers again. Jack explains that he got some pictures for Wes Wise down at the wreaths, but he also took one himself. He could get other things for them too, as he did yesterday. There were crowds down at the wreaths, and this might hold up the time of Oswald's transfer. Does Ken know anything on that? No? Well, perhaps Jack can find out for them, from Henry. Henry Wade, the man I got for you last night. And, whatever happens, "you know I'll be there." Yes. "Would you like me to cover it, because I am a pretty good friend of Henry Wade's, and I believe I can get some news stories." (And *give* Henry some — those box numbers.) Good.

Dowe puts the phone aside and turns on the studio intercom. Does anyone on the news staff know a Jack Ruby? "Of course." Can he be any help in gathering information? "Sure, he knows everybody in town, and may be able to help us." Ken tells Jack they will appreciate anything he can do for them. The reporter is redeputized.

Jack puts back the receiver, asks the parking man, named Hallmark, if Abe is closed yet. Hallmark does not know. "Well, they won't have the nerve to stay open after they see my ad." Jack strides off past Abe's, but soon returns; hesitates, outside the office, anxious to let Hallmark in on past and impending scoops, but decides he has too much to do. Back in the car — Henry is more likely to be at the Courthouse than at City Hall. But he is not at either place, not, at any rate, where Jack can reach him. Well, that can wait.

He drops in at Sol's (the Turf Bar). Frank Bellochio, a competitor of Milt Joseph's in the jewelry business, is at the bar, deeply depressed. He has the Weissman ad with him, he clipped it out; he is outraged at the thing, and saying so to anyone who will listen. Just then Jack shoves in between Frank and Speedy Johnson: "Jesus Christ, I have just been down to the Dallas *Morning News* and there is no such bastard [as Weissman]." Jack looked for his name in the telephone book just before he went to bed this morning. Besides, Jack can show them a link with something as bad as the ad. He produces his pictures; Bellochio, his feelings about Dallas confirmed and deepened, takes the Polaroid shots around to others in the bar. But just as he is hitting his stride, denouncing a city that accepts such things as normal, Jack takes his breath away with a sudden attack: "You've made a good living in Dallas; it gave you everything. Why turn on it now?" Bellochio cannot follow this AC-DC indignation; he does not understand that Jack is working *for* Dallas — for Henry Wade, Bill Alexander, Gordon McLendon. Weissman is not Dallas. Frank himself, and Jack, are Dallas. They are not guilty of what Weissman did — if there is such a man.

If. Stanley would know. Jack has been trying to reach Stanley Kaufman, a lawyer friend who helped him with his tax problems. Stanley is a member of the B'nai B'rith, he knows all the Jewish community. What of this Weissman? Does he exist; and, if so, where can Jack reach him? It is not a new question for Mr. Kaufman. Friday morning, before the President's death, he was speaking to the Jewish Welfare Federation, and many people asked him who would sign such an ad.

But now, Saturday afternoon, Kaufman still has not found out, and cannot help Jack. Has he looked in the phone book? Yes. Why not go to the library and check the city directory? Good idea. Jack tells him he is tracing the clues — the black border, the ad's box number, the Warren sign. The Jews of Dallas need not worry; Jack is defending them.

He is, all afternoon, "a-churnin' " Dallas streets as usual; only more so. Early in the evening, he cannot go to the closed unlit club, it would depress him to see it empty and profitless. He goes back, instead, to Eva's apartment, paces out his bitterness talking to her — Oswald the creep ("the Commie," Eva adds), Weissman the traitor. "I bet Weissman is a Communist," he tells her. She agrees: "He is a Commie straight with Oswald." A Commie, and probably a Bircher too. All the unpatriotic things. After all, there is that clear link with the Earl Warren sign.

There is a loose end to this problem, though, which he must tie up without embarrassing himself. Just to be sure. He does not want to ask someone like Gordon McLendon, but it must be a man who knows.

How about Russ Knight? For all his weird whiskerage, Russ is a knowledgeable radio personality — just the man: Jack calls, pulls one string tight in his cat's-cradling conspiratorial theory: "Say Russ, just who is Earl Warren?"

Eased of this uncertainty, he collapses for a nap on Eva's

bed. He does not even pull down the spread (a new one, it cost over twenty dollars). "There is a big oil spot from his head," Eva remembers, "and I was going to give him hell on Sunday."

Jack Ruby, amateur cop, has had many imitators in the years since he killed Oswald. They pursue him as imaginatively as he hunted Bernard Weissman. He would recognize the type. Police buffs, who like to give information. Some even seem his Doppelgängers — a woman, for instance, who has been arrested for carrying a gun, who likes to help out cops, who has lived in the seamy club world yet strives for class. She boasts of all the important people she knows; she became as persistent in her efforts to help the Warren Commission as Jack was to help Henry Wade. Her name changes frequently, but its most stable element is Nancy. We will call her that.

On June 1, 1964, an F.B.I. agent took Nancy a plane ticket, paid for by the Commission, and drove her out to Logan Airport. The man saw a thirtyish woman, very nervous, with obtrusive facial tics, quick in her speech, articulate despite a minor lisp, and full of information — on the family of Prince Faisal of Saudi Arabia (for which she served as interpreter, since she speaks five languages, including two dialects of Arabic), on the civil rights movement (she is prominent in CORE), on her lifelong career as an undercover agent for various district attorneys and the F.B.I., on counterfeit cases she has cracked, on the difficulty she is having as a housewife (after her exciting days underground), on her first husband (a writer) and her present one (too old for her).

Next day, testifying in Washington, she revealed an even more extensive range of accomplishments. She was trained to be an IBM operator; she is a writer who has published under a pen name. As an advertising executive, she just "ran" a recent convention. She was almost hired as a boat hand, to run guns into Cuba, because of her extensive acquaintance with lobster boats. Everything else paled, however, by comparison with her few brief months in Dallas, when she worked for Jack Ruby as a bartender; was fired; became a prostitute; joined a group that would bring exiles out of Cuba; attended three meetings, at one of which (the second one) Jack Ruby arrived, said "Hi" to several people but went directly to a back room, then came out disencumbered of something that bulged his jacket, and silently left. At this meeting, Nancy found out the Cuban adventure was pro-Castro, and she was too patriotic to go further in the plot; she only went to a third meeting to get information for the authorities (she is, after all, a trained undercover agent of the F.B.I.). But when she recognized Vito Genovese's son at this third meeting (not from anything said there, but because she had once seen a picture — not of Vito's son, it is true, but of Vito himself), she became so frightened for her personal safety that she and her husband fled Dallas and said nothing more — until Ruby killed Oswald. Once she did speak out, she was followed by suspicious cars (but perhaps that was for breaking up an abortion ring) and received threatening phone calls meant to deter her from testifying.

The Warren Commission reprints this fascinating testimony (baroquely figured over with subsidiary plots and police work Nancy has been prominent in), but the Report of conclusions reached by the Commission omits all mention of Nancy. Mr. Mark Lane finds this a proof of the Commission's remissness, and tries to mend the error (or worse) by devoting a whole chapter of his book to the rich leads furnished by this single witness.

That makes all the more striking Mr. Lane's own remissness. He does not mention several stories just as interesting as Nancy's, and intimately connected with hers.

Take the Oakland phone call. It came to the California office of the F.B.I. a mere three days after Ruby killed Oswald. A girl known as "Julie" had information about Ruby. Could she bring it in to them? She arrived five minutes after the phone was put down. Her story was important. Agents went over it several times, at her home and in their offices, during the next week.

This woman had been a "lobbyist" in New Hampshire, playing "hostess" to legislators who might vote in favor of various liquor firms. She knew J. D. Tippit; she too had worked for Ruby, and attended meetings of a group meant to run guns into Cuba and exiles out. But Ruby attended more than one of the meetings she was at; he even made an impassioned pro-Castro speech, pounding the table and getting red in the face. Mr. Lane, for some reason, does not mention this important story, though it was told immediately after the events of 1963.

Perhaps he does not do so because this witness's testimony has so many internal contradictions. At one session, she told agents she had been to four meetings (Ruby present at three); at another, it was three (Ruby present at two). In one and the same interview, she said that she had fought with Ruby, and quit working for him, before any of the meetings took place — only to add that she was fired between the second and third meetings because Ruby caught her looking through the keyhole of his office while he talked to a Chicago hood named Nick. But such contradictions must not trouble Lane. Nancy herself gave, in her Washington testimony, two entirely different reasons for her departure from Ruby's employ — first, he decided he did not need a bartender (a strange decision for one running a champagne club); then, when he decided that he *did* want one, she returned (in a matter of a week or so) and got fired because she did not keep the glasses clean enough.

Perhaps Mr. Lane does not rely on the Oakland witness because her polygraph test (taken December 5, 1963) indicated to the operator that she was lying — though the test could not yield clear-cut results because the witness suffered from chorea (St. Vitus's dance) and low blood pressure, and took several drugs for these ailments, and had a history of psychiatric disturbance (attempted suicide, commitment to a state hospital's psychiatric ward). Nonetheless, this story is so relevant to Nancy's that it deserved some mention in his chapter. As a matter of fact, this witness resembles Nancy in many ways. She,

too, knows important people — Jacqueline Kennedy, for instance, and Teddy Kennedy (with whom she danced at Harvard).

Nor is that the end of such witnesses. The Oakland caller did
not know anything about the route of the rifles her group
meant to smuggle into Cuba. An important link was added to
the story when a witness called from Boston, early in 1964, to
report that *she* had attended pro-Castro meetings at which
Jack Ruby showed up; and *this* witness knew where the rifles
were to be gathered — in Guadalajara. Furthermore, this witness had also seen Vito Genovese — well, no; she guessed,
after all, it was only his son. Not at the Cuban meeting, however, like Nancy. *She* saw Genovese *fils* at The Carousel Club
talking to Jack Ruby. This witness, too, knows important people — including a prominent politician who is about to get her
pardoned from a prostitution charge.

Amazingly, Mr. Lane is mum on this corroborative witness
linking Jack Ruby with Cuba — absolutely mum, even though
she added vital information not supplied by the other two.
Well, not so amazingly: he *must* neglect these stories (close as
they seem to the version he places so much reliance on) — because they were all told by the same girl. What would be
corroborative coming from three different witnesses is destruc-
tive of all credibility when the same girl rushes forward with
tales so disparate.

Nancy, in whichever of her many guises, is an unfortunate
young woman — one who left high school to get married at
seventeen, had a child (whose whereabouts she no longer
knows), was divorced at nineteen, attempted suicide at
twenty; married again, but saw her husband only in intervals of
his psychiatric care, and separated after eight months; at
twenty-three, got a Mexican divorce and married her "first"
husband of the Logan Airport conversation — a "writer" who
also had a history of psychiatric treatment and who killed himself, with arsenic, in 1962. This man had as colorful a mind as

Nancy's own. He told her he had been a mercenary on both sides of the Spanish Civil War, piloting a boat that ran guns to the armies — all at the age of sixteen. He knew many prominent gangsters. This is the husband Nancy somehow lost track of in Boston, though he left a note saying he would be in Dallas (he was not). Nancy called the police to see if he was there; then came to Dallas, though he was not there. Guess who answered her phone call? J. D. Tippit. When she came to Dallas, she went straight to the police station. Guess who was the first man she saw behind the desk? Good old J. D. Nancy's stories preserve an admirable economy; most of the cast is known from other contexts. In a space of three or four or five months, she works for three or four clubs, including two months at The Carousel. From Dallas, she and her husband (retrieved, at some point, from South Bend, where he has been living, Nancy tells us, "with my secretary") move to New Orleans, where the writer dies. Nancy, alone again at twenty-six (except for four children scattered somewhere), goes to California and, by her own account, helps various district attorneys solve crimes, using the name Julie Ann Cody. She marries a fourth time in 1964, a fifth time in 1966.

Mr. Lane's Nancy is, by comparison with the real one, a very sedate creature. He tells us only this about her background (in such a way that any irregularity actually contributes to her credibility): she "frankly told Commission counsel that for two years she had led a disturbed and unsound life." (Two!) With a great sense of decorum, he clears her tale of messy inconsistencies (she jumps back and forth between 1961 and 1962 for the time when she was in Dallas — Mr. Lane sticks to one year, the wrong one, 1962) and unartistic extravagances (J. D. is a little too much for anyone to swallow, so he simply disappears from Lane's account — though he is surely "relevant" by standards Lane uses elsewhere; he loves to arrange meetings between principals in the assassination).

A discreet veil is drawn across Vito Genovese's son and

Nancy's strange way of recognizing him. It sounds much better this way: "At the third meeting a person was present whom [Nancy] thought she recognized as someone associated with syndicated crime." Nothing wild about that is there? Lane neglects not only Nancy's earlier sworn statements, and multiple depositions, and phone calls, and polygraph test. He omits the background to her story supplied in the Washington testimony itself. Although she claims she worked as a bartender not only at The Carousel but also at Barney's Theatre Lounge, none of the dancers, musicians, or waitresses we talked to knew her under any of her several names — or even remembered a woman bartender at The Carousel. Nancy's account of her work at The Carousel is ludicrously vague or inexact. Asked what time she went to work every day for two months, she said it was at three — or four — or five — or six — or seven. (Safe enough.) She always calls Ruby "Mr. Ruby" (we never heard an employee call him anything but "Jack") and claims he regularly wore a shoulder holster (he did not). She remembers none of her addresses in Dallas; she never heard of Ralph Paul; at first she does not recognize Andrew Armstrong's name, then vaguely recalls him as her helper at the bar — "You don't notice people like that" (Andrew never heard of her or worked for Jack other than as bartender himself). Her chronology fluctuates wildly from sentence to sentence, marriages and divorces and childbirths slipping forward or backward on the scale of years. None of the references she gave called her reliable. The lawyer she called a personal friend described her as "an habitual liar." Police agencies to which she applied as a paid informer never used her more than once, and said they could not trust her — she had a habit of solving nonexistent crimes committed by all the famous gangsters.

Poor Nancy, the Pasionaria of some Warren critics, would hardly deserve mention were it not for Mr. Lane's deft presentation of her as a dire threat to Commission findings. Mr. Lane told us he was very impressed with her and placed great reliance on her memory — something she must have sensed, for she revealed to him that the apartment at which the Cuba meetings took place had an ammunition depot, "probably half a dozen land mines, and, why, twenty or thirty packing cases of hand grenades." Why did she omit this in her Warren testimony? She did not leave it out — Mr. Griffin told the reporter to strike it from the record. (Her deposition ends with the question, "Is it not a fact that all that has occurred between you and me in this interview, with Mr. Griffin, is on the record?" To which Nancy answered, "That is correct.")

We tried to talk to Nancy, but her present husband pleaded with us not to do so: "There's a couple of kids involved here." (We respected his wish; that is why we do not use her present name.) But what does he think of his wife's interview with Mark Lane? "Well, I talked to Lane, and I asked him at the time of the interview what he thought of it, and he told me he didn't see how he could use any of it. Then that book comes out." He added that the Warren Commission judged her story better than Mr. Lane did: "She is very nervous and imaginative. Things build up pretty easy like."

Nancy, so anxious to please the cops, so easily used by others, wanting fame and being maneuvered into notoriety, an instrument, now, for attacking Ruby — she reminds us of Sheriff Decker's words: "I've got two hundred men in that jail; and there's probably another Jack Ruby among them — one who would take a crack at him to be a hero." It is even more depressing to reflect that there are men ready to prod on and exploit this drab endless series of displaced people who can be duped onto the stage of history.

...
iii

Ruby's prison theories developed naturally from his first suspicions about Weissman. He thought Weissman was implicated, knowingly or unknowingly, in an unpatriotic act meant to harm the Jews. But then a more useful scapegoat blundered into their hands. *Jack* lurched onto the assassination scene. If they could connect him with the supremely unpatriotic act, with killing the President, they would go far beyond their original plan — not only discrediting Jews, now, but moving on to their extermination.

The purge was already under way. Quietly, at first. When Emmett Colvin came to visit Ruby while preparing the appeal brief, Jack could not be kept to that subject. He pulled cards and papers out of his coverall pocket, flipped through them, gave him a slip of paper with telephone numbers on it — looked the numbers over, scribbled some others down from memory, and said: "Call these people — you won't get any answer." Though some were long distance numbers, Colvin felt obliged, that first time, to place the calls. The first time. After that he mumbled *mmn-hmn*, like everyone else, and forgot about the numbers. It was a routine all his guards and lawyers knew: "Call Earl — you'll find out he's dead." The purge was beginning with the other Rubensteins, his family first.

When Clayton Fowler came to jail, Jack took his long yellow pad and scribbled: "Johnson is behind them all the way." Earlier, in the Warren interview, Ruby said Johnson could still be warned, though perhaps they had reached him. But as the plot mushroomed in Jack's sunless mind, all hope of snatching Johnson from its clutches vanished. A plot this size could not go forward without the aid of "our beloved President." He has traveled the circular conspiracy route: the plot is invisible because so vast, the plotters so skilled at camouflage; and it could not be this well hidden unless it were protected by authority; so the very unobviousness of it shows how established it is, omnipresent. The less evidence there is for it, the more it is to be feared.

Then see how it all fits! Who gained most from Kennedy's death? Why, President Johnson, of course. He had to be in it from the start. Jack's note to Jim Martin says:

This country has been overthrown by the Nazi's. Johnson is a Nazi, the worst sort, that is why they won't let anyone come talk to me. They know that I know too much and don't want me to talk to anyone.

The lawyers tried to argue with him. When the Warren Report came out, Fowler told him: "See, Jack? They don't say you killed the President." But everything is equally interpretable to the conspiratorialist, for whom there *cannot* be contradictory evidence: Jack nodded his head sadly and told him this was a ruse to lull his people into confidence. Abe Fortas and Arthur Goldberg are being used for the same reason:

Johnson appointed these Jews to high office, to show he is not prejudiced, and so people will not suspect him for what he really is. Later one [sic], everything I'm telling you will out [sic] the truth.

Johnson is lulling Israel with false gestures of alliance. His plot rolls on, unchecked. Only a few people know the real truth — among them, Jack. There is a double meaning to everything Johnson says and does in public. The code name of the conspiracy is "The Great Society."

At his habeas corpus proceeding, Jack told Judge Davidson: "Well, I am sorry to say this. It is strange that a person like

Harvey Oswald, who never worked a day in his life (and I have reason to think of these things because I know all the things that are going on), a man who has never worked in his life is able to secure a job in a bookstore weeks prior to the anticipated arrival of our beloved President. Who else could know that our President was coming to Dallas?" One note he scribbled held the awful truth: only Johnson could have known. On the way out of a public hearing, Jack said to a reporter who aimed a microphone at him, "If Adlai Stevenson had been Vice President, there would have been no assassination."

Jack was worshipful of authority — he felt that any successful plot must control the right officials. He thought the world was run, like Dallas, out of the offices of a kind of global Citizens Council. That was all right; the Citizens Council are good guys, they are for Dallas. President Kennedy was a good guy, too. He was all but all-powerful, and using that vast power for the good of the country. Who could kill *him* but a group that is *entirely* in control, and using its power for evil? The authoritarian (or his counterpart, the compulsive rebel obsessed with a suffocating Laius of power over him) is the born conspiratorialist. Life resists him; it is not tractable. And not by accident. Others are pulling the strings that make him a puppet ("I am the fall guy," Jack moaned). Malevolent dim enemies are manipulating him. For Jack, life had always been a matter of "contacts," of "who you know," of buttering up important people — *they* can do everything, punks can do nothing.

One of the first conspiracy theories to emerge after Ruby's own was produced by the John Birch Society. That society also worships authority, discipline, and patriotism. It feels that any setback America suffers must be the result of plan and cooperation. Authority cannot simply err, meet situations that admit of no perfect solution. It is more bearable to think authority has been diverted to evil ends than to suppose it is fallible, weak, living in darkness like the rest of us. The Birch theory — aired in the society's magazine early in 1964 — posits a struggle with men "phenomenally intelligent and unutterably evil."

The theory was hatched from an intricately learned mind, then tricked out with all that mind's polyglot skills. Even the man's name is a little verbal labyrinth — Revilo Oliver; run it backward ("palindrome" it), read it forward, it is all the same. And so with his theory. He also thinks the Warren Commission was meant to lull America into a false sense of security; he also sees the CIA as a tentacle of the worldwide plot. There is no such thing as coincidence in his planned meshing crushing world, the hideous tank about to roll him under. Like Jack, he hears the music of infernal spheres, the grind of all the plot's gears toward him.

No coincidence. Did Oswald buy a mail-order rifle? That was part of the plan to introduce gun legislation, to discredit Minute Men and leave Americans unarmed against the traitors in their midst. Was Kennedy killed in November, not December? — ah yes, to prevent the sordid revelations about to boil over: "the vast cess-pool in Washington was leaking badly. . . . There are rumors that an even more filthy scandal, involving both sadistic sexual perversions and the use of governmental powers for the importation and distribution of hallucinatory narcotics, is simmering dangerously near to the surface. . . . For aught I know to the contrary, the assassination of Kennedy may have been necessary as the only means of avoiding, or even long deferring, national scandals so flagrant as to shock the whole of our brainwashed and hypnotized populace back to sanity." The Conspiracy, being all-powerful and evil, *absorbs* every evil — from murder to sexual perversion to gun legislation.

Plurality of minor plots, perhaps; but *the* Conspiracy is single and exclusive, a jealous god: "I cannot believe that two wolves are peacefully munching one rabbit." Professor Oliver's world resembles Ruby's (whom he refers to as Jakob Rubenstein) in that it has a towering Olympus of divine authority somehow obnubilated by diabolic schemes, while, around the flanks of the mountain, vile punks and "characters" are creeping:

You can see fledgling Oswalds in the flesh whenever, as occasionally happens, a loyal American is permitted to speak on or near a college campus. The young "progressives" will be there to jeer and quibble. It will be instructive to observe how many are deformed in body as well as mind [*the plot absorbs all evil, even physical ailments*], and if you approach near enough, you can see the hatred glistening in beady eyes.

The Professor thinks Oswald looks just like Corky Crawford.

Like Jack, the Professor refers to his enemies as "degenerates" — though Jack could not deal easily in trisyllabic curses, as the Professor does when describing the internal wars of the Conspiracy: "The purulent blob of anti-human protoplasm called Nicolai Yezhov was blotted out and replaced by the equally loathsome thing called Lavrenti Beria" (later referred to as "the Beria-thing"). Jack, according to Dr. Guttmacher, refused to think of Oswald as a person rather than a thing. That is why he avoided using his name. Professor Oliver is as adept as Jack was at pyramiding fantasy to a skeletal culmination — Oliver's top man is a "necrophilic degenerate." The perfect reversal of the authoritarian's world — a punk, a "dee-jee," somehow sneaked to the *top* of the mountain (burrowing up through the middle, no doubt; decent folk would have kept him from rising up the slopes).

Once detectives of this sort get onto a favorite theory, they seem to take a melancholy satisfaction in the confirmation of its most gruesome details. Bad as things are, they at least show that the theory is right — which is a kind of victory for the human mind. Revilo Oliver found in the horrors of the assassination a proof that the Birch timetable of imminent takeover is confirmed: "We have come to the year of decision." That was 1964, but apocalyptists never seem to mind the uneventful passing of their favorite doomsdays: Mr. Lane predicted in

April of 1967 that James Garrison would have revealed the truth about the assassination "in four or five months." He promised: "It will be impossible when Garrison presents the evidence, it will be impossible to hide any longer."

Jack, in the same way, found confirmation in everything that seemed to refute him — in the very skepticism he met with. You wouldn't *expect* the plot to be visible, would you? How could it be successful if it were? It is like the earth — too big for men to see its shape. It is only powerful because it is hidden: "You wouldn't understand a thing this big," he used to tell guards and lawyers. And even Justice Warren: "Don't register with you, does it?" In the same way, Mark Lane finds confirmation for his theories in the very fact that political analysts he most admires do not agree with him: "I. F. Stone knows what it means if the Warren Report is a fraudulent document. It means that everything he has been writing about for years has been confirmed, and he can't stand that. He knows what that means we are in, and he can't face that possibility." Those who know most about our society realize what a monstrous Evil is oppressing us if hoaxes like the Warren Report can be perpetrated. Does this mean that Lane agrees with those on the left who would implicate President Johnson? No: "It's very nice, if you don't like President Johnson, to say he was involved in the assassination. But it's good also to look at the facts. And if the facts are presented, it's more shocking than that . . . and we'll know very quickly." It is the year of decision. ("Time is running out," Jack would tell those who came to him. He wrote to Jim Martin: "Don't ignore what I am saying, but if you wait a few days and I prove that I am right in what I'm telling you, then I'm no doubt right in everything else. . . . Jim, if find [*sic*] out what I say is true, that they are doing away with the Jews. Then I am right about a lot of things.")

Jack's certainty of disaster could not be shaken. Every brake-screech heard through the prison's soft walls, the grind of every floor-buffer danced along by trusties, became the cry of tortured Jews, the scream of power saws. Sawing men limb from limb in the Dallas jail, boiling them down, shipping them out by train in huge vats of melted human stuff. With an odd relish he seemed to dwell on the details: Jews dragged in and castrated (Jack tried to prove they have balls, so the Plot will make sure they have none). *Power* is still there, but power directed to the wrong ends. Still, even this is more imaginable, more to be lived with, mentally, than a world bereft of power, drifting senselessly, hacking at Jack Ruby by accident, not caring or knowing who he is.

Professor Oliver, too, is important; near the center. Dallas, in his view, is the hub of the assassination sequence because an important leader lives there, perhaps the most important in the world, General Walker. Oliver also finds a kind of relief in the idea that power is at work in the world, though perverted to the ends of torture: he describes "the numerous vermin that have been living for years in ill-concealed anticipation of the glorious day when they will be able to hack Americans to pieces and drag bodies through the streets." He forebodes "nice rubber-lined chambers, . . . in which the hated Americans could be scientifically tortured into 'confession,' and the remains of those who proved 'uncooperative' could be efficiently washed down the drains" — or boiled and carted off in trains.

Grisly, all of it; the guards thought Jack must be faking, he could not believe such horrors and be, for part of the time at least, so placid or even chipper (shrewd at cards, and cheating them). They did not understand; if authority is against him, at least it is *aware* of him, wary, on guard — from Bill Decker and Henry Wade all the way up to Earl Warren and Lyndon Johnson (and whatever vaster rulers move these lesser powers as their pawns). They are, you will notice, shipping the thousands of Jews all the way to the *Dallas jail* — and that takes money. No matter how widespread the web, Jack is at or near its center. In his way, the most important man in America.

Ruby's sense of importance, of odd comfort drawn from catastrophe, is not unique. Marguerite Oswald, for instance, seems to take a complacently proprietary attitude toward the case. She was on the verge of writing Her Book even before the assassination — a book on Lee Harvey's defection. But before she could get started, he returned. Now her role has grown in importance, and so has her impending Book. "After all," she told Jean Stafford, "I am responsible for two Presidents." She refers to Mrs. Kennedy, Mrs. Tippit, Marina, and herself as "four women in history." And her importance grows as The Plot spreads: "So were they all subversive and in a plot? Or were they all humanitarian and in a plot? The same people, though." Communists, or Birchers. Or both.

You find this preening of men under imagined showers of gore in the *frisson* with which conspiratorialists speculate on which one of them the Conspiracy must kill in order to maintain its secret. Revilo Oliver promises a crowd great revelations in his very next lecture — if the Communists have not killed him by then. And once the fantasy begins, it acquires garish subtleties — technicolor, as it were (sawn Jews, castration, boiling oil). Oliver, in *American Opinion,* imagines how, if the plot had been just a little more perfect in Dallas, "all the leading American patriots could have been dragged in chains to Washington. The 'Federal Marshals,' fresh from Alcatraz and the like, whom the juvenile Czar had used for his invasion of Mississippi, could have been counted on to beat some of them to death or murder them while 'trying to escape.' "

One of the conspiracy theorists is so frightened of the consequences of his work that his vast research on Dealey Plaza has all been done on a scale model. He has never seen the original, since that would involve entering Dallas, and They would never let him leave the scene alive. Others fear for Robert Kennedy, the next man on the assassins' schedule — though most reserve their solicitude and admiration for each other: Mark Lane told us, "Penn Jones [of the Midlothian *Mirror*] is a very brave man. . . . He lives right near Dallas, and he is conducting a very serious investigation, and it takes a brave man to do that."

Mort Sahl told us, in Mr. Lane's Palo Alto home, that he does not know how Mark has survived, after risking so many ventures into Dallas. "Mark Lane is the most important man in America," he assured us. Turning to Mr. Lane, we asked if he felt the same way. Not any longer, he admitted; though he was disturbed during his first visits to Dallas. It would not make sense to kill him now, after his book has already appeared. The man he worries about is New Orleans District Attorney Jim Garrison. Garrison first met Lane in the wine cellar of a New Orleans hotel, carrying a gun; but when Lane went to the D.A.'s home, he noticed there were no guards, and asked why. Here is Garrison's answer, as Lane repeated it on television: "You know who killed the President, what force is involved. What good is a guard out here? They killed the President when he was surrounded by the Secret Service, in the midst of the greatest security precautions in the history of this country. If they want to kill me, I cannot stop them. We know that." Mr. Lane's opinion of such a person? "Jim Garrison is the most important man in America." Mr. Garrison, for his part, thinks David Ferrie "was one of history's most important individuals."

iv

Ruby's guards all knew what to do when he put his ear to the wall and said: "Shhh! Do you hear? The screams! They are torturing the Jews again, down in the basement."

"O.K. Jack, cut the crap or we won't play cards with you anymore."

"Oh, you sonsabitches," Jack would say, and try to con them

out of some minor privilege. That made every guard, and some of Jack's own lawyers, think he was putting on an act.

There is one important episode that tends to confirm their view. During the polygraph test administered to Ruby, most of the questions were aimed at satisfying the Commission on his role in the assassination. But Dr. Beavers had been called in ("Bunny" Beavers, Alexander calls him), and he took the opportunity to suggest three questions asked late in the day. Beavers was sure that Jack believed in his fantasies; and if the prosecution ever tried to use the test in a new trial, he wanted them to cope with three unpalatable parts of the record tending to establish Jack's insanity.

So Beavers had the machine operator, Bell Herndon, ask whether harm had come to Jack's family because of what he did; whether they were in danger of harm; more specifically, whether Clayton Fowler was endangered. (Jack's attempts at proving the efficiency of the plotters had centered, in recent days, on warning Clayton: They are after you, flee, go to Israel.)

During the explanation of the questions, Jack answered all three items. Have his brothers or sisters been hurt? "Not up to this point." Are they in danger? "Yes, sir." Is Fowler? "Yes." He asked for no clarification or qualification, as he had with other questions that made him hesitate. Yet, during the actual run, with the chest-tube and arm-cuff and finger-bands on, he did something unparalleled all that long day. To the first question he said "May I interrupt?" and the needles jittered. Herndon said he must keep his answers, here as elsewhere, to yes or no. To the second and third questions he gave no reply at all. Herndon wrote on his chart, during a pause after the third question, "Visibly pondering." When the instrument was off, before Alexander's return to the room, the operator asked Jack to explain his reaction. He said, of his family: "Well, they are always exposed to it, so I don't know how to answer that." (He had no problem understanding the question when it was first posed — if they are in danger, now or always, the answer would be a Yes.) "The same with Fowler. I know when he's representing me, he's putting himself on the spot." (Then why not answer Yes?) Alexander and Tonahill came back, but Jack was still trying to explain: "Well, number one, this is quite a notorious thing, and don't forget, it's just like I specified when Earl Warren was in danger, you know, so he is — in other words, people have a dislike for me, and Mr. Fowler is trying to defend me, and this won't make him too popular a person — too well liked of a person, I should say."

Jack's evasiveness here runs counter to his frequent boasts, all that day, of openness, readiness, candor; his preference that the questions be shot at him unprepared, as many as possible, "no punches pulled." In fact, before this very series Jack had emphasized again his readiness and promptitude. Herndon mentioned, for the record, the subject's fine effort to concentrate by closing his eyes to all others in the room. Jack responded: "That's why — if I were guilty of something or if I were trying to evade something, certainly closing your eyes would be less advantageous for you to cover up something. Do you follow me? In other words, closing your eyes means that I do want to tell the truth." Yet Fowler's eleven-page memorandum on the test states that, at the question about harm to him, "Jack did not answer *and turned and looked at me*." Alexander, in the report on the test he submitted to Henry Wade, wrote: "My own interpretation is that his so-called delusion regarding his family being in danger is for the purpose of an insanity plea and that he did not wish to jeopardize this test by giving an untruthful answer even in regard to these questions regarding the safety of his family and his lawyers." These are the only questions he did not answer at all — as opposed to some he answered with confusion, or the one on jail terms which he told the man beforehand would "embarrass" him.

After the test, Dr. Beavers was sworn, then asked to give his interpretation. Though he himself still thought Jack sincere in his protestations, he admitted: "It possibly could have been his trying to protect in some way an answer from the polygraph."

Yet Alexander's skepticism is unjustified. Jack's fantasies rise too clearly from his lifelong preoccupations. The D.A.'s office thought Beavers and other psychiatrists were coaching Jack on how to feign insanity — a laughably perilous thing to try with this transpicuous, unstable, suspecting man. In a mood of conciliation or fear, he would surely tell "my Chief" or "Bill" if they were doing anything of the sort. And it would be as foolish as dangerous: Jack was not the brightest of pupils. Even if he could be counted on to hold his tongue about such lessons, it takes no psychiatrist to see how unlikely it was that he could *learn* them.

Furthermore, Jack did not *want* to be considered crazy. Why should he? To help him at a second trial? He long ago lost interest in his own defense; he would not cooperate with the lawyers preparing it, he "gave things away" to his jailors constantly. Did he do it for sympathy? The talk of Jews brought nothing but derision from the guards he spent all his time with. As part of some private scheme of deception? If so, it went undetected by prosecution as well as defense lawyers, and by his family. He resisted attempts to remove him to a mental ward. He wanted people to believe him, to get his story out. For that, he needed to be sane.

Men did not see how a man truly convinced of the horrors Jack claimed to live with could rebound, at times, to levity; be frivolous, almost slaphappy; show such ability to forget what haunted him moments earlier. But we all have things we half believe, private myths that make life easier. When these come into conflict with things dearer to us, nearer to the core — when they make life less rather than more tractable — we abandon our illusions (not necessarily forever), as Jack did in his lie-detector test. The important thing to realize is that Jack held onto his fantasies *because* he needed them. For comfort. They made him still important; still the object of authority's regard; central to the scheme of things.

More than that, they gave sense to what would otherwise be

a senseless chain of bafflements. Everything turned back on him, his city, his friends, the cops; his schemes, lawyers, aims. He killed the punk, hired Belli, pleaded epilepsy, called for Warren — all to please others; and each thing made him more hated. What could explain this? Some grudge of the universe against Jack? Annihilative darkness, evil fate, hostility of gods? At times this seemed to be true: he told Earl Warren he had ceased to pray, told others he no longer believed in the God of his people, in any God. Yet he was sure he would descend to hell when he died. Belief in his personal devils survived belief in God.

Or — as the vision of positive evil pressed on him — could there be another explanation? The universe was *not* against him for some quirky unthinkable reason, some giant evil whim or joke, vaster for its devotion to such tiny prey. What if the hostility made sense? Not *good* sense — the reasons were petty, and based on deception. Still, a human plot, with thinkable human motives and chartable historic causes: men planning, as they have planned in the past, to harm the Jews, out of revenge, envy, ambition; taking coordinated steps toward this end, seducing some people, deceiving others. Horrible as it seems, this is a blessedly *human* vision for anyone with Jack's dark, nihilist alternative.

It should not seem strange to us. It is, in some measure, our choice. We all live — and shall live for years, till our many wounds heal themselves — with hints of plotted malevolence that shattered a golden lad's head as easily as a drunk in the alley brains a chimney sweep. We live apparently undisturbed by suggestions that coordinators of such darkness are uncaught, still moving among us (against us? — why not? why did they move at all, if not toward further goals, a prize to match the stature of that crime they started with?). Polls show, month after month, that a majority of the American people believe there was a plot of some kind to kill the President, yet do not worry over its undetected continuing existence — do not

believe the Warren Commission, yet do not want a new commission to investigate. This frightens Mr. Lane, who character-
izes the people's response as: "My Government, I know you
have lied to me, but for God's sake, whatever you do, don't tell
me the truth."

Mr. Lane and the other theorists take credit for the disbelief
greeting the Warren Report, even as they lament the apathy
toward other solutions (an apathy their own growing stridency
seems meant to redeem). But deeper things are at work, here,
than *Rush to Judgment*.

In the direct shadow of the killings, days after they took
place, the National Opinion Research Center undertook an extensive survey of America's response to the whole experience.
(These and similar tests are reported in *The Kennedy Assassination and the American Public*, brought out in 1965 by Stanford University Press.) The NORC questionnaire showed that
a large majority of people believed Oswald did not act alone,
yet Paul B. Sheatsley and Jacob J. Feldman, in their treatment
of the survey's results, note that "the majority who do say 'other
people were involved' do not seem to take this belief very seriously," because "few people seemed particularly concerned
about discovering their identities and capturing them." This
was true even when the atrocity had just been committed and
national anxiety was, one would expect, at its very peak. Like
Jack, we liked to think of plots — up to a point. In areas where
the thought of them was more distressing than comforting, we
conveniently stopped believing (or took the belief without accepting any of its concomitants). Logic has little hold on us in
a crisis of this sort.

The psyche's maneuvers are made clear in another survey
reported in the Stanford book. James D. Barber summarizes
the group interviews he taped on Monday and Tuesday after
the President's funeral. Six of the eight groups interviewed
were searching for a conspiratorial interpretation of the death.
Significantly, the other two groups showed fewer signs of recovery and communal stability under the weekend's disruptive

threat. Barber thinks the "need for an interpretation" allowed people to regain a sense of cause-and-effect; to overcome their first panicky feeling that chaos had broken loose and "anything can happen"; to work out, in a political model, their personal fear that life's normal laws had been abrogated with unknowable consequences for them.

The bullet from the Book Depository (or from "the knoll" or from no matter where) suggested to us dangers more disintegrative than any conspiracy could manage. It was a bullet out of nowhere, striking anywhere, a sign of "what can happen," any moment, to any of us. One man's life seemed a dream, roamed into daylight, of everything we strive to be — sophisticated, but not jaded; realistic without cynicism; serious, not stuffy; and, above all, young. There is an almost universal feeling that Kennedy's achievement lay not so much in specific political measures but in his magical attunement with the newest forms of man's oldest aspirations — in the resiliency of his youth under stress, in that combination of poise with endeavor for which no term has been found but "style." And if his achievement touched the springs of myth in us, so did his death — tapped subterranean streams that well up darkness. It was necessary, when *they* began to flow in us, to return the myth to "reality," to politics and hard scientific fact, to ballistic reports and witnesses, clues and plots.

In its least guarded moment, from its most vulnerable side, the nation looked, unexpectedly, on Night — the obliterative irresponsibility of death. So much human promise so easily erased. Is it true then, after all, that depth on depth of reason in the mind of Socrates can be idly sealed up with a sprig of hemlock? The youth, hope, vitality of a nation were encapsuled in a man; and man must die. Saturday, in tears, Jack called Bill Willis: "How could it happen? — a *nothing* like that killing a man like the President!"

> Golden lads and girls all must —
> As chimney sweepers — come to dust.

All our private hells — surviving our beliefs — arose out of the national catastrophe, invaded us in privacies we did not know we had. A shrewd instinct of self-preservation made us drive the threat back out, make it public, reduce it to "a plot."

This explains the widespread audience the theorists enjoy, the willingness vaguely to believe it is "all politics," that in some such terms it all makes sense. Human ambition, venality, greed, crime — all these we live with and can handle; no matter how criminal, such acts are at least conventional in their sequence of cause and effect; things done by man, and so within man's power. There is this much, at least, of reason and light in the darkness of the darkest plot. Better that than the vision of total night, of superhuman or subhuman forces revealing themselves, at last, as *anti*-human, erasing all man's pretensions, all reason, order, law.

And this explains why the audience is, for conspiratorialists, such a frustrating one — why there is no more (indeed, a good deal less) acceptance of any *other* theory, once the Warren theory is discounted. The populace is, for theorizers, infuriatingly bored with details of the plot — so long as the plot is dimly, reassuringly *there,* protecting them from darker things.

It is not surprising, then, that Ruby should be used for men's comfort. We are only doing, in our way, what he first did. He typifies our whole range of response — not because he is a typical American (not at all); because he was so unchecked, obvious and almost primordial, in those days of primitive gestures toward self-preservation. He was the buried child or savage in us all. Surveys show that children were as profoundly disturbed as their parents by the death of Kennedy; but they were very little upset, or were pleased, when Ruby killed Oswald. The wife of Justice Douglas told an interviewer she shouted "Good! Give it to him again!" when she saw Oswald killed on her screen. That was the Ruby impulse. Most of those who felt it stir in them inhibited it; they may not even know, in retrospect, that it kicked, a child in the psychic womb. A brief sputter of applause greeted Sheriff Decker's announcement, outside the County Court House, that the prisoner they were awaiting had just been killed at City Hall. Ruby said he did it to spare Mrs. Kennedy the ordeal of a trial. Ruth Paine, who befriended the Oswalds, is a Quaker who does not believe in violence; yet she too said her first reaction to Ruby's act was "Good!" — it would spare *Marina* the ordeal of a trial. We all wanted to spare ourselves that trial.

But we could not. We would not bless the Ruby impulse in us, even if it slipped out for an instant. *It* is a danger also. Violent retribution breeds violence. If the first need was for some kind of revenge on that which had outraged our world of order, the second need, dawning more slowly, was for escape from violence. So Ruby, the Ruby in all of us, must be rejected.

Besides, he lent himself so conveniently to our emotional demand for a conspiracy. The "silencing" of Oswald raised doubts even in those who had not, to that moment, thought of plots. The first killing was abrupt; itself and alone; a Mystery. The second was merely suspicious — more sordid (robbing evil of its majesty); in retrospect it would seem almost inevitable (reintroducing calculation). It put the startling death of Friday in a *series*, a pattern; freed the mind to take up again its patternfinding role — Jack searching for Weissman and, behind Weissman, for the others (Hunt? Walker? the Birchers?). Eva repeated what he said to her: "I don't know why I want to connect that sign and the mail box with Oswald, but I do."

And still, behind these coolest theorizings (*deduction*-dear-Watson) moves a blind mute Ruby-need to deny it all, get rid of the challenge, wipe it away. William Manchester takes up, incredulously, Jack's protest that this *could* not be — a *nothing* kill a man like Kennedy: "It is not too much to say that he was the diametric opposite of John Fitzgerald Kennedy. . . . Kennedy, for example, was spectacularly handsome. Although Oswald's voice hadn't yet lost its adolescent tone, he was already balding, and he had the physique of a ferret" (the punk! creep!

little weasel of a guy!). Ruby could not bring himself to call the thing by name. It is the instinct that kept Sandburg from using Booth's name in his long description of Lincoln's death. When he must refer to the assassin, he calls him "the Outsider." Manchester, too, is sickened by the need for naming Oswald: "Noticing him, and even printing his name in history books, therefore seems obscene. It is an outrage. He is an outrage. We want him Out." So did Ruby.

Jack had only one way to get a man *out* — by simpleminded force, as he threw the punks and pimps and creeps down The Carousel stairs. But others will find subtler ways to exorcise this affront to human reason. They too will turn him into a thing, an instrument of more logical agencies hidden somewhere behind him — just a hired gun. The CIA, or Cuba, or Russia, or the mobs, or *somebody* did it for a reason. It does not matter who they were — Communists? Birchers? both; who cares? — so long as there was a reason.

But no matter what finesse they use, we recognize these men. Returning to the mystery over and over, trying to "solve" it, to limit, to dispel it, poring over the volumes of clues, all the odd things that "do not fit" (not yet — the assumption is they *will* fit if we only arrange them better), pinning their hopes on a new book, on better photographic sleuthing, more debate, examination, science, *reason,* these men — we know who they are (we should, we *are* these men) — would like to find a simple, clear, demonstrable explanation; ferret out some individual, some group that logically set the thing in motion, which can be traced with the weapons of reason, identified, pointed to, disposed of. Such men are out, intellectually, to get rid of the assassin; still driven by a need to "shoot" him with words, talk, theory, proof — we all know them. They are Jack Ruby.

Sources

Most of the taped interviews used as the basis for this book were conducted by Mr. Demaris, who was standing close to Jack Ruby when he shot Oswald. Demaris was the first newsman to identify Ruby, even to local radio and newspaper men, and his account of the assassination was televised to European audiences. He had been in the city a year earlier doing research on Dallas crime for his book about Las Vegas, *The Green Felt Jungle* (which is the last book Ruby is known to have read as he lay on his deathbed).

When President Kennedy was assassinated, Demaris returned to Dallas and began questioning eyewitnesses to the assassination. He was one of the first men to record interviews with Oswald's landlady and with Tom Howard, Ruby's lawyer, as well as with nightclub strippers and bouncers who had known Ruby. He returned to Dallas late in 1966, when Ruby lay ill in Parkland Hospital, and spent another seven weeks talking with officials and entertainers, lawyers, policemen, prison guards, friends and acquaintances and enemies of Jack Ruby. He spent time in Jasper, Texas, questioning Joe Tonahill, in Los Angeles and San Francisco questioning Melvin Belli, in Palo Alto questioning Mark Lane. He held long telephone interviews with Earl Ruby and Marguerite Oswald.

Written sources were also acquired during these interviews. Notes written by Ruby during his trial and imprisonment were loaned to the authors by Melvin Belli, Joe Tonahill, Jim Martin, and Clayton Fowler. Bill Alexander furnished transcripts of the Ruby trial and the Candy Barr trial. Many defense lawyers loaned briefs, the records of hearings, and other instruments in the legal struggle — Mr. Elmer Gertz was especially helpful here.

The twenty-six volumes of Warren Commission material were consulted throughout, usually in conjunction with taped and written records acquired by Mr. Demaris. The section on Ruby's polygraph examination, for instance, was drawn from the following sources: the complete transcript of proceedings on pp. 504-599 of Warren Volume XIV; the tape-recorded memories of participants Joe Tonahill, Clayton Fowler, and Bill Alexander; the eleven-page memorandum written after the test by Fowler; the seventeen-page report drawn up by Alexander; the reflections of Sol Dann and Earl Ruby on their roles in that day's events. A similar confluence of testimony was relied upon for all the major events treated here.

Drawing on this range of sources, on two weeks spent viewing Dallas and meeting witnesses with Mr. Demaris, and on trips to Detroit and Chicago for consultation with Ruby's lawyers, Mr. Wills wrote the book.

The authors express their gratitude to all those who cooperated with them; and they feel a special debt to Harold Hayes, the editor of *Esquire* magazine, who conceived and commissioned the two articles on which the first half of this book is based.

About the Authors

Garry Wills, born in 1934 in Atlanta, Georgia, was trained as a classicist, receiving his Ph.D. from Yale, and taught ancient Greek at the Johns Hopkins University for five years before becoming a free-lance writer and a contributing editor of *Esquire* magazine. He is the author of *Chesterton, Politics and Catholic Freedom,* and *Roman Culture.*

Ovid Demaris, born in Biddeford, Maine, received an A.B. from the College of Idaho and an M.S. in journalism from Boston University. He was a reporter with the Quincy *Patriot-Ledger* and the Boston *Daily Record* before joining the United Press, and later became Ad Copy Chief of the *Los Angeles Times.* For the past nine years he has been a free-lance writer. Mr. Demaris is the author of sixteen paperback originals, which have been translated and published in eighteen countries, and the bestseller *The Green Felt Jungle* (with Ed Reid). His study of the alliance between organized crime and politics in Chicago will be published this winter.